How to Understand the Sacraments

*The Crossroad Adult Christian Formation Program*

**The Crossroad
Scripture
Study Program**

*How to Read the Old Testament*
*How to Read the New Testament*

**The Crossroad
Theology and Church
History Study Program**

*How to Read Church History: Vol. 1*
*How to Read Church History: Vol. 2*
*How to Understand the Creed*
*How to Do Adult Theological Reflection*
*How to Read Christian Theology*
*How to Understand Church and Ministry
in the U.S. Experience*

**The Crossroad
Christian Living
Study Program**

*How to Understand the Liturgy*
*How to Understand the Sacraments*
*How to Understand Marriage*
*How to Understand Christian Spirituality*
*How to Understand Morality and Ethics*

**Crossroad
Special Interest
Courses**

*How to Understand Islam*
*How to Read the World*
*How to Understand God*
*How to Read the Church Fathers*

Some "How To. . ." texts, and accompanying study guides,
may be in preparation. For complete up-to-date
information, please write: The Crossroad Publishing Company,
370 Lexington Avenue, New York, NY 10017.

Philippe Béguerie
Claude Duchesneau

# How to Understand
# the Sacraments

CROSSROAD · NEW YORK

1994
The Crossroad Publishing Company
370 Lexington Avenue, New York, N.Y. 10017

Translated by John Bowden and Margaret Lydamore from the French
*Pour vivre les sacrements*
published 1989 by Les Editions du Cerf,
29 bd Latour-Maubourg, Paris

© Les Editions du Cerf 1989

Translation © John Bowden and Margaret Lydamore 1991

*Nihil Obstat:* Father Anton Cowan
Censor

*Imprimatur:* Rt. Rev. John Crowley, VG
Bishop in Central London
Westminster, 12 April 1991

Printed in the United States of America

Library of Congress Cataloging-in-Publication Data

Béguerie, Ph. (Philippe)
[Pour vivre les sacraments, English]
How to understand the sacraments/Philippe Béguerie,
Claude Duchesneau.
p.     cm.
Translation of: Pour vivre les sacraments.
ISBN 0–8245–1026–7 (pbk.)
1. Sacraments—Catholic Church—History. 2. Catholic Church–
–Doctrines—History. I. Duchesneau, Claude. II. Title.
234',16--dc20                                        91–13221
                                                          CIP

# Contents

## PART TWO
## The Church Celebrates the Sacraments

That which was from the beginning,
which we have heard,
which we have seen with our eyes,
which we have looked upon
and touched with our hands,
concerning the word of life –

the life was made manifest,
and we saw it,
and testify to it,
and proclaim to you
the eternal life
which is with the Father
and was made manifest to us –

that which we have seen and heard
we proclaim also to you,
so that you may have fellowship with us;
and our fellowship is with the Father
and with his Son Jesus Christ.
And we are writing this that our joy may be complete.

I John 1.1–4

# Introduction

This book invites you to make a journey. If you follow it step by step, it will lead you to discover a rich world, that of the sacraments. Rather than launching into definitions and then deducing logical applications from them, we have thought it better to examine the life of Christian communities throughout their history.

The word sacrament took on the meaning that we give it today only after centuries of church life. But from the beginning, the new communities practised baptism and met together for the breaking of bread (the name Christians gave to the eucharist, as we shall see in Chapter 3). Here we have at least two realities which have always been lived out by the different churches. They still are, in spite of the variations which can divide the churches on a number of other issues, especially over how many sacraments there are. That is enough to enable us to embark on our enquiry.

In actual fact, the sacraments are in the order of practice: they even form part of the customary practices of those men and women who throughout the centuries have called themselves Christians. On the day after Pentecost, the apostles did not begin by working out a theological plan, or a catechism, or a handbook of theology. They had a message to proclaim, and a mission, and they went out along the roads to announce the Good News. As the apostle Paul said, they carried out 'that which they had received from the Lord' (I Cor. 11.23). Life brought them step by step to a richer discovery of 'that which they had received from the Lord'. Meeting with other people encouraged them to express themselves. And the church subsequently worked out a theological explanation of these sacramental realities. But receiving them from the Lord has always had a much more solid basis than rational explanation or theological reasoning.

It has been the same for every generation of Christians, and in particular for our own. The ritual acts of our community have been passed on to us by those who went before. We carry them out, and they mould us even before we are able to place them in a theory or a theology. This is a good thing, because Christianity is first and foremost a way of life, a practical exercise, an ethic, before it is a philosophy or a theology.

When we say 'a practical exercise', we do not just mean a religious, liturgical or sacramental practice, but a type of behaviour, a way of living amongst other human beings. And we want to find out how the sacraments are not only religious and liturgical exercises, but belong even more to the realm of everyday living and our relationships with other people.

### Before and beyond rites

As soon as we think of the word 'sacrament', we might imagine a ceremony in which the priest performs certain rites over one or more Christians. It is the rite itself which, in common parlance, is a sacrament. We all know quite well why a marriage is more than a church ceremony which lasts for an hour. It expresses itself throughout a whole lifetime; it lasts much longer than the time of the celebration; it lives beyond the boundaries of the church. So the sacrament consists just as much in life outside as in the ceremony. How much connection we shall be able to make between the two, we shall see during the course of our journey. For now, let us get into the habit of not limiting the word sacrament to the rite.

But we need to go further. Do you know that Vatican II several times referred to the church as the 'universal sacrament of salvation' (for example, in *Lumen Gentium* 48; see also p. 16) It is also worth remembering that St Augustine said: 'The only sacrament is Jesus Christ.' Such language shocks many Christians. Their catechism has not prepared them for it. And yet that is the tradition of our church. Cardinal Ratzinger has written: 'In the early church, the word sacrament was used of historic events, words of scripture, elements of religious worship which allow the saving action achieved by Christ to show through, thus enabling the Eternal to reveal himself in history and even to be present there as its true inner reality.' And Mgr R. Coffy, in a report to the Plenary Assembly of the French Episcopate at Lourdes in 1971, commented: 'We have to realize that we have been conditioned by definitions of sacrament which are extremely succinct but which, through this very succinctness, imprison the richness of the sacramental mystery in narrow limits . . . When we use the word sacrament to define the church, we must make the term wider and more subtle.'

### The stages of our journey

Don't let us begin our study at the end – the fact that there are seven sacraments. Let us grasp the reality at its very beginning, as it arose, and try to understand how it is possible for us to say with St Augustine that the Lord Jesus Christ is the first sacrament, or, more precisely, that he is the original sacrament, from which all the others derive. In doing this, we shall immediately avoid the problems of ritualism, in the pejorative sense of the word. By the same token we shall once again discover the direct link there is between the sacrament and the Christian life, between the sacrament and the proclamation of the Good News.

To discover Jesus Christ as the sacrament of God is at the same time to recognize once again what was unique and completely new about the 'event of Jesus of Nazareth'. That is where we shall begin. Then we shall trace how the Christian community carried on the Lord's work. In doing this we shall discover a new definition of sacrament. That is the object of Chapter 1.

In Chapter 2 we shall take up that definition to see how it applies to Jesus himself, to the church as the sacrament of salvation, and certainly to the realities of our lives which we today call sacraments.

Our journey will then involve us in looking at how the authors of the New Testament expressed themselves. Each of them was the spokesman for a group of Christian communities. And so Chapter 3 will enrich our perception of the life of the sacraments in the early church.

Faith in the resurrection of Jesus of Nazareth and the certainty of his presence is at the heart of the witness of the first disciples. To live in this presence is to see what is really at stake in the sacraments. The evangelist Luke will guide our thinking on this in Chapter 4.

This preliminary survey will allow us to recognize the basic links between what is given in the New Testament and the world of the sacraments. In the second part we can work out our thinking in more detail through what we can learn from the history of the church and the pastoral work put into practice after Vatican II.

In the third part we shall place each of the sacraments in its relationship within the group of seven.

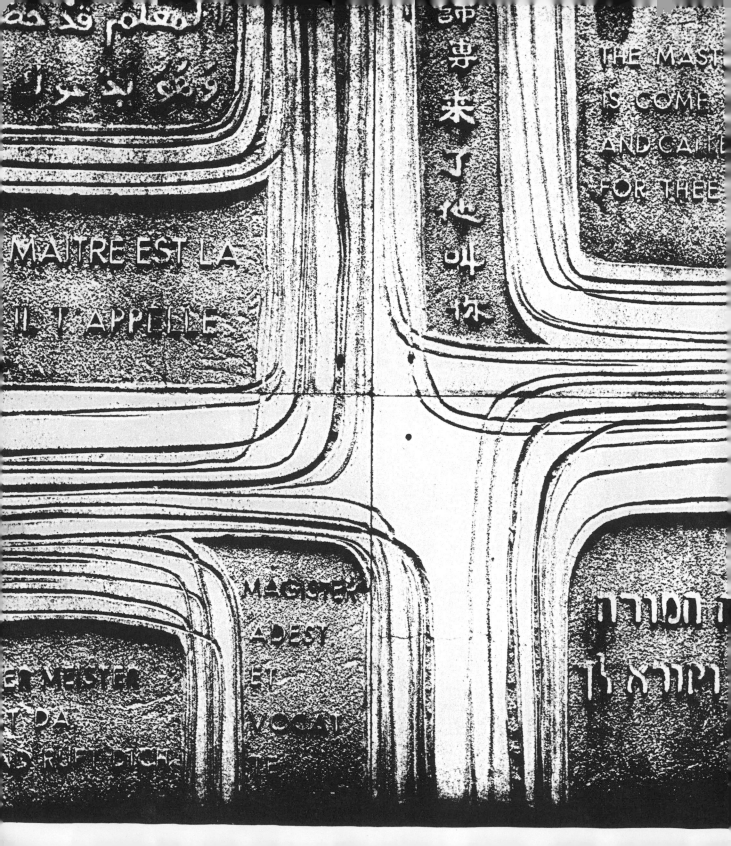

# PART ONE

# *Discovering the Sacraments*

# 1

# Jesus Christ, the First Sacrament

*'In many and various ways God spoke of old to our fathers by the prophets; but in these last days he has spoken to us by a Son . . . He reflects the glory of God and bears the very stamp of his nature.'*

Heb. 1.1–3

## The originality of Jesus Christ

'Philip, whoever sees me, sees the Father.'

To discover Jesus Christ as the sacrament of God is at the same time to recognize again what was unique and completely new about the 'event of Jesus of Nazareth'.

For us as Christians this represents a unique fact in the history of the world. Of course, every person who has lived is unique, but what we say about Christ is much stronger than that. There is nothing that can be compared with him. We can even say that he alone is the Saviour: 'for there is no other name under heaven given among men by which we must be saved' (Acts 4.12).

That affirmation is not easy to sustain in a world where many of our colleagues and friends do not have faith in Jesus. It is uncomfortable for us, even, to face the consequences. Let us tackle them on just one point, that of the human discovery of God.

## *The image of God*

On the evening of Maundy Thursday, during that very important time when Jesus was saying farewell to his disciples, a surprising dialogue took place. The Lord said: 'I am the way, and the truth, and the life; no one comes to the Father, but by me. If you had known me, you would have known my Father also; henceforth you have known him and have seen him.' Then Philip asked the question which was on everyone's lips: 'Lord, show us the Father, and we shall be satisfied.' Jesus' answer still takes us by surprise: 'Have I been with you so long, and yet you do not know me, Philip? He who has seen me has seen the Father' (John 14.6–9).

Doesn't that dialogue illuminate in some respects the basic experience of the disciples during the three years of their life with Jesus of Nazareth? Everything becomes clear! In Jesus, they have discovered the true face of God!

1

That is the originality of Jesus Christ. God came to reveal himself to human beings. The Word became flesh, the face of God took on human form. Jesus of Nazareth, a human being like us, lived in the midst of his own. The disciples searched his face, were astonished at his behaviour, gathered together his words. The words of God were heard in our human tongue.

The apostle Paul relates the same experience when he claims that 'Jesus is the image of God' (II Cor. 4.4). From now on humankind is no longer searching in the dark for evidence of God. We find it in the life of a man, in human life.

### The search for God

Philip's request, 'Show us the Father, and we shall be satisfied', is one which the world still makes today. We cannot escape it; it is the question of humankind in all times and in all places. As Christians, we are bound to welcome it. It is voiced as much by those who seem to turn their backs on God as by those who seek God and hope to be illuminated. It is enough that we are able to show God to men and women. All the rest is superfluous.

In an era like ours, for many of those who do not belong to any religious community, any religious group, any confession of faith, God remains a question, a quest, a search. Some people are unwilling or even refuse to use a language which speaks too easily of God. If we call God the 'Absolute', we are able to say that, whether we are aware of it or not, he is present in all life. In all of life there is a desire to which everything can be sacrificed. There is a reality which is put above everything else. This can be money, or power, or honour, or success, motor cars or even myself!

There exists within many of us this thirst, this mysterious dissatisfaction, quite incapable of pin-pointing its object, but building up like a nostalgia which troubles our existence, to the extent that we try to drown it in a whirl of activity. Men and women are not only creatures with needs, they are creatures with desire. The needs can be satisfied; the desire stretches towards infinity.

## The Image of God

*Jesus said: I am the way, and the truth, and the life.*
*No one comes to the Father,*
*but by me.*
*If you had known me,*
*you would have known my Father also;*
*henceforth you know him*
*and have seen me.*
*Philip said to him:*
*'Lord, show us the Father,*
*and we shall be satisfied.'*
*Jesus said to him:*
*'Have I been with you so long,*
*and yet you do not know me, Philip?*
*He who has seen me has seen the Father.'*

John 14.6–9

### On being mistaken about God

But in their quest for the Absolute, human beings creep forward with difficulty, as if in the dark. It is not the sayings of wise men and philosophers which have the last word. The French philosopher Blaise Pascal remarked: 'God! Not the God of the philosophers and the wise, but the God of Abraham, of Isaac and of Jacob, the God of Jesus Christ!'

It is possible to be mistaken about God. Human beings can be mistaken about the Absolute. Christians themselves can mix up a good deal of rubbish with the image of God. And in the course of the centuries we have seen the church carry out acts in the name of a God of a kind which we renounce today, actions which we are not always proud of having done in the past. Nothing is more dangerous than for human beings to be mistaken about the Absolute; in that way we sow the seeds of death. Nothing is more alienating.

The god who can be falsely blamed is not a saviour. The god of war and revenge is not a saviour. The god of chance and necessity, the god of luck, the god of money . . . and all those false gods conjured up incessantly by fundamentalists, whether they be Christians or non-Christians. All through the year the media broadcast talk about God which revolts us because it is so simplistic and so little resembles the God we would like to make known.

And so we welcome the originality of Jesus Christ with joy. 'The people who walked in darkness have seen a great light; those who dwelt in a land of deep darkness, on them has light shined.' In Jesus, God shows himself to us. That was the testimony of the first generation of witnesses.

## On the evening of Good Friday

But then came the drama of Good Friday. Jesus was dead. Had God's countenance, which had shined through a man's face, disappeared for ever? The question is all the more painful to the degree that, as the centuries have passed, so the figure of Jesus has become blurred. Each person is at liberty to reconstruct Jesus according to his own pattern; to make him an object to be talked about instead of a face to be gazed upon. We can seize on his words to make them justify our behaviour, to safeguard our interests. Do we have to carry on our search for God in the dark, scarcely allowing the recollections of that group of men and women who were at one time the disciples of Jesus of Nazareth to illuminate our way at all?

Nevertheless, Jesus said: 'It is to your advantage that I go away' (John 16.7). 'I will pray the Father, and he will give you another Counsellor . . . I will not leave you desolate . . . Yet a little while, and the world will see me no more, but you will see me; because I live, you will live also' (John 14.16–19).

## On the morning of Easter Day

And then came the resurrection. Humankind's night was illuminated by the light of Easter. Jesus is alive and the incarnation goes on. The adventure of Jesus of Nazareth is not an episode in the history of the world. It was the beginning of a new relationship between God and the world, and between humankind and God. That relationship has to be followed up: He who was dead is alive again; he is risen! The face of God is always turned to the world, and shines out on the face of humankind. That is the work of the Holy Spirit.

---

## Some questions people ask themselves

Do we need Jesus Christ in order to reach God?
Do we need the church in order to reach Jesus Christ?
Do we need the sacraments in order to be a Christian community?

These three questions are of a kind. We all know men and women who are deeply religious, sometimes true mystics, and yet are not Christians. However, John the Evangelist records these words of Jesus: 'No one comes to the Father but by me' (John 14.6). If it does not seem right to us to restrict the number of those who are truly travelling towards God to those who know Jesus, how are we to understand these words of Jesus?

Others recognize Jesus as a way, but nevertheless do not join one of the Christian churches. Still others call themselves Catholics, but are not 'practising'. So, of what use is the church?

Each of these questions is linked to a more basic one: can we know God directly, go straight to him? Must I accept a mediator, that is to say, an intermediary (Christ, the church, the community) between myself and God?

When we say that Jesus is a 'sacrament', we begin to discover the role that he plays to show us the way to God.

When we say that the church is a 'sacrament', we are also affirming that it is carrying out the missionary work of Jesus Christ.

When Christians live out the sacraments, they in their turn become signs of the meeting between God and humankind.

## The first Christian community

Open the book of the Acts of the Apostles. The first narrative that we find after that of Pentecost is the story of the curing of a lame man at the Temple (chs 3; 4). For the first time, the church is confronted with a request which is made to it from the world.

Peter, accompanied by John, had gone up to the Temple to pray. There was a lame man there, near to the Beautiful Gate, who asked alms of the apostles. Then Peter looked at him and said: 'I have no silver and gold, but I give you what I have; in the name of Jesus Christ of Nazareth, walk.'

Peter, under the influence of the Holy Spirit, understood what was asked of him. It was then given to him to reflect the face of Jesus. He did what his master had often done, and healed the sick man.

He did not do this in his own name, as if the power were his own. He did it 'in the name of Jesus Christ'. And the author of Acts deliberately draws our attention to this expression, because he repeats it seven times within the course of the same narrative (3.6, 16; 4.10, 12, 17, 18, 30).

In the same way, on the day after Pentecost the first Christian community discovered both what was asked of them and what was given to them when, faithful to the Spirit, they presented to the world the main features of God's face, as these were reflected in the face of Christ.

The Holy Spirit is the Spirit of Jesus. The place where he most desires to be is within the community of believers. Both the community as a whole and each of its members ought to welcome him. It is he who gathers them together and makes them into the Body of Christ.

If today there were no longer any visible body of the Lord, there could be nowhere where God's face could make itself known. But the Holy Spirit transforms and transfigures believers. 'And we all, with unveiled face, beholding the glory of the Lord, are being changed into his likeness from one degree of glory to another; for this comes from the Lord who is the Spirit' (II Cor. 3.18).

And so it gradually dawned on the first Christian community that they were not only to talk about Jesus, and proclaim what he had done, but even more importantly, they were to be witnesses of their Lord who was alive within them. He is as it were the head of the body.

If Jesus had not loved, how would anyone have understood the way in which God loves? And if the Body of Christ does not today reflect the riches which it has received from its Lord, how can humankind come to know the face of a loving God?

This brings us to the heart of any theology of the sacraments:

- a sacrament is always performed in the name of Jesus Christ;
- all sacraments are the work of the Spirit, and are both a gift and a call;
- they are to be found at the heart of human life, and they carry on Jesus' mission, which was to reveal the true face of God to the world.

This recollection of what happened on the morning after Pentecost will lead to a better understanding of a new definition of a sacrament.

Human life, when strongly motivated by faith and under the guidance of the Holy Spirit, becomes as it were the bearer of the face of God. It proclaims the news of God and his kingdom from the moment it accepts this kingdom as a gift from God.

In the report given to the Plenary Assembly of the French bishops at Lourdes in 1971, Mgr Coffy offered this definition: 'A sacrament is a worldly reality which reveals the mystery of salvation, because it is its realization.' We shall adopt this definition, and try to understand it better.

We shall begin by noticing that though the words are different, we can easily recognize in them the definitions of our childhood catechism. Then we used to say: 'a sacrament is an efficacious sign of the grace of God.' Let us compare the two:

- 'a worldly reality which reveals' is what we call a sign;
- 'because it is its realization' is what we mean by efficacious;
- 'a worldly reality which reveals the mystery of salvation' is certainly a sign of God's grace.

## Definition of a sacrament

A sacrament is a worldly reality which reveals the mystery of salvation, because it is its realization.

We are thus still keeping to a very traditional way of looking at things. But at the same time we are opening up the possibility of a deeper and broader meaning of the word sacrament.

St Augustine said that the first sacrament is Jesus Christ. In a way he is the source of all other sacraments. And Jesus was certainly 'a worldly reality'; for was he not 'the carpenter, the son of Mary and brother of James and Joses and Judas and Simon' (Mark 6.3), Jesus 'reveals the mystery of salvation' because he himself is salvation. He reveals salvation by realizing it. He alone truly deserves the name 'sacrament'. Jesus is the 'sacrament of the Father'; the Belgian theologian Edward Schillebeeckx has described him as 'the sacrament of the encounter with God'.

The church, too, is 'a worldly reality'; it 'reveals the mystery of salvation' – that is in fact its mission. 'It is its realization' in so far as it allows itself to be controlled by the Holy Spirit. But the church is not a sacrament in addition to Jesus Christ. It is not of the same order of magnitude. It depends on Jesus Christ. One could say that Jesus is the 'sacrament of the Father', while the church is the 'sacrament of Jesus Christ'.

There are also realities in our own lives which we call sacraments; the Catholic church today identifies seven of them. These various sacraments come to us as our main meeting points with the kingdom of God. They are elements of our life, but our life as it is transfigured by the Spirit of the Lord. They reveal salvation, since our life has to reproduce the main features of Christ's face, to mark out the path for men and women in their search for God. The sacraments ensure that the whole of our lives is a proclamation of the gospel. They allow us to speak of God not only in learned terms (the God of the philosophers and wise men) but within the fabric of our existence (the God of Jesus Christ).

*Of you my heart has said*
*'Seek his face!'*
*Your face, Lord, I seek;*
*do not turn away from me.*

Ps. 27.8

## Is it still possible to speak of God?

Speaking of God has always been difficult. Between Christians, it is certainly an easier matter, because we have a common language, the same cultural references, closely related thought-modes. We can understand one another. But as soon as we step over the boundary of the quite limited group to which we belong, the words which we use to speak of God are the source of a great deal of misunderstanding. Many parents nowadays suffer a great deal through not being able to pass on their faith to their children.

If words betray us, how can we speak of God to the world? When we say that Jesus is a sacrament, we confirm that he reveals God by showing his face. It is not what we say that is important. In the church, we too become the sacrament of Christ; we show his face. To speak of God through the way in which we live our lives is more real than to speak of him in words.

Ten or twelve years ago, a baptism was being held among a young Christian community in North Cameroun and the first candidate to be baptized was a deaf-mute. For his brothers, he was the one who had best proclaimed the gospel! The next chapter will help us to understand this point better.

# 2

# The Church, Sacrament of Salvation

*Father, the hour has come.*
*Glorify your Son that the Son may glorify you,*
*since you have given him power over all flesh*
*to give eternal life to all whom you have given him.*
*And this is eternal life, that they know you the only true God,*
  *and Jesus Christ whom you have sent.*
*I glorified you on earth, having accomplished the work which you gave me to do.*
*I have manifested your name to men.*
*Now they know that everything that you have given me is from you.*

John 17.1–8

The previous chapter ended with a new definition of sacrament. That is not enough. We must take time, too, to renew our way of thinking, to find a richer vision of sacramental reality, to discover its practical implications in the life of the Church and of Christians.

## Looking on Jesus Christ

To start with, let's look at Jesus. In saying that he is the sacrament of the meeting between God and humankind, we affirm that he is the sign of this meeting, and moreover that he makes real what he signifies.

*Different kinds of signs*

In Chapter 6, we shall be examining in more detail the question of rituals and the world of symbols. But it is necessary to say something more precise about signs at this point.

Most signs that we use are human inventions, and are called 'conventions'. The red light, the 'no entry sign' or the decorations on an officer's epaulette are of this kind. One must know the code in order to work out the meaning. In the same way, the words in our language are conventional signs, and a child has to learn its own language to know the meaning of terms like 'door' or 'horse'.

Such signs are not efficacious. We have proof of this every day when we see cars jump a red light or

7

go past a 'no entry' sign. The efficacy does not derive from the sign, but from the co-operation of those who obey it.

There are also signs which come into being of their own accord, and which experience teaches us to decipher. Smoke means fire; a black cloud comes before a downpour. It is the same with human behaviour. It makes itself known in a natural way; the sign is the result of an emotion that is felt. Laughter is a sign of joy, tears of sadness. And so there are several kinds of sign in the world in which we live.

But it is possible to push the analogy still further. A mother who hugs her child does not need to teach it the meaning of this gesture; it springs from love and is understood as such. In this latter case the sign performs an action. It is not content to show love, but brings love alive. It is not just an indication, but makes present what it shows. Using more technical language, one could say that, in this kind of sign, 'reality presents itself, becomes present'.

## Jesus, the presence of God

Jesus is not just a man who signifies God: he is the presence of God. When we say that he is the sacrament, the effective sign of salvation and of the kingdom, we do not just mean that he brings news of this salvation and this kingdom, or that he shows the way. Over and above this, he is the realization of it. He is Emmanuel, God with us, and that is the kingdom.

That is why Jesus does not reveal God only by his words and his teaching, but by the whole of his life and his mystery. God gives himself to the world by means of the Christ. Jesus is the Living Word of God, the Word Incarnate, the Word made flesh, the Image of the Father. The words which Jesus spoke are not the most important part of his message. His presence in the midst of us says more, as does his way of doing things. As soon as he acts, the reality which he signifies shows itself to be present. That is how we are able to say that Jesus is an efficacious sign.

## Jesus, turned towards the Father

What is signified is always more important than the sign. When a mother kisses her child, the love has value over and above the action which accompanies it.

In the same way, Jesus said to his followers that he is not an end, but the way. To get to the Father, we have to go through him. We could say that all the time Jesus effaces himself before his Father.

The evangelist John tries to highlight this behaviour of Jesus: 'The words that I say to you I do not speak on my own authority; but the Father who dwells in me does his works' and 'The word which you hear is not mine but the Father's who sent me' (John 14.10, 24).

The most significant episode in this respect is the one in which John recounts the appearance of Jesus to Mary Magdalene after the resurrection. Jesus frees himself from Mary; he does not allow her to hold him prisoner in any way, but turns her towards the Father. 'Do not hold me, for I have not yet ascended to the Father; but go to my brethren and say to them, I am ascending to my Father and your Father, to my God and your God' (John 20.17).

Jesus even goes so far as to say, 'The Father is greater than I' (John 14.28). This humiliation of the Christ, his effacement in front of the Father, is an important part of his mystery. It is really this attitude which allows us to say that he sees himself as the sacrament of God (see the table on the following page).

Jesus draws us in his wake in this movement towards his Father. That is the reason why the liturgical prayer of the church is not usually addressed to the Christ but is, for preference, a prayer made to the Father, through the Son, in the Holy Spirit.

## Jesus, the servant

'God so loved the world that he gave his only Son' (John 3.16). Jesus did not live on his own behalf, but so that the world might be saved. He said: 'I came that men may have life, and have it abundantly' (John 10.10).

'Christ Jesus, though he was in the form of God, did not count equality with God a thing to be grasped, but emptied himself, taking the form of a servant' (Phil. 2.6f.). He was God's servant, certainly, but at the same time servant to his brothers and sisters, to give them life by showing them the Father.

The world needs God to show himself, needs God's action to become visible, to be a physical reality in our life. This is what every sacrament accomplishes.

We can pick out three things from this examination of Jesus Christ:

Jesus is sacrament because he is God's effective presence in our daily life, and as such he is truly an efficacious sign.

Jesus is sacrament because he always points to his Father as the source of his work, as the end of his road, and in doing so, he proclaims the gospel.

Jesus is sacrament because he is at the service of the life of the world, and as such he is the presence of salvation.

---

### Jesus and his Father

*For he whom God has sent utters the words of God,*
*for it is not by measure that he gives the Spirit.*
*The Father loves the Son, and has given all things*
*into his hand.*

John 3.34f.

*My food is to do the will*
*of him who sent me,*
*and to accomplish his work.*

John 4.34

*Truly, truly, I say to you,*
*the Son can do nothing of his own accord,*
*but only what he sees the Father doing.*
*For whatever he does,*
*that the Son does likewise.*
*For the Father loves the Son,*
*and shows him all that he himself is doing;*
*and greater works than these will he show him,*
*that you may marvel.*
*For as the Father raises the dead and gives them life,*
*so also the Son gives life to whom he will.*

John 5.19–22

*I can do nothing on my own authority;*
*as I hear, I judge;*
*and my judgment is just,*
*because I seek not my own will*
*but the will of him who sent me.*

John 5.30

*My teaching is not mine,*
*but his who sent me.*
*He who speaks on his own authority*
*seeks his own glory;*
*but he who seeks the glory*
*of him who sent him is true.*

John 7.16, 18

*The words that I say to you*
*I do not speak on my own authority;*
*but the Father who dwells in me*
*does his works.*

John 14.10

*The word which you hear is not mine*
*but the Father's who sent me.*

John 14.24

We can see from these sayings, or others like them which can be found in John's Gospel, how Jesus speaks of the relationship which unites him with his Father. And so we have a better understanding of how Jesus can be spoken of as the 'sacrament' of the Father. He makes known the works of his Father; he does not seek glory for himself.

## The church, sacrament of Christ

The manifestation of God in Jesus of Nazareth lasted only for a limited period. For the people of our own day, Jesus is almost as far removed as God. We cannot see or touch him. It is the church's mission to carry on what Christ started, to ensure the continuity of his presence as history unfolds. That is why, according to the Second Vatican Council: 'Rising from the dead Jesus sent his life-giving Spirit upon his disciples and through him set up his Body which is the church as the universal sacrament of salvation' (*Lumen Gentium* 48). What does it mean to say that the church is sacrament?

For the world, the Christ is the sacrament of God, and similarly the church is the sacrament of Christ for the world. 'By virtue of an analogy which is not without value, the church may be compared to the mystery of the Incarnate Word. Just as the nature taken by the Word is at his service as a living organ of salvation . . . so the social entity formed by the church is at the service of the Spirit of Christ who gives it life with a view to the growth of the body' (*Lumen Gentium* 8).

The three elements which made an appearance when we considered Christ the sacrament must reappear when we consider the church.

---

### A part of humanity

The church is not the whole world, but it is truly in the world; moreover, it is made of the flesh of the world. It is not the whole of humanity, but it is human, in all senses of the word. It is made up of men and women who live in the world and take part in its history, in the way that they live and in what they do, in their joys and hopes, their sorrows and their disillusionments, their inter-dependence and their struggles. It is *that part of humankind which confesses that God has intervened in history in the person of his Son Jesus of Nazareth, who died and has risen*, and *which lives looking to the kingdom*. That is why we say that it is the sacrament of salvation for the world.

---

'Go therefore and make disciples of all nations, baptizing them in the name of the Father and of the Son and of the Holy Spirit, teaching them to observe all that I have commanded you; and lo, I am with you always, to the close of the age' (Matt. 28.19, 20). This is how the risen Christ spoke to his apostles. But he had already said to them: 'For where two or three are gathered in my name, there am I in the midst of them' (Matt. 18.20).

Just as Jesus was not content to speak of the Father, but was the presence of God amongst men and women, so the church cannot be content to relate the life of Jesus and pass on his teaching, but has to be the place where the presence of the Risen Christ is recognized and welcomed. In this way it becomes the effective sign, the sacrament of Christ.

It is not enough for the church to reveal God's face through its words; it has to embody it, like Jesus, in its very being. Christ gives himself through the church. The church is not just the proclamation of the kingdom, but is already the place where the kingdom is coming into being. The church's effectiveness does not come from within itself, but from the Spirit which has been given to it. 'Those whose lives have been transformed enter a community which is itself a sign of the transformation, a sign of the newness of life; this is the church, the visible sacrament of salvation' (Paul VI, *The Proclamation of the Gospel*, 23).

### The church, witness to Jesus

The church is not an end in itself; it is a way. It has no other function than to show someone other than itself, to point to Jesus Christ as the saviour of the world and the one who saves it from its own sin. It leads men and women to Christ, who leads them towards the Father. It is simply the body of which Christ is the head.

Like Jesus, it does not speak its own words, but those of the one who sent it. It does not do its own works, but those of its Lord. This is why the church always has to efface itself before the one who is head of the body. It is the means of salvation, and even more the outward sign of that salvation to the world. The kingdom is partly made real in the church, and yet the church must not be confused with the kingdom. It is both saved and needing to be saved. It has within it the holiness which God has given it, but it is also intrinsically sinful because it is made up of sinful men and women.

People sometimes talk of fighting against a certain triumphalism in the church. This triumphalism happens when Christians believe it more important to further the church than to show the way to God. They forget that their community is only a way and not a goal.

The greatness of the people of the covenant has always been its proclamation of a Word which judges it as well as the world. It is the same with Christians. Indeed, the gospel which we proclaim denounces our own sin as much as that of all human beings. We are bearers of this Word, even when we are incapable of listening to it or putting it into practice. Within our weakness, we go on pointing to Jesus Christ as the source of all strength, all justice, all truth. The church is simply the sacrament of Jesus Christ.

### The church, servant of the world

The church cannot close in on itself. It only has meaning as a witness to the Good News. It is given by God to the world, as the Son is given by the Father.

In order to carry out its task, it has to become a servant, just as its Lord became a servant. And just as Jesus was only the servant of his Father by becoming the servant of his brothers, so the church can serve God only by serving humankind.

Every Christian community will always find itself confronted by this question: how much of its resources, strength and time is turned in on itself, and how much should be put at the service of humankind? Is it a club providing only for its members, or is it concerned to be the leaven in the dough, a light for the peoples of the world? In the course of the centuries of its history, there have

---

### Salvation

The basic event of the biblical tradition is the departure of the people from Egypt under Moses' leadership. This departure, this *Exodus*, is thought of as a liberation, a journey from slavery to freedom. It becomes the prototype of God's action in the world. It is the image of salvation.

And so the God of the Bible is always thought of as a Saviour God. He is the God who makes people free. But in Hebrew, the verb 'to free' means 'to bring out'.

It is a fine image, and the language is forceful: the human being, the creature who was fashioned from clay, has a constant need to 'get out' or, to put it more strongly, to be set free. But freedom is not given ready-made; it is a process of bringing to birth. In this constant birth of humankind, God is at our side, is the source of the freedom for which we are continually striving.

As far as history is concerned, Jesus is the archetypal free man, and we bear witness that the Spirit which he gives us is the source of true liberty. For it is there that salvation lies: freedom from idols such as money, power, violence, appearances, domination, and doubtless even more: freedom from self and from this enclosed world which we are incessantly rebuilding.

The body of Christ is this place where the Spirit calls us and leads us along the paths of liberty.

On the day after Pentecost Peter, having cured the paralysed man in the name of Jesus Christ, declared: 'There is no other name under heaven given among men by which we must be saved' (Acts 4.12).

---

been periods when the church has closed in on itself, locked in its internal arguments, and times when it has been concerned to proclaim the gospel at the risk of impoverishing itself. These have been the greatest periods for the church.

As we did for Jesus of Nazareth, after our look at the church as sacrament we can remember the following points:

The church is sacrament when the Spirit allows it to welcome its Lord's presence and to live in him. Then the Spirit makes the church an efficacious sign.

The church is sacrament when it effaces itself before its Lord and Master. It points to him as head of the body. It proclaims the gospel of Jesus Christ.

The church is sacrament when it is not turned in upon itself but undertakes to carry out its role as servant to the world. It puts salvation into practice.

---

## A question

If Christians are no better than other people, how do they have the temerity to proclaim the gospel to the world? The one, holy, catholic and apostolic Church is just a utopia. What exists in real terms are Christian communities, often made up of not very brilliant people, who ought to have enough humility not to hold forth at length about God! There is too much of a gap between what the church says and what Christians do!

We welcome this question. A healthy reflection on the church as the sacrament of salvation can help us to see the difficulty more clearly.

We know that the church will always be made up of sinners. Jesus did not come for those who are well but for those who are sick. The dream of a perfect Christian community is even dangerous. A self-satisfied group of human beings can only proclaim itself!

But the church is not salvation; it is only its sacrament. It is not for the church to put itself forward as an example, but to point to Jesus Christ as the only possible saviour of the world.

And so the church, whose unity is very crippled, cannot be satisfied with its divisions. It knows that it is always called to conversion, to be faithful to its Lord's commandment. It turns towards him to affirm that in him alone is found the leaven of unity.

A Christian community, even if it is crippled and sinful, goes on being a sign as long as it does not see salvation in itself, but in the Christ. The church does not depend on its own perfection for its effectiveness, but on its reception of the Spirit.

---

## The sacraments of the church

The church in itself is not visible. Christians are scattered in the world where, according to one of the earliest Christian writings, known as *The Epistle to Diogenes* (second century): 'they live in the same houses as other people, carry on the same trades, wear the same clothes as everyone else'. They are only recognizable as Christians when they have the courage to demonstrate in their own lives their faith in the Lord Jesus. It is precisely this to which the sacraments of the church call them.

We say that there are seven sacraments. Since seven is a figure with great symbolic meaning, this is already a way of saying that our whole lives ought to become sacramental. To confess one's faith in the Lord Jesus does not prevent one from leading the same life as other people, but it means leading it in a different way, just as Jesus lived a human life, yet in a completely new way. 'If anyone is in Christ, there is a new creation; the old has passed away, behold, the new has come' (II Cor. 5.17).

There are seven sacraments, but it is possible to establish a hierarchy among them. At the centre we must place the eucharist, as the sacrament of the body of Christ, the sacrament of the church. Baptism, confirmation and first communion are called 'sacraments of initiation'; they are as it were the way which leads to the eucharist. The sacrament of order is the service of the body of Christ. The sacraments of reconciliation, of marriage and of anointing the sick let us live out the Lord's Pasch, his death and resurrection, in the most important situations in our lives (see the third part of this book.)

And so the first of the church's sacraments is the eucharist. When the community meets around the Lord's table it becomes visible. This is the very place and time when it manifests itself in the very reality of its mystery, the body of Christ reunited by the Lord who is its head. So we can say that if Jesus is the sacrament of the Father, the church is the sacrament of Jesus Christ and the eucharistic assembly is the sacrament of the church. Each of these realities corresponds closely in its own way to the idea of sacrament that we have given.

# God reveals himself to the world

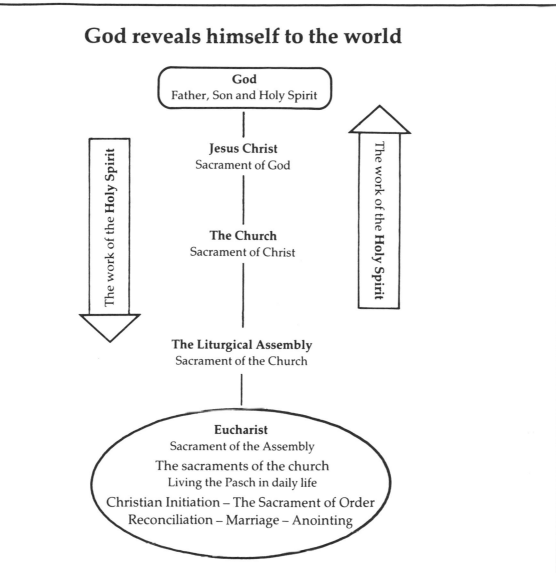

The downward-pointing arrow shows how at each stage we draw closer to daily life. God becomes visible in history. But each time the field narrows.

The upward-pointing arrow shows how human life goes back step by step towards the revelation of the true face of God.

The sacramental life keeps this two-way movement constantly in motion: God comes towards humankind and humankind goes towards God. Through his church, Jesus then really appears as the path which links humankind with God.

## The sacrament, presence of the Spirit

The sacrament is not a pure language adopted by Christians to proclaim Jesus Christ. It is not a declaration of intentions or a proclamation; it is a time and a moment when human beings welcome the Spirit, and accept that the Spirit is doing its work. Then it allows the face of God to be made visible in the lives of men and women. This presence of the Spirit leads us to speak of an efficacious sign.

It is important to grasp that the sacrament is a reality in human lives before it is a religious ceremony. (In the second part of this book we shall see the importance of celebration.)

Reconciliation does not take place first and foremost in a confessional; it is a reconciliation between people, between ourselves and God. The sacrament consists in accepting the Spirit to enable us to live in reconciliation.

In the same way, the sacrament of marriage is not confined to a church ceremony. When a man and a woman decide to make a covenant, and to live this covenant in faith, in the light of the Word of God and under the guidance of the Holy Spirit, they accept and live the sacrament. Their union becomes sacramental.

Similarly, when members of the community live out an illness or suffering as a way of faith, when they accept the Spirit in their very lives, they are living out the sacrament of the sick.

Baptism is not confined to a ceremony which is more or less solemn; it extends over an entire lifetime lived out in the light of Easter, in the mystery of the Lord's death and resurrection.

God gives himself in the sacrament: he gives himself to be known through the realities of our lives; he gives himself to be *seen*. In the sacrament Christ, through his church, gives us his Spirit so that we may wear his face and live his life. That is why the sacraments are not only something to be *received*; they are also to be *lived*.

## The sacrament, submission to the Spirit

Just as Jesus guides us to the Father, and just as the church effaces itself before its Lord, so the sacrament bears witness to a richness which comes to us as much from another as from ourselves. It is the welcome of God's gift, the Holy Spirit.

So when a man and a woman join together in the sacrament of marriage, they have no intention of setting themselves up as a model of the full realization of the covenant between God and his people. They simply recognize that the covenant that they have to live out is only its reflection. Their wish is to welcome the Spirit so that God may make real in them the mystery of his love.

Similarly, when the church meets together for the eucharist, it does not own what it celebrates, but proclaims the coming of someone other than itself, and gives thanks for that coming.

Sacraments cannot be truly lived out except by those who have accepted the status of being the poor. 'For what have you that you did not receive? If then you received it, why do you boast?,' said St Paul (I Cor. 4.7). Sacraments put us into the situation of being humble, because they are the welcome of someone greater than us. They invite us to give thanks, that is, to give back to God the gift that he has given us. This is the opposite of the attitude of the Pharisee in the gospel, who sought to justify himself.

## The sacrament, the service of the world

Christians do not use sacraments to enrich themselves. They are put by them into the position of servants. We do not receive Christ in order to keep him, but to give him to the world. One does not marry in church in order to do the right thing, but to accept the mission of showing to the world belief in the God of the covenant.

Those who have not understood that sometimes set the sacrament and the proclamation of the gospel against each other, even though the sacraments are 'the source and the climax of the church's life', including its mission. It is not enough to say that they are a force which allows the gospel to be proclaimed. They are the very form which that proclamation takes.

When I forgive my brother or sister, I become the sacrament of forgiveness; I unveil the face of God who forgives, as Jesus himself did.

This missionary concept of the sacraments is undoubtedly the one which Christians lack the most. They will not be able to discover it if the sacraments are presented to them only as means of salvation for themselves. They are indeed a means of salvation, but of the salvation of the world. They are a revelation of God, the presence of God in our affairs.

Only by looking upon Jesus as a *servant* can Christians be cured of such a misconception. In living out the sacraments, they ought to learn that they themselves become servants.

In the sacraments we find the features which we have already picked out in relation to Jesus and the church:

Every sacrament is the presence of the Holy Spirit in the life of the believer. That is how we can say that it is an efficacious sign.

Every sacrament makes us point to the Holy Spirit as the source of what we do. In that, it is a proclamation of the gospel.

Every sacrament puts us at the service of our brothers and sisters. In that, it contributes to the salvation of the world.

We are beginning to perceive the richness of the idea of sacrament. We started from Jesus Christ and his relationship to God the Father. We then considered the church in its relationship to its one Lord. But all that has only one goal: to allow us to give human life its full dimension. In order to focus our thoughts, we must again investigate the first Christian communities, as we shall do in the following two chapters.

## The proclamation of the gospel and the sacrament

One might believe that mission, the proclamation of the gospel, is an activity of the church quite separate from the life of the sacraments. And in fact, in those areas where traditional Christianity is well established, there are regular Sunday churchgoers who seem to have little interest in proclaiming the gospel during the rest of the week.

Can that be held against them? They are only the descendants of past generations when everyone thought of themselves as more or less Christian. In those days the missionary activity of the church seemed confined to those ready to leave their homeland to travel to distant countries, where the message of Jesus Christ had not yet been proclaimed. On the other hand, the very way in which the sacraments had been presented and celebrated did not encourage people to discover the direct link they have with evangelization.

The Christian era is now a long way behind us,

and if the important book by Fr Grodin and Fr Daniel, *France, Country of Mission*, seemed provocative when it appeared in 1943, it soon became a classic, and no one is any longer surprised by such a perspective. Today we know that the division into a mission church and a sacramental church is fatal for both. However, it is not easy to avoid this, and requires great effort on the part of Christian communities to ensure that they are well integrated into contemporary life.

It also demands a theology of the sacraments which has been renewed in the light of the thinking of the last Vatican Council. In the end, it calls for a pastoral approach and a way of celebration which are in tune with the realities of human life.

The church needed to reconcile two of its activities which seemed too much opposed to each other or mutually exclusive. Vatican II achieved this by speaking of 'the church, sacrament of salvation' (see the box on page 16).

# 'The church as the sacrament of salvation' according to Vatican II

For anyone who has read the various documents of the Second Vatican Council, the concept of the church as 'the sacrament of salvation for the world' is not a new one. In fact it appears in all the important texts: at the beginning of *Lumen Gentium* (Dogmatic Constitution on the Church, 1 and 48), at the beginning of the Decree on the Church's Missionary Activity (1 and 5) and of the Constitution on the Sacred Liturgy (5 and 26), and at the conclusion of the first part of the famous Schema 13, *The Church in the Modern World* (42 and 45).

Fr Guillou, a member of the International Theological Commission and an expert on Vatican II, was able to write:

'If anyone were to ask me what is the key concept of Vatican II, I would reply without hesitation that it is the concept of the church as sacrament. This idea of sacrament embraces all the schemata to their very depths. It unites all the conciliar documents, whether constitutions, decrees or declarations; it consecrates the unity of the church's action from the first evangelization to the celebration of the eucharist. In allowing the church to take its unity from its source, Jesus Christ, it allows it to hold to this, a living tradition and an opening for mission' (*La Maison Dieu* 93, 1968, 13 and 15).

And it was undoubtedly no coincidence that in his first homily, Pope John-Paul II declared: 'We must first of all get in step with the Council to make real in our lives what it sets out . . . For that we must return to the constitution *Lumen Gentium* with a view to a new and strengthened meditation on the function, the mode of being and acting, of the church.'

'The church, the sacrament of salvation for the world', is not a new expression. It can be found in the Roman Missal of Pius V (for example in the prayer after the fifth lesson for Holy Saturday) and it already appeared in the Church Fathers (for example in Cyprian, *De cath. Eccl. unitate*, 7). But it has to be acknowledged that before the Council it was not in the vocabulary used outside theological circles. It had no influence on the way in which the sacraments were referred to in the catechism.

# 3

# The First Christians

## *The first Christian community in Jerusalem*

*So those who received his word were baptized, and there were added that day about three thousand souls.*

*And they devoted themselves to the apostles' teaching and fellowship, to the breaking of bread and the prayers.*

*And day by day, attending the temple together and breaking bread in their homes, they partook of food with glad and generous hearts, praising God and having favour with all the people.*

*And the Lord added to their number day by day those who were being saved.*

Acts 2.41–47

## *I received from the Lord*

*For I received from the Lord what I also delivered to you, that the Lord Jesus on the night that he was betrayed took bread, and when he had given thanks, he broke it, and said, 'This is my body which is for you, Do this in remembrance of me.'*

*In the same way also the cup, after supper, saying, 'This cup is the new covenant in my blood. Do this, as often as you drink it, in remembrance of me.'*

*For as often as you eat this bread and drink the cup, you proclaim the Lord's death until he comes.*

I Cor. 11.23–26

On the day after Pentecost the new Christian community which had just been born did not find itself the possessor of the seven sacraments as we know them. That is obvious. The word sacrament itself had not yet entered its language.

However, let us take a look at the Acts of the Apostles, and follow the disciples step by step. When the Twelve and their companions had been filled with the Holy Spirit they set out 'to proclaim in diverse tongues the mighty works of God' (Acts 2.11). As the multitude gathered, Peter got up to make the first proclamation of the gospel: 'This Jesus God raised up, and of that we are all witnesses . . . Let all the house of Israel therefore know assuredly that God has made him both Lord and Christ, this Jesus whom you crucified' (Acts 2.32, 36). And when people asked what they ought to do, Peter replied: 'Repent, and be baptized every one of you in the name of Jesus Christ for the forgiveness of your sins, and you will receive the Holy Spirit' (Acts 2.38).

Immediately after this Pentecost narrative, the book of Acts gives as it were a résumé of the life of this first community: 'And they devoted themselves to the apostles' teaching and fellowship, to the breaking of bread and the prayers' (Acts 2.42). This term 'breaking of bread' was, together with 'the Lord's Supper', one of the first names given to the eucharist.

And so we have evidence that baptism and the eucharist were part of the very earliest Christian practice. It is usual to begin any enquiry into the sacraments in the New Testament with them. Taking up the witness of the first Christians we will see if there were other actions on the part of the church, or other features of life, which can be compared with these first two elements.

From the beginning, the practices could differ, depending on the various communities. In the interests of accuracy, we shall find it best to examine separately each of the witnesses who are the main authors of the New Testament.

## Pauline communities

Paul's letters are the oldest written evidence of the life of the first communities, and were set down about twenty years after Jesus' death. The first letter to the Thessalonians can be dated to the year 51, and Paul went on writing up to his death in 67.

In the first letter to the Corinthians Paul speaks of baptism and the eucharist as if they were well-known practices. But he does not put them at the forefront of his concern. He even states: 'Christ did not send me to baptize but to preach the gospel' (I Cor. 1.17).

### The Lord's Pasch

The oldest narrative relating to the evening of Maundy Thursday can be found in this letter, and Paul concludes: 'For as often as you eat this bread and drink this cup, you proclaim the Lord's death until he comes' (1 Cor. 11.26). We also find there a parallel being drawn between baptism and the death of Christ: 'Was Paul crucified for you? Or were you baptized in the name of Paul?' (I Cor. 1.13). To be baptized, like taking part in the eucharist, is to travel again with Christ along the

---

### The sacraments in the New Testament

One sometimes hears it said that the sacraments did not appear until late on in the church's history. What do we know of the first Christians? What significance did they attach to the sacraments? In the Acts of the Apostles and in the Epistles, we find a number of passages which testify to the presence of certain sacraments in the life of the Christian communities:

Numerous allusions to *baptism*: Rom. 6; I Cor. 1.13–17; Acts 2.41; 8.12, 38; 9.18; 10.48.
The *eucharist* as described by Paul: I Cor. 11.20–34 ('breaking of the bread'); Acts 2.42–46; 20.7.
*Marriage* according to St Paul: I Cor. 7; Eph. 5.21–33.
Prayer with the *anointing of the sick*: James 5.14.
Numerous allusions to the rite of the *laying on of hands*: Acts 6.6; 8.17; 13.3.

---

path of the Pasch, to pass through death in order to attain life. The rite of baptism itself was especially symbolic, being a journey through water, an immersion from which the candidate arose as if from the dead.

And Paul went on to develop the comparison between Christian baptism and the crossing of the Red Sea with Moses (I Cor. 10.11–12).

### Marriage

For Paul, baptism and the eucharist are means of expression written into human life to state and proclaim the death and resurrection of Jesus.

Are they the only ones? It would seem not. The love between a man and a woman, that gift of self which each gives to the other in marriage, is also presented as a means of proclaiming the paschal mystery. 'Husbands, love your wives, as Christ loved the church and gave himself up for her, that he might sanctify her, having cleansed her by the washing of water with the word' (Eph. 6.25–26). This washing of water accompanied by the word is baptism. In Paul's eyes, the love between a man and a woman involves an identification with Jesus Christ, in the gift of himself which he made to his church.

We are well into the sacramental order. There was no talk of a rite or of a ceremony, but of the reality of human life which comes to wear the face of Christ. Christians are called upon to live as companions to Christ in his journey to Easter, when he involves himself in a mutual covenant.

How can we take the way of Christ on his journey to Easter? How can that be woven into our lives? In order to understand Paul's thought we must re-read many passages from his letters and follow him on his own journey. In this way we shall discover the progression of his thought over the years. In the early epistles the apostle is above all preoccupied with the mystery of death, which was an immediate reality to communities exposed to persecution. Subsequently he realized that the paschal mystery is at work from now on in the lives of all believers. It expresses itself in 'death to the flesh and to sin' and a participation in the resurrection which has already begun. 'If with Christ you died to the elemental spirits of the universe . . . If then you have been raised with Christ, seek the things that are above, where Christ is. When Christ who is our life appears, then you also will appear with him in glory' (Col. 2.20; 3.1, 4).

---

### Pasch

The first great Christian festival of redemption was a transformation of the Jewish Passover, and was a combined commemoration of both the crucifixion and resurrection of Jesus. In the Christian passover, the Hebrew name, *pesach*, took on the Greek form *pasch*.

In the fourth century there was a process of development, and the two aspects of the *pasch* were divided into Good Friday and Easter Day, commemorating the crucifixion and resurrection to some degree separately.

Use of the old word *pasch* reminds us that the death and resurrection of Jesus and our celebration of them belong inextricably together.

---

### *The sacraments according to Paul*

Celebrating the presence of the risen Christ is not just a matter of carrying out actions such as baptism or the breaking of the eucharistic bread.

It is to take into everyday life the way of the true life.

It is to welcome the Spirit who is at work through the Lord's resurrection.

Without using the word sacrament, Paul unfolds what it means.

## Matthew's communities

### *Baptism*

In Matthew's Gospel, baptism makes a solemn appearance. When Jesus meets with his disciples after the resurrection, he sends them out on a mission: 'All authority in heaven and on earth has been given to me. Go therefore and make disciples of all nations, baptizing them in the name of the Father and of the Son and of the Holy Spirit, teaching them to observe all that I have commanded you; and lo, I am with you always, to the close of the age' (Matt. 28.18–20).

The baptism which the church celebrates goes back to the Lord's command. It is normal to refer to it in the classical formula of theology: it was instituted by Christ. The Lord is certainly the one who acts with authority, and the Christian community finds in him its justification for what it does. So we are not surprised to find the Lord's assertion witnessing to the reality of his presence among his disciples throughout history.

We find the same air of authority in the narrative of the baptism of Jesus by John the Baptist (Matt. 3.13). The Master asked John to baptize him, but John, who was only a forerunner, recognized that his action did not carry the weight of Jesus' actions. However, it is clear that he is already proclaiming the future practice of the Christian community. In undergoing a rite which was well known in his circles, the Lord in a way made a gift of it to his disciples.

> *Do you not know that all of us who have been baptized into Christ Jesus were baptized into his death? We were buried therefore with him by baptism into death, so that as Christ was raised from the dead by the glory of the Father, we too might walk in newness of life.*
>
> Rom. 6.1–3

### The eucharist

Like the writers of the other Synoptic Gospels, Matthew records the narrative of the institution of the eucharist (Matt. 26.26–29). He does not include, like Luke and Paul, the brief phrase 'Do this in remembrance of me', but Jesus' words when he takes the bread and cup into his hands are more than just a sign: 'This is my body' and 'This is my blood of the covenant'. In that way again the Lord gives a commandment to his church. Matthew is the only evangelist who has Jesus say, 'Take, eat' and 'Drink of it, all of you.' And so, as in baptism, the church is not just an institution which carries on something which it has seen its master do. It carries out the mission entrusted to it; it follows the instructions it has been given.

### The forgiveness of sins

Matthew is the only evangelist to have linked the celebration of the Last Supper with the forgiveness of sins: 'Drink of it, all of you; for this is my blood of the covenant, which is poured out for many for the forgiveness of sins.' It is not surprising, therefore, that when he speaks of forgiveness, he is also the only one to evoke the particular presence of the Master amongst the community of believers.

This happens in chapter 18. Look at the passage which runs from v. 12 to v. 35. It begins with a parable, that of the lost sheep, and ends with another about the unforgiving servant; the whole extract is given a symmetrical structure which brings out the central passage, as the following table shows:

12–14: The lost sheep
  15–18: Forgiveness offered by the community
    19–20: The presence of Christ when people are gathered together in his name
  21–22: Forgiveness offered by a brother who has been wronged
23–25: The unforgiving servant

It is a solemn passage, like the one which gives the command to baptize and make disciples. As there, the presence of the Lord amongst his own is strongly affirmed. We also have an instruction given by the Master to the community which is being formed: 'Whatever you bind on earth shall be bound in heaven, and whatever you loose on earth shall be loosed in heaven.'

It is obvious that this Gospel passage was not addressed primarily to Jesus' contemporaries. He was with them, and had no need to emphasize his presence when they met together. Those to whom this message was aimed were the communities which formed after the resurrection. Their life, which showed itself in particular through forgiveness and the meeting of all people in prayer, was truly the place where the special presence of the Lord was felt.

### The sacraments according to Matthew

For Matthew baptism, the eucharist and forgiveness all correspond with the instructions given by Jesus of Nazareth, and all three are linked with the presence of Christ in the midst of his church.

Therein lies the originality of the sacraments. The emphasis is not on the paschal mystery, as with St Paul. It is more on the Lord's command, on his presence and on the life of the community.

## The life of the communities according to Luke

Luke is the author of two books, or, if you prefer, of a work in two volumes: the Gospel and the Acts of the Apostles. A good historian, he is careful to relate events as they actually happened, and he states that he has listened meticulously to witnesses. But he is not merely a chronicler; he takes care to link events to one another, and to put an interpretation on them.

As one might expect, baptism and the eucharist figure in his work. They are placed within coherent groups, which reflect their insertion into the practices of the church. Baptism is one of the rites of integration into the community, and the eucharist is part of its permanent life.

### Integration into the community: baptism and the gift of the Spirit

On the morning of Pentecost, there was not more than a handful of men and women who had pledged their faith to Jesus of Nazareth. When the Acts of the Apostles was written, thirty years later, Christianity had spread throughout the Mediterranean basin. On several occasions Luke shows the entry of new members into a group which already exists. He does this according to a plan which is almost always identical. There is first of all a happening which is often surprising, even miraculous. Then one of the apostles takes the floor and proclaims the gospel. His speech inspires new disciples to join, who then receive the signs of acceptance into the community: baptism and the gift of the Spirit.

The first story takes place at Pentecost. These are the first baptisms held by the church, as we saw earlier. The plan is simple, and consists of three elements, which involve different partners.

- repentance: an inward movement on the part of the new believer;
- being baptized: an action by the community;
- receiving the Holy Spirit: a gift from God.

Luke does more than tell us a story; he discloses the true meaning of the rites of his community.

We can see a similar plan being followed right up to the foundation of the community in Samaria. One of the Seven, Philip, was proclaiming the Word of God there. His preaching brought about the conversion of the Samaritans, and they received baptism. Peter and John were then sent out from Jerusalem and laid their hands on the new converts, who received the Holy Spirit (Acts 8.5–17). Two actions are mentioned here: baptism and the laying on of hands. Two ministries are exercised: that of Philip, who proclaimed the gospel and baptized, and that of the apostles, who confirmed the baptism by the laying on of hands.

In the case of the conversion of the centurion Cornelius and his family, the natural procedure is reversed. Peter's preaching brings about conversion and adherence to the faith. But God intervenes directly to give the Spirit, and Peter welcomes this initiative on the part of God by giving baptism.

The circumstances are different in each case, but the three parts are always there: the personal spiritual process, the action of the church, the gift of God. In each case, the preaching clarifies the essential relationship between this entry into the faith and the proclamation of the death and resurrection of the Lord.

### The regular life of the community: the breaking of bread

For the eucharist, Luke retains the old vocabulary of the first Christian communities and speaks of it as the 'breaking of bread'. It is the repetition of Jesus' action on the evening of Maundy Thursday. It is also the sign of recognition given by the Risen Christ to the pilgrims on the way to Emmaus (Luke 24.30, 35), and is found again on the occasion of Paul's visit to Troas (Acts 20.7, 11).

It is interesting to see that Luke inserts it into the life of the community. In one of the brief descriptions he gives, he makes this clear: 'And they devoted themselves to the apostles' teaching and fellowship, to the breaking of bread and the prayers' (Acts 2.42). This sentence indicates four characteristics of the community. It may even be that it gives a description of the assembly, the ancient source of our liturgy: the teaching of the apostles followed by a kind of sharing of goods, then the reenactment of Jesus' action in breaking bread and finishing with prayer.

And so the breaking of bread appears very close to the daily life of the community, which is made up of sharing, of poverty and joy. In Acts, Luke does not give any further explanation of its meaning. But we must remember that, in the story of the disciples on the way to Emmaus, it is the sign of the presence of the Risen Christ in the midst of his own people. We shall see that in the next chapter.

In Luke, the sacramental acts:
- form a real part of life and of the spread of the gospel;
- cannot be separated from the discovery of faith through preaching;
- proclaim a new style of life which flows from conversion to the Risen Lord.

## The sacraments in John's Gospel

John's works are amongst the last in the New Testament to have been written. They were actually composed around thirty years after the great epistles of Paul, and allow us already to encounter the second generation of Christians.

Oddly, John gives no account of either the baptism of Jesus or of the institution of the eucharist. And yet his Gospel is permeated with a symbolism which constantly recalls these two sacraments. It is unthinkable that he either was unaware of them or played down their importance.

Jesus said to Nicodemus that it is necessary 'to be born of water and of the Spirit'. The cripple at the pool of Bethesda is dipped in the water, which cures him. The man born blind recovers his sight after being washed. From the pierced side of the crucified Jesus there flows water and blood. Jesus promises the water of life to the Samaritan woman . . . From the first centuries the church has used these narratives as rich sources of material for its teaching on baptism.

The wine at Cana already proclaims the new wine of the eucharist. The multiplying of the loaves is followed by a discourse on the bread of life. The foot-washing and the allegory of the vine enable us to understand Jesus' action on the evening of Maundy Thursday.

Why this apparent lack of interest in the original action, together with such richness in the development of its significance? No doubt there are several reasons.

Sixty years after the crucifixion and resurrection, the Johannine communities already had long experience of the practices of the church. They knew quite well that these derived from the first disciples. They knew in what circumstances they had come into being. John chose to lead them towards a richer, more spiritual meaning.

Jesus already seemed remote. This new generation who had not known him, missed him. Some thought that the first witnesses were more fortunate, those who had been able to see and touch the Lord. It was undoubtedly for them that Jesus' speech to Thomas was recorded: 'Have you believed because you have seen me? Blessed are those who have not seen and yet believe' (John 20.29). The evangelist always seems to be fearful that his readers will stop at the external signs, and not let themselves be led to a deeper understanding. There were those who saw Jesus of Nazareth and the signs that he did, and did not understand the life that he brought. John does not draw the disciples' attention to the Master performing the first actions which were to become the sacraments; he tries to uncover their deeper meaning.

The two passages which have most to say on the sacraments are, without doubt, for baptism, Jesus' conversation with Nicodemus (John 3), and for the eucharist his sermon on the bread of life (John 6.22). Nowadays a relationship is found between these two texts. Jesus is presented in them as 'the one who comes from above'. That is undoubtedly the key to the Johannine interpretation of the sacraments.

For Paul, faith and the sacraments make us participants in the death and resurrection. Jesus was laid in the tomb in order to be raised to life again. We were 'baptized into his death' and celebrate the eucharist in order to 'proclaim his death until he comes'. But, at the same time we were raised with him, and became a member of his body.

For John, the movement is a similar one, but it

takes its origin in the very nature of the Word of God. Jesus has come down from heaven, from God, and he goes back to his Father. The cross becomes the moment of Christ's glory; he is raised up, and from his pierced side flow blood and water. This is the origin of the two sacraments of the eucharist and baptism. Through them we are associated with the movement which was that of Jesus' life.

His whole life was a baptism, an immersion in our humanity in order to return to God. And we are being carried along the same path: 'Unless one is born of water and the Spirit, one cannot enter the kingdom of God' (John 3.5). 'No one has ascended into heaven but he who descended from heaven, the Son of man . . . so must the Son of man be lifted up, that whoever believes in him may have eternal life' (John 3.13–15).

His whole life is a eucharist, bread come down from heaven to give life to the world, a liturgy of praise in which everything returns to the Father. 'I am the living bread which came down from heaven; if anyone eats of this bread he will live for ever' (John 6.51). Our celebration of the eucharist involves us in this: 'He who eats my flesh and drinks my blood has eternal life, and I will raise him up at the last day' (John 6.54).

The whole life of Jesus of Nazareth is a revelation of God. 'No one has ever seen God; the only Son, who is in the bosom of the Father, he has made him known' (John 1.18). And it is in this way that he gives us life: 'And this is eternal life, that they know thee the only true God, and Jesus Christ whom you have sent' (John 17.3).

For John, the sacraments:
- come from above;
- allow us to live in deep communion with the Lord;
- and so introduce us to the life and knowledge of God.

## In conclusion

From the beginnings, the first Christian communities lived with the riches of the sacramental realities. Each one had its own way of speaking of their importance; in this way they were aware of calling to mind the heritage which their Master had entrusted to them. In that, the main authors of the New Testament were privileged witnesses.

For Paul, the sacraments are a way of living out the Pasch. They link us with Christ's death in order to make us partakers in his resurrection. Married love is associated with baptism and the eucharist.

For Matthew, the sacramental rites have been given by Jesus the Christ as a sign of his presence in his church. The forgiveness of sins is associated with baptism and the eucharist.

For Luke, it is the Holy Spirit which accompanies the work of the church and makes it fruitful. It is he who makes certain that the gospel is successfully proclaimed and leaves his mark on the community of believers, who express themselves in the rites of baptism, of the breaking of bread and of the laying on of hands.

For John, baptism and the eucharist make us partakers of the true life, that of the Word which came among us to reveal the Father and lead us towards him.

### Born from above

*Truly, truly I say you, unless one is born from above, he cannot see the kingdom of God . . .*

*Truly, truly, I say to you, unless one is born of water and the Spirit, he cannot enter the kingdom of God. That which is born of the flesh is flesh, and that which is born of the Spirit is spirit. Do not marvel that I say to you, 'You must be born from above.' The wind blows where it wills, and you hear the sound of it, but you do not know whence it comes or whither it goes; so it is with every one who is born of the Spirit.*

John 3.3–8

### Bread from heaven

*I am the bread of life; he who comes to me shall not hunger, and he who believes in me shall never thirst.*

*I am the living bread which came down from heaven; if any one eats of this bread he will live for ever; and the bread which I shall give for the life of the world is my flesh.*

John 6.35, 51

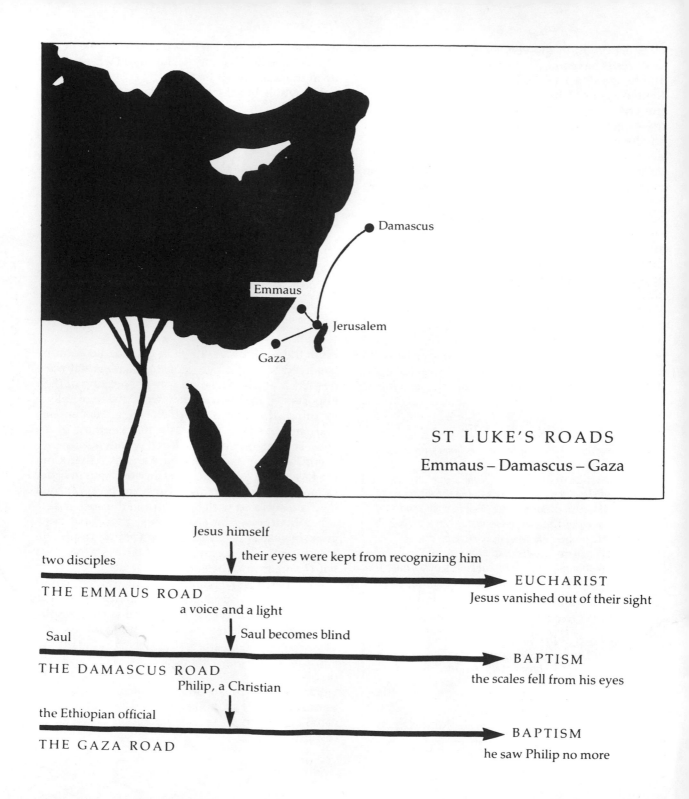

Damascus

Emmaus

Jerusalem

Gaza

ST LUKE'S ROADS

Emmaus – Damascus – Gaza

Jesus himself

two disciples — their eyes were kept from recognizing him

THE EMMAUS ROAD

EUCHARIST

Jesus vanished out of their sight

a voice and a light

Saul — Saul becomes blind

THE DAMASCUS ROAD

BAPTISM

the scales fell from his eyes

Philip, a Christian

the Ethiopian official

THE GAZA ROAD

BAPTISM

he saw Philip no more

# 4

# The Presence of the Risen Christ

*'Stay with us, Lord, for it is toward evening and the day is now far spent.' So he went in to stay with them. When he was at table with them, he took the bread and blessed, and broke it, and gave it to them. And their eyes were opened and they recognized him; and he vanished out of their sight.*

Luke 24.29–31

## Appearances of the Lord, and recognition of the Risen Christ

'Lo, I am with you always, to the close of the age.' That is how the Gospel of Matthew ends. Christ is present on the human road. Risen from the dead, he gives us his Spirit and causes us to live out his Pasch, to lead us towards true life.

Through the sacraments we welcome the presence of the Risen Christ in our everyday lives. And the Spirit calls us to relive the discovery made by the first disciples at the time of the birth of the church, which extends from the Ascension to Pentecost. At the tomb, Mary Magdalene recognized the Lord in someone she had first of all taken for a gardener. Peter and his friends were fishing on Lake Tiberias when a mysterious presence appeared on the shore. It took them some time to realize that it was the Master. It was the same for the apostles who met together in the Upper Room. And the pilgrims on the way to Emmaus had their eyes opened only at the breaking of bread.

Each of the Gospels ends with several narratives telling of the appearances of the Risen Lord to his disciples. Jesus is not only a figure of the past, he is alive, mysteriously present in the world.

This encounter with the Christ is so important that we must take seriously those men and women who were the privileged witnesses of this incredible fact: the Christ who rose on the morning of Easter Day is the very same who walked along the roads of Galilee, and yet he cannot easily be recognized.

Our personal experience will no doubt be different from theirs, and yet it will be very close to it. The Risen Christ does not appear in front of our eyes as a visible reality, but the path that we have to tread in order to recognize his presence is similar to that of the first witnesses. There is a transition to make.

We are invited to make this transition by living out the sacraments. They call us to recognize the presence of Christ in our lives, which are then transformed by them. We discover the Lord by welcoming him through the Spirit. We remain the same, and yet become something else.

As we reread the pages of the Gospels which relate Christ's appearances, we discover an affinity between them. Let us take St Luke as our guide, knowing that he will lead us along the road to Emmaus.

## St Luke's roads

Amongst the oldest Christian teachings on the sacraments we must include three accounts from St Luke: one from the Gospel (the disciples going to Emmaus) and two from the Acts of the Apostles (the conversion of St Paul and the baptism of the Ethiopian official).

Oddly, each of these events takes place on a road, and each one leads to the experience of a sacrament. The road to Emmaus leads to a eucharist; the roads to Damascus and to Gaza end with a baptism.

Is this by chance, or is it part of Luke's plan? These three roads represent the three main routes from Jerusalem! The Emmaus road comes down from the hills and goes towards the coast, allowing travellers to embark at Caesarea or Joppa, and so to reach the whole of the Mediterranean area. The Damascus road goes on to Asia Minor and Mesopo-tamia. The Gaza road carries on in the direction of Egypt, Ethiopia and Africa. There are no such routes of communication towards the east, as one all too quickly comes up against the Arabian desert.

The three narratives have an identical structure. They can be lined up as parallels. However, a development from one to the other is traceable. The Lord increasingly disappears, and the church assumes a more important place. On the Emmaus road, Jesus himself joins the disciples and presides over the eucharist. On the Damascus road, Paul 'sees a bright light, and hears a voice', and it is a Christian, Ananias, who baptizes him. On the Gaza road, the Ethiopian official is joined by the deacon Philip, impelled by the Spirit, and he receives baptism from the hands of his companion. It seems that Luke's intention was to lead us slowly from the resurrection experience of the first community to the experience we share in the life of the church after Pentecost. We relate more easily to the Ethiopian official than to the disciples on the way to Emmaus.

The structure which we find in these three narratives is close to that which underlies the accounts of the appearances of the Risen Christ in Luke as well as in John. We shall refer to them later on. Let us take the most developed narrative, that about Emmaus (Luke 24.13–35), and examine this ancient catechesis on the sacraments.

---

## How the sacraments work

A certain kind of common talk seems to make the sacraments into something quasi-magical. There is sometimes the feeling that it is enough for an action to be performed or a word to be spoken by someone who has the 'power' (a priest, a minister of the sacrament) for the result to be achieved.

That has never been the attitude of the church. It is obvious, for example, that God's forgiveness in absolution cannot be effective without co-operation from the person who receives it. What is the effect on someone baptized at birth who has never afterwards been aware of this baptism? God alone knows. But Vatican II reminded us that the sacraments are sacraments of faith. We must therefore get out of the habit of thinking of the sacraments as magic, and rediscover the place of human freedom; this recognizes the action of God in the dialogue of faith. The sacraments are effective because they express our life of faith. They are there to awaken our faith, to provoke it. And that is not done instantaneously. We have to take time over our journey. Luke suggests this in his story of the pilgrims on the road to Emmaus.

---

## The Emmaus road

This story is very well known. Let us look at it closely in order to grasp the details. Between the time that the two men are walking disconsolately along the road which leads away from Jerusalem and the time when they find themselves reunited with the other disciples, something has happened. They have lived through a slow evolution. We can set it out in three stages.

- a mysterious presence
- a difficult recognition
- the birth of the church

## A mysterious presence on the human road

That very day two of them were going to a village named Emmaus, about seven miles from Jerusalem, and talking with each other about all these things that had happened.

'That very day': we have only to look at the beginning of the chapter to discover that this means 'the first day of the week', the one which was to become the Lord's Day, Sunday. That is the day of the resurrection, the one on which the Lord appeared to his disciples.

These men walking along the road, talking between themselves about what had happened, are ourselves, are all humankind. And it is on our journey that the Lord makes himself known.

While they were talking and discussing together, Jesus himself drew near and went with them. But their eyes were kept from recognizing him.

It is not that men and women go towards the meeting with Christ; it is the other way round. We are surprised to find him there where we did not expect him. Each of us is occupied with our own concerns and is not thinking that the Lord can appear in front of us. The travellers to Emmaus were returning home, Mary Magdalene was weeping over a dead man, the apostles were fishing on Lake Tiberias. Later on, Paul left for Damascus for a police operation and the Ethiopian official was going back to his own country. The Lord is there, at a bend in the road. He gets involved in everyday life. He converses with the disciples going to Emmaus, he questions Mary Magdalene. He waits on the shore for the fishermen to return. And yet even those closest to him do not recognize him!

Here we have valuable pointers to the sacraments. If we look at the plan on page 24, we see that the horizontal arrow represents the human road upon which, at any moment, someone might appear. We show this meeting by the vertical arrow. In all our pastoral teaching on the sacraments we must respect the two arrows, or we run the risk of two diversions.

The first is to forget that the meeting must take place on the human road. The sacraments are administered without regard for the individual history of each one. When they are not related to life, their use is artificial, and they have about as much effect as a poultice on a wooden leg!

The second diversion is concerned with the vertical arrow. We sometimes carry on as if a human life lived out faithfully must necessarily lead to God. That is to forget that the initiative comes from God and that we are only the servants in a meeting.

Let's take an example. A boy and a girl love each other and want to get married. That is the road on which the Lord joins them. When insufficient attention is paid to how they live, the sacraments appear impersonal to them. They will not taste their riches. But if we believe that the fact of their loving each other will always lead to Jesus Christ, we forget the vertical arrow; we do not disclose the Lord as the one who comes to disrupt the quiet surface of their life.

## The difficulty of recognition

'Their eyes were kept from recognizing him.'

Here we have one of the recurring themes of the accounts of the appearances of the Risen Christ. Mary Magdalene believed him to be the gardener, the apostles in the upper room thought that he was a ghost. On Lake Tiberias, Peter and his friends had difficulty in identifying their mysterious companion. The end of Mark's Gospel even says: 'He appeared to them in other forms.' In this way, the first witnesses wanted to alert us to the difficulty we always come up against in recognizing this presence of the Lord.

We should remember this in all sacramental life. As old Christians we too easily forget this difficulty and we speak of the faith as an obvious truth. Ought we not to respect a slow development, in which a number of hurdles have to be cleared? It is only at the end of his account that Luke says: 'Their eyes were opened and they recognized him.' We can easily detect the stages of this development in the Gospel. Let us pinpoint them.

Jesus begins by accompanying them on their journey. He becomes involved in their concerns. To share someone's journey means sharing their hopes and their disappointments as well: it is being involved together in the same adventure.

'What is this conversation which you are holding with each other as you walk?' And they stood still, looking sad . . . We had hoped that he was the one to redeem Israel. Yes, and besides all this, it is now the third day since this happened.

If in present-day meeting with the Risen Christ, the church has to assure the real presence of the Lord along the road human beings have to travel, Christians have to share the journey with them. The sacraments can only be the signs of the Lord's presence in so far as the community, which is the body of Christ, shares in the hopes and disappointments of other people.

The text includes a detail which is not without humour. It is perhaps to get over the difficulties posed by the proclamation of the resurrection that Luke records:

Moreover, some women of our company amazed us. They were at the tomb early in the morning and did not find his body; and they came back saying that they had even seen a vision of angels, who said that he was alive. Some of those who were with us went to the tomb, and found it just as the women had said; but him they did not see.

For those who judge by external appearances, the proclamation of the resurrection easily seemed like 'old wives' tales', daydreams. And as for the apostles, those of the present day as well as those of the past, they could not say much, because they had not seen anything themselves!

*Re-reading life in the light of scripture*

The second stage is that of re-reading life. How can one progress in one's recognition of the Risen Christ without allowing one's life to come face to face with the Word of God? That is what Jesus did with his companions on the way to Emmaus. The disciples had lived with him, they had shared a common past. Everything that concerned him concerned them. That is what they were talking about on the road.

And he said to them, 'O foolish men, and slow of heart to believe all that the prophets have spoken! Was it not necessary that the Christ should suffer these things and enter into his glory?' And beginning with Moses and all the prophets, he interpreted to them in all the scriptures the things concerning himself.

Here was no theoretical course on the necessity of suffering before entering into glory. Jesus was thinking of his own life. The Gospels often emphasize how he himself was accustomed to read his own life in the light of scripture.

This is why, on the cross, he cried, 'My God, my God, why have you forsaken me?' Many will not grasp the allusion. If one were to tell them that he had said, 'Our Father', they would go and search in the rest of the prayer to discover what Christ was thinking at that particular moment. The opening words of Psalm 22, 'My God, my God, why have you forsaken me?' shed light on our understanding of the whole of the crucified Jesus' suffering and loneliness. But this same psalm ends with a great declaration of hope which imparts its whole dimension to the drama of Calvary:

I will tell of your name to my brethren;
in the midst of the congregation I will praise you.
All the ends of the earth shall remember
    and turn to the Lord.
Posterity shall serve him;
they shall tell of the Lord to the coming generation,
and proclaim his deliverance to a people yet unborn,
that he has wrought it.

In the sacramental life, it is up to the church, to us, to understand human life in the light of scripture. That assumes that we are capable of doing it as far as we ourselves are personally concerned, and also that we are solidly for other people.

And so in the sacrament of marriage, for example, it is quite normal for there to be Christians who are already married, living their partnership and their love in faith, who will put themselves at the disposal of engaged couples to help them discover the light of God's word.

### The presence of the paschal mystery

It is not surprising if, here as in the other accounts of the appearances of the Risen Christ, we find an allusion to the drama of the Passion:

Was it not necessary that the Christ should suffer these things and enter into his glory?

In the upper room, Jesus showed the marks of the nails and the hole in his side. He would say to Paul on the Damascus road: 'I will show him how much he must suffer for my name's sake. And Luke recorded that the Ethiopian official was in the act of reading the Song of the Suffering Servant (Isa. 52.13–53.12).

Imagine people who have been separated for a long time, such as those whom war or exile have forced to live apart from each other. When they are reunited at last, they have to 'recognize' each other again. Day by day, over the years, they have lived unrelated life stories, and different sufferings and joys have left their mark on them. Much patience is needed for them to meet again, for them really to recognize each other. Each one has to try to travel part of the journey made by the other. Now between the evening of Maundy Thursday and the morning of Easter Day, Jesus has lived through an abyss. He has passed through death. How would his friends be able to recognize him unless they undertook to travel the same road with him?

It is the same for us. In order to recognize Christ on our way there will always be a passage through death. Therein lies faith. That is the law that governs a grain of wheat, which does not bear fruit unless it dies. The Lord said: 'If anyone wants to be my disciple, let him take up his cross and follow me.'

Every sacrament is participation in Christ's Pasch. So marriage inscribes the paschal mystery on human love. The project of fidelity which comprises a true covenant is the presence of death and resurrection. Faithfulness borders on the absurd. It proclaims that a love which is to survive has always to be rising from its ashes.

### The invitation

So they drew near to the village to which they were going. He appeared to be going further, but they constrained him, saying, 'Stay with us, for it is toward evening and the day is now far spent.'

Nothing would have happened had that invitation not been given. Human freedom depends on that. For Christ indicates his presence. But the moment comes when we have to jump that hurdle. There is no certainty, unless it is that growing conviction: 'Did not our hearts burn within us while he talked to us on the road, while he opened to us the scriptures?' We do not yet know who he is, and yet already we want him to stay longer with us.

Every sacrament contains this part of ourselves. Let us take an adult's preparation for baptism. A time is needed for development. The day comes when the Christian community believes that baptism is possible, but the decision still belongs to those who are offering themselves. They alone are able to 'invite' the Lord to enter into their lives.

In the same way, by Lake Tiberias, Peter threw himself into the water to join the mysterious stranger who waited on the bank.

### The sign of recognition

So he went in to stay with them. When he was at table with them, he took the bread and blessed, and broke it, and gave it to them. And their eyes were opened and they recognized him.

This is how we take part in the liturgical celebration. There is always a sign which is put like a seal on the long road towards recognition. In the evening at Emmaus, this was the breaking of bread. On the road to Damascus, it was the baptism given by Ananias to Paul, and 'immediately something like scales fell from his eyes and he regained his sight'. On the road to Gaza, it was also the sign of baptism.

Similarly, we are able to discover this sign in the

other narratives of the appearances of the Risen Christ. For Mary Magdalene in front of the tomb it was the single word 'Mary', and she realized that the man she had taken for the gardener was the Lord. At the lakeside, Jesus cooked the fish and invited the disciples to eat, and no one dared ask him who he was 'because they knew it was the Lord' (John 21.12). In the upper room, Jesus said: 'See my hands and my feet, that it is I myself.'

This sign is taken from everyday life. It is usually a sign of something lived out with Jesus of Nazareth before his passion which is relived after the resurrection, as a kind of link between the before and after of the Lord's Easter. Jesus had to say quite firmly, 'It is I myself!'

In our day, through the sacramental sign, those who did not live in Palestine with Jesus of Nazareth have the means of recognizing him in their turn. In all our sacraments there is a sign. It is made use of in the liturgy. To begin with, it was equally a sign from everyday life, but it assumed new significance through its use by the first Christian community who saw it as a remembrance, a memorial, of something they had lived out with Jesus. So it is with the breaking of bread, and also with the immersion of baptism or the laying on of hands.

Has not the mission of the church throughout the ages been to keep alive the signs which allow men and women to recognize the Lord's presence in all ages and in all places?

### The birth of the church and its mission

And they rose that same hour and returned to Jerusalem; and they found the eleven gathered together and those who were with them, who said, 'The Lord has risen indeed, and has appeared to Simon!' Then they told what had happened on the road, and how he was known to them in the breaking of the bread.

The liturgical celebration is not the end of everything. It is a new starting point.

Everything had changed in the life of these people. They had been discouraged, they were

---

## Emmaus and the liturgical celebration

The structure of the Emmaus story also allows us to discover that of all our liturgical celebrations.

- The Christians meet together again. They need to take time to *'talk together about what has happened'*.
- The Lord himself *'interpreted to them in all the scriptures the things concerning himself'*. That is the liturgy of the word.
- We invite him to sit at table with us. That is the occasion of the offertory.
- It is the Lord who presides: *'he takes bread and blesses and breaks it, and gives it to us'*. Then our eyes are opened and we recognize his presence. That is the eucharistic liturgy.
- *'Our hearts burned within us, while he opened to us the scriptures'*, but we have to take to the road again to proclaim to our brothers and sisters that the Lord has risen. That is our mission to the world.

---

joyful. They returned to their homes, they went out into the community. They travelled the same road, but in a different direction.

The recognition of the Risen Christ built the church up into a confession of common faith. Each one related to the others how he or she had recognized the Lord. The certainty of the meeting with the Christ was reinforced by the faith of the community which rested on the witness of its first member, the rock, Simon Peter. It was like a new liturgy which gathered all the world together. And this is what is needed to rediscover the presence of the Lord.

And as they were saying this, Jesus himself stood among them and said to them, 'Peace be to you!' But they were startled and frightened, and supposed that they saw a spirit. And he said to them, 'See my hands and my feet, that it is I myself.'

We glibly say that 'the church makes the sacraments', but it is just as correct to say that 'the sacraments make the church'. The Risen Lord builds his church, and brings his disciples together in a common confession of faith. They proclaim a gospel amongst themselves, the good news, that of the presence of the living Lord in the world where they are.

The birth of the church is intimately connected with mission. The Holy Spirit sends the disciples out into the world to be witnesses to the resurrection.

> Thus it is written, that the Christ should suffer and on the third day rise from the dead, and that repentance and forgiveness of sins should be preached in his name to all nations, beginning from Jerusalem. You are witnesses of these things. And behold, I send the promise of my Father upon you.

## Conclusion

This teaching of the early church makes us realize how the sacrament cannot be instantly reduced to the moment of its celebration. It comprises the whole road, and not merely the moment of the breaking of bread. If there had only been that liturgical action of the Christ, would the disciples have recognized Jesus? Would their road have been transformed? It was necessary for all the preceding stages to be passed through for the end to be achieved.

It is the same for the church today. We shall see more clearly the importance of the length of time needed to establish the relationship between faith and sacrament when, in the next chapter, we study the significance of the sacramental stages and the celebrations which mark them.

# The sacraments of faith

The second Vatican Council thought to describe the sacraments thus: 'Not only do the sacraments presuppose faith, but by words and objects they also nourish, strengthen, and express it. That is why they are called "sacraments of faith"' (*Constitution on the Sacred Liturgy*, 59). And Cardinal Villot affirmed: 'The sacrament, as a sacrament of faith, requires a preliminary evangelization which prepares the faith of the one who is to receive it to be in a position to understand it, to live it out, and to translate it into reality' (Letter to the Bishops' Conference of Latin America, *Observatore Romano*, 16 August 1977).

The church has always held that the sacraments ought to be lived out within the faith. But that is easily assumed when one is in a time and place where almost everyone belongs to the believing community. That is often called a state of *Christendom*. Education in faith is then carried out by the family and by the environment, and anyone who attends a sacramental celebration is thought of as a participant who knows what he or she is doing. Fifty years or so ago, when a family asked for a child to be baptized, one could be almost certain that this would be followed up by a Christian education. This is still the case in some areas.

But contemporary civilization has altered the terms of the problem. A majority of the people around us live outside any explicit confession of Christian faith. Religious practices are sometimes kept up more or less out of habit, without any clear perception of their significance. And so we encounter young people who come to be married in church, partly under pressure from their families, partly to do the 'done thing', and partly, too, to take their commitment seriously, but without having the intention or the means to live out their commitment as Christians. Out of concern for the truth, the Church then asks them to take time to prepare themselves. Either by sessions with a priest or by evenings spent in marriage prepara-tion classes, it is possible for them to make progress in the discovery of faith. That is what Cardinal Villot calls 'a preliminary evangelization'.

Relevant here is the declaration made by a working party consisting of experts from the Congregation for the Doctrine of Faith and experts from the French Conference of Bishops:

'It is common for engaged couples to apply to the church as their marriage approaches, saying honestly that they are acceding to the wishes of their families or others, but that they do not consider that they belong to the church community or confess faith in Jesus Christ. Even the meaning of a sacrament is alien to them, and moreover they have no intention whatsoever of participating in the other sacraments of the eucharist and reconciliation at their wedding.

It is necessary to find a way to enlighten them so that, if possible, they change their attitude, or give up this request in order to keep faith with themselves and with the church community. The priest ought also to help the family to see the matter from his perspective, and respect the consciences of the engaged couple.'

The sacraments presuppose an attitude of faith. At the very least, this is the willingness to carry out a religious act laid down by the Christian community. This community often welcomes participants who are only at the start of their journey. That is why they are asked to take their time, only accept Christ as their companion on the road, and with simple trust set themselves to listen to the Word of God. It is a suggestion which can be made equally well to engaged couples preparing for marriage, to parents considering the baptism of their child, or to adults asking for baptism. It is not an indoctrination; it is the journey of the Emmaus pilgrims. In this way, we can say that the sacraments nurture faith.

# PART TWO

# The Church Celebrates the Sacraments

So far we have been looking mainly at the New Testament. We have gathered together the witness of the first Christian groups.

Now we must return to the life of the Christian communities that we know and in which we share. Today the church lives out the sacraments and they provide the structure for its liturgy. Today all Christians have their lives marked by celebrations which are like mileposts along their way.

Some recur regularly, like the eucharist on Sunday or the practice of reconciliation. Others mark the great moments of life: baptism marks entering the church, marriage the start of a home, ordination appointment to the service of the community, anointing of the sick the afflictions of suffering and illness.

Common to all these celebrations is that they are expressed in a ritual universe. Now our 'technological' world is often ill at ease with rites and particularly with religious rites. Some people ask whether these rites should not be seen as sheer survivals of an outmoded world, a stage of humanity that will never return.

At the same time, the progress of the human sciences over the last thirty years has rehabilitated this whole appeal to a symbolic universe which is a human characteristic and the mark of all civilizations.

In this light it is good to take one's bearings. That is why this second part is concerned with the liturgical activity of communities of the Roman rite and the way in which they express themselves during the celebration of the different sacraments.

We shall first look at the actual moment of celebration, which for every sacrament is the action in which everything comes together and takes form: that is Chapter 5.

Chapter 6 brings together some facts from the 'human sciences' to help us see the importance of the symbolic universe.

The presence of the sacraments is attested from the beginning of the church, but the word came into use only gradually and the content of the notion of sacrament has become more precise down the centuries. Chapter 7 will allow us to locate the sacraments in the history of the church.

Chapter 8 will then resume theological reflection, in the light of the texts of the Second Vatican Council, to provide a context for the different persons involved in the celebration. In every sacrament it is Christ who acts through his church.

# 5

# The Sacrament is a Way

## Stages

The yachts which leave for a round-the-world race have their route marked from port to port. Great races and great rallies, like great voyages, need to have a route which is broken down into successive stages.

There is nothing more human than this way of dividing a test, for our lives themselves often appear as a series of stages, each of which has its riches and its demands. The route changes, the horizon varies, and the travellers themselves mature and progress, acquiring a greater mastery.

There are also stages along the way on which God leads us. And this image of a route to be covered is as ancient in the biblical tradition as the old stories which told of the journey of the people of God in the desert of Sinai when they left for the Promised Land.

Everything takes place over a period: there is no waving of a magic wand, but a slow maturing. One of the riches of liturgical reform promoted by Vatican II is the way in which it has allowed the deployment of this sense of time in sacramental life. So we rediscover the intuition of the first Christians that we indicated when speaking of 'St Luke's roads', in particular the discovery of the risen Christ on the way to Emmaus.

## The sense of 'time' in the sacramental process

*Homo viator*, says the old tradition of the church: human beings are travellers. They constantly accomplish a Pasch. God accompanies them on their way. God reveals himself to them, gives them the light of his word, the power of his Spirit.

If the sacraments transform our lives, they cannot do so without our collaboration. They become a place of permanent dialogue between God and human beings. God comes to meet us, but we must discover God and live for God. This transformation of our lives, this 'transfiguration', to take up an image of the Gospel, calls for co-operation between individual men and women, with all their faculties, intelligence, will and dynamism, and the Holy Spirit, a co-operation which is always reborn. The sacrament has to be given time to do its work. Liturgical celebration is a point in time, but it only takes place in a history which goes on. The time which precedes the celebration and that which follows it are also part of the sacrament.

The church is this people of God on the way, and within it each person can follow his or her own route. Liturgical celebrations are not the 'whole' of the sacramental life. They are its 'source and climax'. Like so many stages along our way, they are like the inn at Emmaus where the Lord made

35

himself known. The mission of Christian communities is to keep these Emmaus inns alive and open, so that everyone can be invited to go in. The Lord has already set the table, where he waits for us to 'break the bread'.

One of the aims of liturgical reform has been to rediscover this sense of duration. Two factors have helped here: the importance which the Council has attached to faith as the bedrock of all celebrations, and the rediscovery, over recent decades, of the adult catechumenate.

---

## Time and the moment

There is the time of the sacrament and there is the moment of its celebration.

The moment is of short duration. It is the half-hour at church for a baptism. It is a marriage feast with its religious celebration. It is the few minutes devoted to a confession.

Time weds the inherent duration of the sacrament to all of human life. The time of baptism is the whole life of the Christian. And all the world knows that a marriage is not just experienced in the singing and feasting, but that it lasts through days, months and years.

The grace of the sacrament is not given solely at the moment when one finds oneself in front of the priest. It is the power of the Spirit, ceaselessly offered, ceaselessly to be accepted, for the way opened at the time of the celebration.

But do we have to believe that the grace of the sacrament begins only with the action of the priest? Is that not too simplistic a way of considering these matters? The Spirit is always at work when two beings meet and decide to make a covenant. It is the Spirit which transforms the human heart so that a process of reconciliation is undergone. And the grace of the sacrament of baptism does not wait for the rite of water to be the source of living water and the riches of the gift of God to the catechumen.

---

*The rediscovery of the stages of the catechumenate*

The church has a long experience of the unfolding of the sacramental stages. In particular it made use of them for the entry of new Christians into the community. That is how Christian initiation was structured over the first centuries, an initiation which took place during a catechumenate.

The catechumenate is this time which extends from the moment an adult comes to ask for baptism to the last part of the celebration of the sacrament. It is of indeterminate duration; that depends on the individual. It is a way which has to be followed, during which the demand becomes more specific, faith becomes deeper, and knowledge of the content of this faith develops. Those who have entered into the catechumenate are already part of the Christian community, but they have a separate place. And the liturgical celebrations are spaced out over this period, marking both the commitment of the community as the companions of the persons about to be baptized, and the progress of these persons in the confession of their faith.

Except in the so-called mission countries, the church had lost the habit of the catechumenate, and thirty years ago the celebration of the baptism of an adult was performed in the course of a single ceremony, which put one after another elements of liturgies which originally unfolded over quite lengthy periods of time.

From before Vatican II, first in Lyons and then in Paris, the catechumenate had been restored, taking its inspiration from the first centuries of the church. The habit was resumed of distinguishing the different ceremonies, called the stages of baptism.

These liturgical stages are all sacramental, but the interval between each of them, with the catechesis and the friendly meetings which it involves, are also part of the sacrament. By this very fact the Christian community lives out with intensity this prolonged time as a treasure as much for itself as for the catechumen.

Without any doubt, this very rich experience has had a great influence on pastoral work, and also on theological thought about all the sacraments.

The fundamental relationship between catechesis and celebration has come to be understood better. Hence the comment by Cardinal Villot: 'The sacrament, as a sacrament of faith, requires a prior evangelization which prepares the faith of the one who is to receive it to be in a position to understand it, to live it out, and to translate it into reality' (Letter of Cardinal Villot, cited in the previous chapter).

A first pastoral effort has been made for young couples: marriage preparation centres have been created to provide appropriate catechesis. Then the same kind of action has been taken, though requiring less time, to prepare parents for the celebration of the baptism of their child.

It is important to remember that baptism is not the only example of a sacrament the celebration of which is spread out over time.

For long centuries, the sacrament of reconciliation was also experienced in stages. Absolution was not given immediately after confession as happens nowadays. The Christian who wanted to be reconciled embarked on penance, went through a process marked by liturgical celebrations, leading up to the great ceremony, often held on Maundy Thursday, when the bishop reconciled penitents. We have kept traces of this in Lenten observances.

The rite of reconciliation arising out of Vatican II allows us to rediscover this way. So certain Christ-

## Stages in the sacraments

To help reflection, we can identify three characteristics which seem necessary for one to be able to speak of sacramental stages.

1. *Stages of faith*
These are not simply stages of life like, for example, engagement and marriage. In this case there are two stages, but they do not involve a deepening of faith. It is not enough to make them the stages of the same sacrament.

Let us see what happens in an adult baptism. The stages relate to faith. They are accompanied by a catechesis. They are moments of conversion. One cannot say to someone, 'For the time being you should have a non-sacramental celebration of marriage, and if you develop you can come back to us.' In the stages of the sacraments the church does not remain in waiting, but takes action through a happening within the community.

2. *Being on the way*
The stages are a progression. It is not just a matter of waiting, in case people want to go on. What needs to be done next is worked out between each stage. There is as it were a way to follow.

Here is an example. If you want to go from London to Manchester you have to take the right road. If when you get to Birmingham you stop there without any intention of saying when you are going to continue the journey, it is difficult to say that you are still on the way. It's the same with the sacraments.

Marriage by stages cannot in any case be a trial marriage, any more than customary marriage is in some African countries. So there is a way of checking how serious the approach is. It is for the Christian community to be the witness to this.

3. *The institution of a way by the church*
The celebration of a sacrament is an official act of the church. It is for the church to fix the discipline. That is what the Council did when it called for the restoration of the stages of baptism and the catechumenate. It is not a matter of the individual initiative of a priest or a team, as was sometimes the case with so-called 'non-sacramental' marriages.

These steps have to be capable of being suggested officially to those who come. They do not have to be compulsory, since situations of faith can be different for each person. But in this sphere the liturgy cannot be uninterested in canon law, for the church has to be able to name the sacraments.

ian communities have adopted the habit of marking the time of Lent by a penitential sequence lasting from Ash Wednesday to the days before Easter (see Chapter 12).

We can also recall that the diaconate and the priesthood form as it were the stages of the sacrament of order. During seminary years they are preceded by the call to other ministries like those of lector or acolyte. The whole process is lived out as a long journey in which everything contributes to a life of faith illuminated by the sacraments (see Chapter 10).

The time of children's catechetical instruction is also that of a real Christian initiation (see Chapter 11) marked by sacramental stages. During these years those who have received baptism at birth receive first communion and confirmation. In their catechism class the others go through the whole process from the 'entry into the community' to baptism in the Spirit given at confirmation.

Concerning the sacrament of marriage, the church has adopted the habit of not suggesting religious marriage unless the customary formalities have been gone through. For the couple, this results in an irregular situation *vis à vis* canon law. And during this time they are excluded from sacramental communion. It is a curious situation for the community when those who are excluded are the best families, those which give life to the community and sometimes even those who distribute communion without being able to take part in it. That raises the question whether a religious marriage could not be celebrated in stages.

## The moment of celebration

### What is the use of celebration?

The sacrament lasts over a period. The celebration of it is just a privileged moment. There is a risk that we should not underestimate. In discovering the relationship of the sacrament to everyday life one can come to find the celebration optional and ultimately without interest, whereas it is the heart of the sacrament. It is the 'source and the climax', as

the Council is fond of repeating.

To understand how this question can arise we shall begin by giving some examples, despite the risk that they may prove caricatures.

Here's a first one. A quarrel between a couple has divided the two partners deeply. However, each of them, after a longer or shorter process, agrees to reconciliation with the other in faith. They truly live out this reconciliation as a work of the Spirit. One can say that their life becomes a sign and realization of God's forgiveness. Through them the face of God is present in our world. Here we have the sacrament of reconciliation in action. But why, once unity has been restored, is it necessary to go to a priest to ask absolution from him? Isn't this pure formalism? Isn't this a lapse into a quasi-magical view of the sacrament? Is God waiting for the action of the priest to give his forgiveness?

Let's take another. We have heard talk of 'baptism of desire'. A person has been preparing very seriously for baptism for several months. She has joined the catechumenate. She has gone through the first liturgical stages. She has been called to baptism by the bishop. But on the way to the Paschal vigil on which she was to be baptized she is hit by a truck and killed. The church has always affirmed that she already had the grace of baptism. She had the baptism of desire.

Is it because she was hit by a truck that she receives the grace of baptism? Surely not. The truck is not the minister of the sacrament. So did she have this grace before the accident? Beyond any doubt. But since when? Does another catechumen to whom no accident happens also have the grace of baptism before the celebration? If that is the case, what reason does he have for joining in this celebration? Doesn't it seem useless and even superfluous?

As with the breaking of the bread with the disciples at Emmaus, liturgical celebration is necessary if one is to speak of a sacrament in a strict sense. It is not an optional moment, but that in which everything takes shape. It polarizes everything; it makes the sacrament.

The sacrament is a whole. 'Sacramental grace' exists before the celebration, but it cannot be dissociated from it. The fullness of the sacrament is lived out because of the very intention of the subject. Like the pilgrims of Emmaus, he or she is really on the way; the Lord accompanies them and gives them his Spirit.

Our plan is not to justify the liturgical celebration of the sacraments, since that is of their essence. Nevertheless it is worth pausing for a few moments and indicating, in an explanatory language which is poorer than reality, something of how they work.

---

## Living the life of God

When I was a child, in the catechism class the priest talked of grace. He did a beautiful drawing on the board. You could see God at the top and man at the bottom.

Between the two, to begin with, there was no continuous communication. That did not prevent God from sending 'help' to people in distress from time to time. It was rather like parachuting in supplies, or like the 'Flying Doctor'. But in normal times, people were reduced to their own resources.

At the moment of baptism, a continuous link was set up between God and man, like a pipeline: a flow passing from God to man. The priest called it 'sanctifying grace'. At that moment man had a permanent relationship with God. If he committed a mortal sin, it was like a bomb blowing up the pipeline. Man lost sanctifying grace. He had to make a repair, re-establish the link with God, and this was done by going to confession. If a person committed a venial sin it was as if the pipeline got clogged, and the fluid flowed less well. With many venial sins the pipeline was almost blocked. It had to be cleaned, always by confession.

There were difficult moments, hard blows. The pipeline was not enough to feed man, and then God had to make more parachute drops. They were called 'actual grace'.

There were also permanent situations in which life placed us, like an arduous task to perform, state duty to fulfil, responsibility to take on. The priest quoted as an example 'the heavy responsibility of parents in the education of children'. God did not abandon his faithful friends and at that time gave them 'states of grace'.

The sacraments were of this kind, like a supplementary pipeline aimed primarily at allowing one to survive a situation. They gave as it were permanent states of grace. The sacrament of marriage gave the family grace to stick together and for children to be well brought up. The sacrament of order helped the priest to do his work well. The sacrament of the sick made it possible to withstand with courage the hard battle before death.

The eucharist was a means put at our disposal every day, or every Sunday, so that the grace of God could abound and allow us to live truly as Christians.

When I became older, I understood that talking of grace was a way of expressing what God tells us constantly, 'I will be with you', as he said to Moses, Jeremiah, the apostles and others. It also took up the image used by Jesus when he said, 'I am the vine and you are the branches.' It was above all an understanding of the promise, 'I will not leave you comfortless, I will send you the Spirit of truth.' Evoking grace is a matter of evoking the generosity of God who gives people power to participate in his riches, to live out his life. It is a matter of discovering that we are allowed to live as true children, in the image of the one who is the Son of God. It is a matter of letting our lives take on a new dimension, that which God can give. It is a matter of being 'reborn from above', of living according to the Spirit, already participating in the resurrection and the new world.

In this sense, the sacraments which are the expression of our life in the light of God and under the guidance of the Spirit are also the moment when God shows himself to us as being very close in Jesus Christ, so that we are truly the members of the body of Christ living out his life.

## Dispossession of the self

The sacrament is a gift, and we need to welcome it as such. We are not the ones who perform the work of God. We cannot attribute merit to ourselves. We live out this dispossession in celebration. The role of the 'minister' is to demonstrate the sacramental act as an act of Christ through his church.

You cannot baptize yourself; you are always baptized by someone. Even if the person who administers baptism is not necessarily a priest but, in emergencies, a lay person, perhaps even a non-Christian, when he or she baptizes they have the intention of doing what the church does and by that very fact manifest this initiative of God.

As soon as the minister is involved there is a celebration, even if this is extremely simple. When a small child is baptized by the midwife at birth that is already a celebration of baptism.

The president at a eucharist acts in the name of Christ. He demonstrates that the community does not own its eucharist, but that it is receiving it as a gift from the Lord.

It is the same with the sacrament of reconciliation. In mutually forgiving one another we take the way of the sacrament. But it also makes us live out this mutual forgiveness as a gift of the Spirit and as an expression of the forgiveness of God himself. 'Whose sins you shall forgive they shall be forgiven, and whose sins you retain they shall be retained.' That is when the celebration takes place, and the absolution given by the priest manifests this part which does not come from ourselves. It gives our reconciliation its full dimension of faith.

## Naming the sacraments

The church needs to name the sacraments, that is, to identify them. The celebration is necessary, since the sacraments have a social dimension, they are the actions of the whole body.

When a baptism has been performed privately, for example at the birth of a child who is in mortal danger (what is called a private baptism), the church asks that later, once the danger is past, there shall be a supplementary ceremony. Celebration at the church makes the sacraments visible.

---

### Grace

In the Bible, grace is primarily a quality of God, 'Lord God of tenderness and grace' (Ex. 34.6). This grace is goodness and mercy. Grace is also the gift which God gives to men and women: it is the fruit of his generosity, the benediction that he gives them. For Christians, grace is the gift which God gives when he makes us participants in his life. It is the work of the Holy Spirit, for the spirit is the gift *par excellence*.

Every sacrament is a gift of God welcomed in faith; it is a part of human life illuminated by the Spirit. It is the reason why we speak of 'sacramental grace'.

---

A couple who make a covenant together by that fact live out the sacrament. One might think that there was no need for them to celebrate it in church, and that has often happened down the centuries (see Chapter 13). However, nowadays marriage has to take place before a qualified witness. In geographical areas where the priest comes only rarely to visit remote communities, marriages must be performed before two members of the community as witnesses.

By this fact the church authenticates the sacraments. Those who have asked for baptism know by its celebration that they have become participants in the community of faith. In their eyes and those of their friends, the long way that they have pursued so far has the character of an authentic Christian process. They need this 'seal' from the official church on their desire to confess faith in Jesus Christ.

## Making the church

The moment of celebration is the moment when one goes to church to receive the gift of God. One then finds other Christians. The members of the community who are present are not simple spectators. They are themselves called to live out a new relationship with the one for whom the sacrament is celebrated.

In the baptism of a new member, the whole community experiences the mystery of the death and resurrection of the Lord. At the moment of a marriage everyone is invited to rediscover the God of the covenant. That is why it is asserted that 'the church makes the sacraments, but the sacraments make the church'. We shall develop this point further in the next chapter, which will deal with the ecclesial aspect of the sacraments.

---

### Presiding

Christ, in the eucharist, gathers and nourishes his church by inviting it to the meal over which he presides.

The sign of this presiding is the presence of a minister.

The minister shows that the assembly does not own the action that it is in process of performing, that it is not mistress of the eucharist; it receives it from another, the Christ living in his church. While remaining a member of the assembly, the minister is also that envoy who signifies the initiative of God and the bond between the local community and the other communities in the universal church.

This text is taken from the document *Vers une même eucharistique*, written by the Dombes group, an ecumenical working party founded in 1937 by Abbé Couturier to work out a formulation of the faith which should be common to the different Christian confessions. The way in which it expresses the role of the minister in presiding at the eucharist can equally well apply to the celebration of another sacrament.

---

#### Confession of faith

Celebration is a communal confession of faith. The profession of faith of the one who receives this sacrament is linked to that of the whole community. All together affirm faith in Jesus Christ. They denote him as the one who acts through the Spirit and through his church.

In this way one meets up with the group of men and women who down the centuries of history have kept alive faith in the risen Lord. This group has its roots deep in the witness of the apostles and the first disciples. They are the ones who have handed down to us the sacraments as visible signs of the presence of Christ in the world.

It is not enough to offer mutual forgiveness for there to be a manifestation of God's forgiveness. It is necessary to proclaim that this forgiveness is given to us; it is necessary to name Jesus Christ over the forgiveness that we are experiencing. Just as when a mother is being reconciled with her child, as often happens in family life, this reconciliation itself becomes a profession of faith when it is lived out again in sacramental absolution.

#### The sacrament is prophetic

The sacrament proclaims a reality which is already there but which has not yet reached its fullness. It leads us towards a fulfilment, it opens a way, it goes forward. It is the announcement of the New Times. That is what the theologians call the eschatological aspect of the sacrament. This tension towards the future has to be expressed in celebration. For each person is aware of not yet having arrived at the goal.

So a priestly ordination is prepared for over long years. On the day of ordination the seminarian officially becomes a priest. But his journey is not over. What has just been proclaimed has to be lived out in everyday life. One could say that he has to become what he is! Like the young couple who, though married in church, have still to 'marry' every day of the lives that they have in front of them.

The texts of the word of God proclaimed during the celebration are not there to tell us what we are living out. They call us, rather, to enter into the mystery of Christ more genuinely. They proclaim the horizon towards which we are going.

When during a marriage the couple want a secular text, a poem, to be read, they often choose it because in their view it is a good expression of their experience of life. But if one proclaims a text of the

Gospel one does so more to speak of Jesus Christ, who alone has fully realized the mystery that one wants to proclaim. Scripture was made to reveal the profound reality of which our life is simply the feeble image. In that respect it is prophetic.

Celebration allows us to put a distance between Christ and ourselves. It reveals the depth of the invisible. If there were not this distance, it would be difficult subsequently to accept what one was able to say in the celebration. For our life will doubtless contain as many failures as successes.

### The rite is always repetitive

Rites are always repetitive; that is a condition of their being rites, and of doing their work (see Chapter 6). Celebrations come one after another in the life of the community. We are often invited to them. From celebration to celebration the life of faith is nourished; the message of the gospel becomes richer and more inward.

Some sacraments are received only once by the same person, yet nevertheless they have an aspect of repetition, for we also experience them when they relate to others. At each baptism we rediscover the content of our own baptism. Young couples have no doubt taken part in many weddings before their own. They have begun to experience in advance what will become their own adventure, above all when they are invited to weddings of friends of the same age. And parents and grandparents relive their own celebration when they are moved by those of the generations which follow them.

### A call to the sacrament

Every sacrament is a call issued to the community of believers for others to participate in the sacrament. If no young people married in church any longer, many others would not even think that this sacrament is also for them.

So in certain parishes, every year there are several celebrations for first communion. When children see their friends taking communion for the first time, they are led to ask whether they too

---

## Eschatology

The word eschatology is formed of two Greek words: *logos*, which means talk about, and *eschaton*, which means the end. Eschatology thus denotes talk about the end of the world or about human destiny at the end of our lives.

So eschatology is tension towards the future, looking towards the fullness of the realities which are not yet there at the present state of our life. It speaks of the future of the human race, of the realization of history when it arrives at the fullness of time.

The New Testament does not see history as doomed to failure, but as directed by God's plan. Human beings are called to become a new creation: in Jesus Christ an old world has passed away and a new world has come (II Cor. 5.17).

'Your life is hidden with Christ in God. When Christ shall be manifested, he who is your life, you too will be manifested with him in glory' (Col. 3.4).

The sacraments are not just the expression of what we live out but also the prophecy of what all human beings are called to live out.

---

should make this decision. In this way each child feels called, while remaining free to give a response at the desired moment.

I remember a rural parish in South-West France forty years ago, where no men ever went to communion. At a diocesan eucharistic congress we were amazed by the reaction of a child in a catechism class who was astonished to see men going to the holy table. He then told his priest that he thought that communion was restricted to women. He would never have thought that he could take communion himself.

### For the world

The Vatican II Constitution on the Liturgy specifies: 'Liturgical actions are not private actions but celebrations of the church. That is why they belong to the entire body of the church, they manifest it and affect it.' The sacraments manifest the church. They reflect its true countenance.

The sacrament is far more than a moment of the liturgy. So it is not simply destined for those who have come to celebrate it. It participates in the proclamation of the gospel in the world. And it does so primarily when it is incarnate in the life of believers. So when couples try to live out the mystery of the covenant in everyday life, they are expressing a particular way of being human. One could say that in living out the sacraments every Christian is at the service of humankind.

But part of this proclamation of the Gospel is also done by the celebration. It often happens that non-believing friends are invited to weddings, baptisms and first communions. The liturgy then becomes a testimony of faith to non-Christians. In our age, when the institution of marriage is somewhat abandoned, we are well aware that any liturgical celebration sought by young married couples is important for the building of tomorrow's society.

All these reflections help us to understand the aim of liturgical celebration. But we have not yet reached the heart of the problem. To get there we have to rediscover the importance of the rite and the symbolic universe. That is what we shall try to do in the next chapter.

## Should secular texts be read in a celebration?

Can secular texts be read in a celebration? The question is often asked during preparations for a wedding. The couple would like to have a poem they have chosen, for example something from *The Little Prince*, or Khalil Gibran.

Sometimes it is a real advantage to read a secular text, but it must not lead to confusion. Care has to be taken so that it is given a different position from the word of God. There needs to be a change of voice, change of place. If the Word is proclaimed from the ambo, why not have this text read from the animator's desk?

It can serve as an introduction. Read before a passage of the Bible, it helps to demonstrate the human roots of the gospel message. Scripture often has a style and vocabulary remote from current language, and a contemporary text helps everyone involved to rediscover themselves in such a ceremony.

It can also come as a counterpoint, as a musical theme superimposed on the main melody. It demonstrates the resonances of the word of God in our lives.

Often it can be put at the end of the celebration. It prolongs the discovery that has just been made. It speaks of joy and hope. It opens up a way for tomorrow to be experienced in truth.

But this text should not be a discourse which weighs down the whole proceedings. Choose a poem, rather than too didactic, too moralizing a passage!

# 6

# The World of Rites and Symbols

*'The sacrament in the broad sense is thus a human reality which realizes and manifests an intervention of God in our world for human salvation. It has a visible face, that which signifies, and an invisible face, that which is signified. As a reality of the world, it is the object of rational analyses; as a divine reality it is the object of faith. However, it is important not to juxtapose the two realities, but to see that one arrives at the signified only through the signifier. The visible reality is read in faith as a saving action of God.'*

R. Coffy, *L'Eglise*

*'All theology is always a theology of secular anthropologies.'*

Karl Rahner

At the point where we are in our study of the sacraments it is time to ask ourselves about what Monsignor Coffy calls their 'visible face'. This is neither a pause nor a parenthesis but a change of perspective through which one is obliged to pass in order to understand the way in which they function. The sacraments are in fact 'divine realities' incarnate in 'the realities of the world'. How are they to be known, explained, celebrated, lived out, unless the two faces which make them up have been examined?

In human terms, the sacraments form part of the world of rites and symbols.

- They are complex realities: it takes time to decipher them.
- They are rich realities: even with the best of analyses they will never be exhausted.
- They are realities which are misunderstood and even decried (rites have not always had a good press!): they have to be rehabilitated.

- They are realities which concern human beings at their most profound depth: to understand them better, it is necessary to know human beings better.
- They are realities which the Lord has chosen, to maintain his active presence in our midst: they relate to the life of our faith, the vital significance of which we understand.

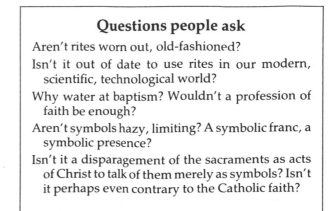

### Questions people ask

Aren't rites worn out, old-fashioned?

Isn't it out of date to use rites in our modern, scientific, technological world?

Why water at baptism? Wouldn't a profession of faith be enough?

Aren't symbols hazy, limiting? A symbolic franc, a symbolic presence?

Isn't it a disparagement of the sacraments as acts of Christ to talk of them merely as symbols? Isn't it perhaps even contrary to the Catholic faith?

45

## Rites and human beings

A difference appears only at the level of identity, and in our age it would be a misunderstanding to suppose that Christianity confiscates for its benefit elements which appear elsewhere, when often it has done no more than restructure them in a specific way (R. Dider, *Les sacraments de la foi*).

Christians of long standing, and above all those who have been part of a Christian milieu for several generations, have a tendency to think that the rite belongs to them, that the rites are naturally Christian: baptism, marriage, mass – they are ours, part of the Christian patrimony.

That is true. A number of rites are part of the continuing history of Christianity over two thousand years.

And it is false. Not only Christians use rites: think of the rites of courtesy among the Japanese, the funeral rites of all religions and even of unbelievers (the burial of a freethinker, funeral rites in the USSR). Furthermore not only Christians use the most specific rites of Christianity; not only Christians marry; not only Christians immerse themselves in water.

In reality, rites belong to everyone; one could almost say that human beings are ritualizing animals. In utilizing rites, Christianity does not invent but borrows a 'mechanism' which is part of the common resources of humanity. To this degree rites can be examined and studied by secular anthropology.

On the other hand, in using rites, the church Christianizes them. It does not use just anything and for just any purpose. And this part of the Christian rite will certainly be taken up by Christian anthropology and theology.

But the rites are one and the same, and their origins and constitutive elements are simply being distinguished for a better analysis.

### *What is a rite?*

A rite is a social operation, programmed, repetitive and symbolic, which, by means that bring into play the sphere of the irrational and the senses, aims at establishing a communication with the occult (the mysterious, the sacred).

A rite is a human approach towards that which goes beyond it but through which it seeks to take form (otherness, the Wholly Other, society, such and such a society). The word derives from the Indo-European root *R'tam* which denotes 'order'. Art, arithmetic, rhythm come from the same root.

*A rite is an operation*   It is an action, a process. It is something that one does. These are neither feelings nor states of mind: engaged couples marry because they love each other, but it is not because they love each other that they are married. Nor is the rite just a rubric which is simply the prescription for the performance of the rite. Ritualism and rubricism are reprehensible deviations, but their existence here or there should not undermine the need for the rite nor its greatness.

*A rite is a social operation*   It is something that one does not do by oneself. One does not clink glasses by oneself! And if by chance one does perform a rite by oneself (a funeral rite on the tomb of a child, the to-ings and fro-ings of a solitary pilgrim), it is precisely so as no longer to be alone, and to enter into relations with others.

*A rite is a programmed operation*   What has to be done is planned beforehand and has to be done as planned to arrive at the effect wanted, i.e. for it to be a rite. The rite of baptism aims at producing the integration of an individual with Christ and the church. To this end it is codified. In fact one has to know at the end of the rite whether the person has been effectively baptized or not, integrated or not.

To that degree the rite is conservative. But to that degree it also provides security and is 'democratic'. It is not invented; it is not the object of creativity in its basic elements. But it is protection against the unforeseen and guards against abuses of power.

*A rite is a repetitive operation*   Since it is planned and programmed, the rite exists only as it is repeated, as it is given as a prelude in which one must engage so as to obtain its effect. It is clear that a dead person only dies once, but one does not invent funeral rites for him or her. In connection with the dead person one embarks on the long chain of what happens when someone dies. In the short term this repetitiveness could seem a weakness. But on closer inspection it reveals the amazing dimension of the rite. By being repetitive the rite says that human beings are not human beings all by themselves, and above all that they are only human beings by integrating themselves into a humanity which is more than they are. Through rites, individuals receive their human identity from beyond themselves and maintain it by integrating themselves to it (it is worth noting that all these observations take on an even wider dimension in the case of the sacraments, as Christian rites).

*A rite is a symbolic operation*    The symbolic character of the rite underlies this social repetitiveness. We shall analyse the symbol at a later stage, but we can already note that the rite is an action which binds and brings together. It does not exist for a particular person, but for the relationship which it allows and establishes. It is necessary, but it is not an end in itself. One does not baptize for the rite of baptism, but for what this rite produces. It is a ritualistic deviation which is satisfied simply by the appropriate performance of the rite, a 'sociological' deviation which mocks the effect but socially needs the rite to be performed.

*A rite is an operation in the sphere of the irrational*    The anthropologist Claude Lévi-Strauss says of rites that one must see in them 'the means of making immediately perceptible a certain number of values which would affect the soul less directly if one tried to introduce them solely by rational means' (*La Croix*, 24 January 1979). Is that not the reason why there is water for baptism and not just a profession of faith?

The irrational is obviously not opposed to the rational; it is complementary to it. The rite involves the whole of a person. It reminds men and women that they are not just thought and intelligence but also body and sensibility. That is why a rite is never just words. In a rite there is always something to feel, to touch, to see, to hear, to undergo, to eat, to drink . . ., because to make a person there has to be both body and soul!

*A rite is a way of communicating with the occult*    The occult is what is hidden, secret, mysterious. It is what escapes us, goes beyond us: the meaning of life, destiny, origin (whence I come) and destiny (whither I am going), divinity, society and even the other – the brother, the friend, the partner, all of whom who always escape me a little, or a good deal, even if I know them well. This occult is fascinating because it makes up the most important things in life, to which are attached happiness, love, freedom, relationships, but it equally causes fear, since there is so much that is inexplicable and inaccessible in it.

---

### Has Vatican II changed the rites?

A rite gives security because it is conservative! The insecurity felt by many Catholics as a result of the liturgical reform arising from the Second Vatican Council may have its explanation here.

It is worth making some comments.

The long period of liturgical stability which preceded Vatican II and the ignorance of the history of the rites of the church meant that many of the faithful confused the rite and the habit of the rite! Whether one baptizes in Latin, Greek, Syriac, French or English, one always baptizes with water and in the name of the Trinity. So the rite has not fundamentally changed.

Besides, it is clear that the lack of explanation from pastors on the occasion of the successive liturgical changes between 1964 and 1968 and the apparently authoritarian way in which these changes took place have seemed to many of the faithful close to a dispossession which brings lack of security, not to mention a seizure of power which abuses authority.

Hence the usefulness of knowing the rites and what is at stake in them.

---

An old man confessed: 'It's amazing. I've been married thirty-five years and I have the feeling that I still don't know my wife!' The occult, finally, is a kind of characteristic of what we call the holy, all those realities which transcend rational experience and the experience of the senses (R. Otto, *The Holy*). But how does one grasp that which cannot be grasped? How does one penetrate the inpenetrable? How does one arrive at the inaccessible? How does one tame it? (At this point it is worth re-reading the episode of the fox in Saint-Exupéry's *The Little Prince*.)

That is the question to which it is the function of rites to respond; that is the problem in life which is continually raised for everyone, even if they are not constantly aware of it, and which it is the aim of the rite to resolve, on great occasions (birth, adolescence, marriage, death) and on everyday ones (relationships, courtesy) or occasional ones (New Year's Day, national festivals).

### A rite is a transition

An observation of a rite will always leave us with our hunger. And just as no characteristic trait will exhaust the mystery of the person, so no anthropology will explain what a rite is, precisely because the rite is part of the mystery of the human person.

However, it is possible for us to go further (deeper!) than the description that I have just given by referring to the work of an English pediatrician, Donald Winnicott, who became a psychoanalyst so as better to cope with the mental disturbances that he discovered among his infant clients.

Winnicott noted that at the moment when the small child felt any threat of a break, especially at the moment when its mother left it to go to sleep, it invented or made an object which would help it accept this break. The object might be the end of a scarf, a curtain, some plush fabric, which the child rubs or sucks to calm the insecurity and the agony which invade it. So the child learns to pass from the warm and reassuring presence of its mother to her agonizing absence. Winnicott calls this object the 'transitional object' and draws three lessons from its use by the child.

1. Here we have the first of all the rites of passage performed by the human being. The use of the object allows the child to follow a transitional itinerary by which it passes from one state to another. And this itinerary is certainly a rite . . . social, programmed, repetitive . . . (see above). In fact the succession of events and the effect sought are precisely the same each evening: caressing, rocking, gentle and encouraging words, putting the child in the cradle, (tears?), grasping the 'object', the mother leaving, putting out (or dimming) the light, last words, separation.

2. On this occasion the first symbolic action also appeared with the child. What, in fact, is this transitional object if not the means by which the child is to re-present (make present to itself) the mother whom it misses: The symbolic object is used as a means of union with the mother who exists but is physically absent. But the object becomes a symbol only because it is used as such. Otherwise it is just the end of a scarf! (The same goes for the water, bread and oil.)

3. Finally, Winnicott says, 'the acceptance of reality is an endless task'. That is to say that human beings must be in transit all their lives. All their lives they have to break with the 'reality within' (their internal world, their reserve, their tranquillity) and pass on to 'outside reality' (the world of others, social life, church life). And it is their ritual life which will allow them to do that, through the rites of the major stages of their existence and the simple rites of their everyday life. But here it is the facts of culture or religion which become the transitional objects of the child who has become an adult.

A rite is always a transition which serves as the way for a person to pass from one state to another.

## The role of the symbol

Our reference to Winnicott's work has already introduced the symbol: it is in a symbolic action that the child uses the transitional object to continue to 'bring back' the absent mother. We must now go further in our analysis of the symbol, its constitution and its role.

A particular feature of human life, and especially religious life, is that it does not cease to allude to realities which exist but at the same time are completely absent from the sense-perception of the person who is talking about them: justice, freedom, one's country, love exist, but these are abstract realities which no human sense can perceive, except by the intermediaries which are charged with representing them. It is the same, and even more so, in the religious life. Believers know that grace exists, that forgiveness and communion exist, but they also know that these are realities of which they have tangible experience only indirectly, through the water, bread, or a particular action.

And God? Is God not as real as cruelly absent from our life, our hearing, our touch? 'No one has seen God at any time' (John 1.18).

Human beings are not just brains: they are bodies, hearts and spirits, and nothing important can affect them unless their whole beings are involved: what is corporeal has to be spiritualized (like work, time and sexuality) and what is spiritual has to be made corporeal. And it is here that the symbol appears, as a sort of embodiment of all that is of the realm of the spirit.

---

### The symbol

'The term which denotes a symbol always implies the bringing together of two halves,' says G. Durand. The word comes from the Greek *sum-balein*, which means 'put with, bring together' (its exact opposite is the *dia-bolos*, which divides).

The symbol was a procedure used in antiquity by two allied cities or countries. A round piece of earthenware was broken in two and each city had half. When a city had a message to communicate to its ally, it gave its half to the messenger who brought the news, and if when he arrived in the other city the half which the messenger held matched the other, it was certain that this messenger came from the allied city and was not a spy.

---

Already in Chapter 2 we saw that there were several sorts of signs·

- The natural signs that people do not invent; they are given naturally when the necessary physical conditions are in place: smoke is the sign of fire, a footprint the sign of a step, etc.
- The conventional signs that people choose or organize into a code: signs of courtesy, a highway code, etc.
- Symbolic signs: one could almost say that human beings do not invent their materiality (one does not invent water) but define and codify the way in which it is used to obtain a broader and richer significance than the original (water is not only an element for assuaging thirst or allowing growth; there is a way of using it which signifies the gift of life or purification).

When people want to enter into relationship with others a long way away (and even more to the point, those who are absent) or to provide information, they set in play a whole system of communication by signs proportionate to the distance which separates the two parties: sound signs (hailing), gestures, luminous signs, telephone, letters. When signs of courtesy are used, the other person is there but the fact that one uses signs (salutations, handshakes, greetings, embraces) reveals that the other person, though present, is always in some way 'distant' by virtue of being the other, i.e. different. And what does one say when this other is the Wholly Other? The sign is always a means of communication.

---

### A biblical example of the symbol

*Tobias replied to his father Tobit, 'I will do all that you have asked me, father. But how can I get this money back (from Gabael) when we do not know one another? What sign shall I give him so that he can recognize me, trust me and give me the money?' Tobit then replied to his son Tobias: 'He has signed a deed, I have countersigned it; I have torn it in two so that each of us should have half, and I have put his with the money.'*  Tobit 5.1–3

---

## The symbol

The symbol is also a means of communication, but it is a communication which extends to communion, since its function is to bring together.

The symbol has in common with the other signs that its starting point is always a physically tangible element:

- smoke, a sign of fire, as a natural sign;
- the road sign, as a conventional sign;
- incense, the sign of prayer, as a symbolic sign.

Like the other signs, the symbol makes use of this physically tangible element to indicate the existence of other things that one does not see and that are therefore absent to the senses:

- the smoke indicates the fire that one does not see;
- the road sign indicates the crossing that one does not yet see;
- the incense indicates the prayer that one does not see in itself.

But while in this way the natural and conventional signs indicate the hidden existence of another tangible element (the fire, the crossing) a symbol relates to quite another reality: a reality which will never be physically tangible because it is abstract, immaterial, spiritual by nature: justice, country, grace.

So the symbol (the symbolic object) is like the material half of an immaterial reality that human beings (body and spirit) can only apprehend through the operation that brings them together.

---

### Three kinds of smoke

The smoke which comes out of a chimney indicates that there is a fire in the house: that is a natural sign.

The white smoke which comes out of a particular chimney in the Vatican indicates that a pope has been chosen: that is a conventional sign;

The smoke which comes out of a thurible in a church shows that the prayer of those who are gathered together is ascending towards God; that is a symbolic sign.

---

### The symbolism of the water of baptism

Water, a natural sign of purification and growth, takes on the status of a symbol when it is used as the material half (the signifier) of the immaterial reality of sanctifying grace (the signified), which human beings can apprehend only by the ritual operation of baptism that allows their being brought together, i.e. the presence of the one (grace) through the other (water).

---

We can also understand that the true symbol is not so much the precise object as on the one hand the way in which it is used, and on the other the 'work' which it accomplishes by being a symbol. A symbol is always matched by external (see, feel, touch, hear, taste) and internal (impressions, emotions, seizures, wonderment) symbolic actions. And while the external action is limited to the act which produces it (letting off a firework), the internal action is limitless and totally open (the effect of the firework cannot be measured).

### The capacity to symbolize

Clearly one has to say of the symbol what we have said of the rite: no science will ever explain it. At least, after this explanation of the mechanism of the symbol, we can try to understand better where the human capacity to symbolize comes from. The psychoanalyst Jacques Lacan can help us here.

At birth, the child is physically separate from its mother, but not yet separate psychologically. For about nine months, it will live in a state of not being able to distinguish itself from its mother. For the child, its mother and itself are one. But soon the awareness of the child will be aroused, thanks to the intervention of a third person, the father, who comes as it were to break up the mother-child couple by bringing out the distinction. For example the child perceives the father talking of 'it' (the child) to the mother as another or the mother speaking 'in the name of the father' who is absent. So the child discovers that its mother is not itself, nor is itself its mother. Above all, the child discovers that there are others than it, that there is it and the rest, and that that which is not it is as real as it is.

This development is what Lacan calls the period of acquiring symbolic function.

Symbolic function is the capacity that a person has to know that there is reality distinct from (other than) himself or herself and to represent this absent reality.

## Symbols, rites and sacraments

By itself, anthropology cannot go as far as saying what the sacraments are. It is faith that does so, and theology which takes account of them. But in that the sacraments are human acts (that they have a 'visible face', as Mgr Coffy says in the quotation put at the head of this chapter), anthropology can decipher the human part of which they are made up.

Then one sees that the way in which the church proceeds with the sacraments brings the symbol and the rite perfectly into play. The church draws them from the common depths of humanity, but evangelizes them by giving them specific meanings and effects.

In the end of the day, symbols and rites, in a Christian regime, take on a meaning and an efficacy which are no longer within the competence of science but that of faith, since they become the place of the action of God. Again it has to be said in the case of the sacraments that God does not intervene without human mediation.

---

## The linguistic explanation of the symbol

'I call a symbol any structure of meaning where a direct, primary, literal meaning denotes in addition another indirect, secondary, figurative meaning, which can only be apprehended through the first' (Paul Ricoeur, *The Conflict of Interpretations*, 16x). Antoine Vergote adds that religious symbolism constitutes as it were a further stage (*Interpretation du langage religieux*, 70).

Structure of meaning

| | | |
|---|---|---|
| Religious symbol | Sacramental bond | Indirect meaning of the word 'bond' based on human symbolism, which is itself based on the direct meaning of the word. |
| ↑ | | |
| Human symbol | Matrimonial bond | Indirect meaning of the word 'bond' which, based on the direct meaning signifies what takes place between a man and a woman who are bonded in marriage. |
| ↑ | | |
| Material character of an act | Bond | The direct meaning of the word which denotes the material act of bonding. |

# God: never without mediation

The Bible reveals to us that God 'whom no one has seen at any time' (John 1.18) nevertheless manifests himself to human beings, but never without mediation.

Adam and Eve: the garden, the tree (Gen. 2.17).

Noah: the rainbow (Gen. 9.12)

Abraham: the oak of Mamre and the three men (Gen. 18.1)

Jacob: the ladder (Gen. 28.12).

Moses: the burning bush (Ex. 3.3).

Elijah: an angel, a jar, water, the breeze (I Kings 19).

Isaiah: the seraphim, the brazier (Isa. 6).

Ahaz: He does not want a sign: God wants it for him (Isa. 7.10–15).

Zacharias: an angel of the Lord (Luke 1.11).

Mary: the angel Gabriel (Luke 1.26).

Finally, the sign *par excellence* that God sends to human beings: his own Son.

No one has seen God at any time, but the only Son who is in the bosom of the Father, he has made him known (John 1.18).

He is the image of the invisible God (Col. 1.15).

He is mediator of a new covenant (Heb. 9.15).

# 7
# The Sacraments in the History of the Church

*'What was visible in our Redeemer has thus passed into the sacraments.'*

St Leo

Twenty centuries of church history, twenty centuries of the presence of the sacraments in this history, is a long time – indeed it is an amazing time!

But at the same time, since this is a history, a life, there is both permanence and change, stability and evolution.

The questions which more or less every Christian asks about the sacraments indicate an interest in a basic part of the life of the church and Christian existence. In the end of the day, what are the sacraments, where do they come from and what do they represent today?

These questions become even more live ones when in catechesis one has to explain the sacraments to children or initiate them into their first celebration and above all when, in pastoral work, one has to prepare young people for marriage or parents for the baptism of their child.

Not all Christians can be historians or theologians of the sacraments, but knowledge of faith must be supported by a minimum of knowledge, particularly history – and that is even more urgent in the present-day world, which is so technical and so precise. 'Always be ready to give account of the hope that is in you,' St Peter said to the first Christians (I Peter 3.15).

That is why, while fully aware of the lack of precision and subtlety that a summary can have, in the following pages we shall try to see how our sacraments have been present in the history of the church. But the aim of this work will not just be to do history. The real concern of the enquiry will be to understand better what the sacraments are so as to live them out better today.

---

**Questions people ask**

I can see that the sacraments are actions of the church, but how can they also be actions of Christ?

Why are there seven sacraments?

Did Jesus Christ institute all the sacraments?

Do all the sacraments have the same importance?

Other questions about the history of the sacraments will be answered in the study of each particular sacrament, for example:

Have the sacraments always been celebrated as they are celebrated today?

In a sacrament, what can change and what should not change?

---

# When it all began

We shall never become the early church again. It would even be unhealthy to involve ourselves in nostalgia over beginnings. On the other hand, we know that our Christian life today depends on the time when it all began, and on our faithfulness to what these first beginnings set in place. What can we say about the sacraments?

The situation of the first Christians was this. Most of them had known Jesus and even gone about with him for three years. Now Jesus had just died. He had been crucified. But God raised him: they were witnesses of this (Acts 2.32). Jesus 'disappeared from their sight' (Emmaus, Luke 24.31). But he was alive: God had made him Lord and Christ (Acts 2.36). The first Christians wanted to pursue their relationship with Jesus, to celebrate the God who had not abandoned his Son to the power of death (Acts 2.24) and to proclaim this good news to everyone.

How were they going to do that? By two activities, different but complementary. The first was turned outwards: missionary preaching (see Peter's speech at Pentecost, then the scattering of the Jerusalem community when persecution broke out, Acts 8.4); the other was turned inwards; baptism as a sign of adherence to Christ and involvement in the community (see Pentecost, Acts 2.41) and the communal meal in the course of which 'bread was broken' and shared to make a memorial of the Lord Jesus (see Acts 2.42; 2.46; 20.7).

---

### Pentecost

*So those who received his (Peter's) word were baptized, and there were added that day about three thousand souls.*

Acts 2.41

### The first community

*And they devoted themselves to the apostles' teaching and fellowship, to the breaking of bread and the prayers.*

Acts 2.42

---

In this activity directed towards the forming (baptism) and maintaining (the breaking of the bread) of the community, there is the basic nucleus of what we now call the sacramental life of the church.

In pursuing our observation of this earliest church, we note that its baptismal and eucharistic life is the result of the combination of three elements: faith, the rite and the memorial.

### Faith

Faith comes first. None of this activity would exist without it. The baptisms of Pentecost took place only because Peter's speech led the hearers to join in: 'What are we to do? Be converted and let every one be baptized' (Acts 2.37–38). The breaking of the bread at home took place only because the disciples wanted to make memorial of the living Lord. The Emmaus episode is an astonishing confirmation of this in its remark that the Lord disappeared from the sight of his disciples the moment they recognized him. One cannot believe if one sees, for in that case there is no room for faith. It is because one does not see that one is led to believe.

### The rite

Neither bathing in water nor sacred communal meals are the inventions of Jesus or the first Christians. These two practices form part of the universal heritage of religion (as anthropology proves) and more particularly of the heritage of the religious life of the Jewish people.

Thus we know (to keep to the period before Jesus) that there was baptism of proselytes (pagans who converted to Judaism), and certainly the baptism of John. Furthermore religious meals were held not only in ardent groups (like the Essenes and the Therapeutae) but in all Jewish families, on the sabbath and all the great festivals. The paschal meal was the most important of them.

Following Jesus, who himself underwent baptism and presided over numerous religious meals with his disciples (of which the Supper was the last), the first Christians resorted to these two ritual practices to give communal expression to their relationship to the Lord.

*The memorial*

Faith, which is the gift of God, and the rite, which is a human action, come together to result in a memorial. The memorial is based on a past event (the death and resurrection of the Lord Jesus), affirming its permanent efficacy and reviving it by the symbolic performance of the rite so as to announce its future fulfilment. As human beings, the first Christians could only continue their relationship with the 'Invisible Living Lord' by the visible mediation of these rites, which were the memorials of baptism and the breaking of bread. These are not rites that they invented – as we have seen – but through Christ and the Holy Spirit they gave them an absolutely new meaning and content.

---

### Anamnesis = Memorial

These words have the same meaning, but one comes from Greek and the other from Latin.

'The Lord, God of your Fathers, God of Abraham, God of Isaac and God of Jacob has sent me to you. That is my name for ever, it is my memorial' (Ex. 3.15).

That day (of the feast of the Passover) will serve as a memorial for you (Ex. 12.14).

Glory be to the Father and to the Son and to the Holy Spirit, to the God who is, was and is to come.

Glory to you, the one who was dead; Glory to you, the one who is alive, our Saviour and our God. Come, Lord Jesus!

---

This new way of using these rites consisted not only of remembering the one who had 'disappeared' (see Emmaus), as Jesus had asked of them (hence the institution), but of 'doing this in remembrance of him', i.e. of allowing the living Jesus to continue to act among them by making them benefit from his Pasch which was historically past, but mystically always present.

It is of the eucharist only that Jesus said, 'Do this in remembrance of me,' but baptism (and all the other sacraments) is as much a memorial of Christ's Pasch as the 'broken bread'.

So what we call the basic nucleus of the sacramental life of the church was in place. This nucleus did not yet have any other name than those of the two acts which made it up, baptism and the breaking of the bread (the Lord's supper, for Paul in I Cor. 11.20; chronologically, he is the first to talk of the eucharist).

However, alongside these, we can see the presence of a certain number of actions in the service of the faith of the first communities. But their practices remain shrouded in the mists of history, and moreover there was still no precise name to designate them or, even more important, theological conception (like that of sacrament) under which to bring them. This is what made Maurice Jourjon, a patristic specialist, say that 'the sacraments were born before there was a term with which to describe them'. To live out all situations of life from Christ and with him was the sole preoccupation of the first Christians.

---

### The sacraments – before the term was used

Some actions of the first Christian communities were already sacraments, even before the term was used:

- acts of exclusion from the community or re-integration into it (Matt. 18.15–18 implies this; I Cor. 5 proves it);
- acts of handing on a responsibility from the leader of the community (Matt. 16.18 to Peter; to bishops or elders (presbyters) in I Tim. 3.2; 5.17, etc.);
- acts of a giving of the Spirit, apparently distinct from baptism (Acts 8.17);
- acts of prayer and the anointing of the sick (James 5.14);
- without forgetting that at this time, as at all others, men and women were getting married, and that Christians married in the spirit of Genesis, which Jesus had recalled (Matt. 19.4), and of which Paul had given a very high Christian interpretation (Eph. 5.32).

---

## The development of sacramental life

Granted that baptism and the eucharist have been constantly lived out by the church down the centuries with a remarkable constancy and fidelity, albeit with unimportant developments in the ritual sphere, we must now ask in connection with the other sacraments how we have arrived at our present situation, after what we have seen of the first Christians.

One might say that in a way necessity was the main factor. It was the life of the church and the vital needs which it came to feel which allowed what was there in embryo in the person of Jesus and the New Testament to come clearly and precisely into existence.

Three factors helped this sacramental development to come about:

the work of history;

the quest for a precise vocabulary:

the need for a definition of the function and number of the sacraments.

### The work of history

Let's take a few examples:

*Confirmation* During the first three centuries of the church, Christianity was essentially urban (Jerusalem, Antioch, Alexandria, Rome, Lyons . . .) and the communities were quite small in size, particularly as a result of persecutions. The bishop was almost the local priest. He was there. He was near. At Easter he baptized the catechumens, performing all the rites which preceded or followed the actual immersion in water. He, too, laid hands on neophytes after baptism, calling on the Spirit, and anointed them with oil. It would not occur to anyone that there were two distinct operations here.

However, when Christianity began to be able to expand into the countryside round the great cities after the peace of Constantine in 313, the bishop came to be increasingly remote from those who were baptized in the distant communities. The priest certainly baptized the catechumens from the community for which he was responsible, but it was necessary to wait for the bishop for him to lay on hands and anoint. It was only in 465 that Faustus, bishop of Riez, spoke of 'confirmation' in this connection.

*Penance* The history of penance is the most eventful of all the sacraments. In the West, penance had at least three different and successive forms (without counting the periods when there was a vacuum), and the general practice of private confession dates only from the beginning of the seventeenth century.

Saint Augustine never had recourse to it between his conversion and his death, but St John Bosco made his confession every day.

*Marriage* Of course Christians have always married, but in the first centuries there was no particular ceremony or religious approach. Faith and law consisted of marriage 'according to the local custom'.

Little by little, it became customary for the permission of the bishop to be asked for the marriage of the clergy and for there to be a mass and a blessing of the bride at the time of a marriage.

But it was only in 1536, and to combat the abuse of illegitimate marriages, that the Council of Trent for the first time produced an obligatory canonical form, which is what is still used: the appearance of the couple before their parish priest and the exchange of vows in his presence.

*Ordination* It was not until 1947 and Pope Pius XII that it was made clear that the act of the ordination of a priest was not the porrection (touching) of the chalice and paten, but the laying on of hands by the bishop and the prayer of consecration that goes with it.

So do we have to speak of the institution of the sacraments by Christ? If that meant that during his earthly life Jesus established the practice of the various sacraments, it would be doubly wrong: first because all the rites which developed into the sacraments existed before him, and secondly because it was not until a number of centuries after Jesus that several of these rites (all of them except baptism and the eucharist) clearly revealed their sacramental value.

That Christ instituted the sacraments means that each of them is rightly considered an act of Christ corresponding to a particular gift of grace which Christ expressly willed, while leaving it to the church to specify the specific forms of human action which would allow it.

### The quest for a precise vocabulary

As we have seen, the first preoccupation of the earliest Christians was to live out their relationship with the Lord Jesus and not to define or classify their actions and gestures. As the years passed, the reflection of pastors and theologians led to questions being asked about a certain number of actions, perhaps because they had to be explained (in pre- or post-baptismal catechesis) or because important questions arose in connection with them (does the church have the right to forgive those who have abjured their faith or committed a murder? Is baptism administered by heretics valid?)

In this reflection, the first word used for all of what we now call sacraments was the Greek word *mysterion* and above all its plural *mysteria*, the mysteries. It is a word which comes from pagan religious vocabulary. The mysteries were the non-public cults to which a person was introduced through rites of initiation which had to be kept absolutely secret and by which the salvation of the initiates was guaranteed.

In fact this word was not new in Christianity. It was already present in the Old Testament, notably in the book of Wisdom, which was originally written in Greek (Wisdom 2.22). But it is above all St Paul who gave it its full Christian sense. For him, the word denotes 'God's plan' (Eph. 1.9), and even Christ in person, as one who reveals this plan (I Cor. 2.1; Col. 2.2).

When one begins gradually to call baptism *mysterion*, or speak of the *mysteria* of the body and blood of Christ, as does Eusebius of Caesarea (267–340) in his *Demonstration of the Gospel* (5.3),

there is a concern to indicate that baptism and the eucharist are bound up with the whole work of salvation which God accomplishes for us through Christ and that they are seen as the privileged realization of this work.

However, from the third century this word *mysterion* and its Latin transcription *mysterium* came to seem suspect to Tertullian (160–240) because of possible confusion with the pagan mysteries. He preferred the Latin term *sacramentum*.

But not all the Latin theologians were as intransigent as Tertullian. *Mysterium* and *sacramentum* were used indiscriminately by St Ambrose and even still by Paschasius Radbertus in the ninth century. It was only with scholasticism that *sacramentum* decisively took on the technical meaning which it has retained to our day. That, however, happened only in the Latin part of the church; the East has always kept the word 'mystery'.

That is how things are and one cannot regret the quest for precision that this development reveals. Each word has its advantages and its disadvantages, and we know that the term 'mystery' is not without its risks. However, it has to be recognized that in its concern to look at the *sacramentum* and the *sacramenta* in increasing detail and in legal terms, the Latin church made them lose something of their openness to the Mystery, sometimes seeing them more as the means (the instrument, the tool, the thing) than the end.

---

### 'Mystery' in St Paul

*For he has made known to us in all wisdom and insight the* mystery *of his will, according to his purpose which he set forth in Christ, as a plan for the fullness of time, to unite all things in him, things in heaven and things on earth.*

Eph. 1.9

*I want their hearts to be encouraged as they are knit together in love, to have all the riches of assured understanding and the knowledge of God's* mystery, *of Christ, in whom are hidden all the treasures of wisdom and knowledge.*

Col. 2.2

If baptism and the eucharist have a clear place in the life of the church of the first centuries, in the midst of other Christian acts which came gradually to find a place in the course of the following centuries, how was it that seven particular rites and only seven came to be called sacraments?

We have seen that first the word 'mystery' and then the word 'sacrament' served to bring out the meaning of certain ritual actions in connection with the whole plan of God. The idea is a fine one. It ended up, for example, in an affirmation by Pachasius Radbertus (790–865) which Vatican II was to take over.

But this admirable theology also concealed a considerable vagueness of definition. What is a mystery? St John Chrysostom replies: 'There is a mystery when we consider other things than what we see.' That is very true and well said. But it is not enough for a systematic reflection.

What is a sacrament? For St Ambrose, both baptism and foot-washing. For St Augustine both the creed and the Our Father, and baptism and the eucharist.

However, it was St Augustine who brought the first clarification in reflecting on the sacrament as a sign. He said that the sacrament is the tangible sign of a holy thing.

With a few nuances, Augustine's definition was to hold until the Middle Ages. But the vagueness

---

## Mystery and Sacrament in Paschasius Radbertus (790–865)

The nativity of Christ and all the economy of salvation form a great sacrament, for in the visible man, the divine majesty accomplishes invisibly and secretly what will serve for our consecration and sanctification. That is why the incarnation of God is rightly called mystery or sacrament.

*Liber de corpore et sanguine domini*, PL 120, col. 1725

---

remained. For St Peter Damien (1072), sacraments are tangible signs of a holy thing, and so the anointing of kings, the canonicate, the dedication of churches, funerals, the monastic habit are sacraments.

It was at this stage that the great theologians of the Middle Ages appeared. First of all, Augustine's definition appeared inadequate to Hugh of Saint Victor (died 1141). It seemed to him that while one can say that every sacrament is a tangible sign of a holy thing, one cannot say that every tangible sign of a holy thing is a sacrament. The sacrament of baptism is certainly the tangible sign of a holy thing, but blessed water, which is also the tangible sign of a holy thing, cannot be a sacrament with the same status as baptism. So he adds to the definition of Augustine the need for the sign to be of divine institution to be a sacrament.

---

## The *sacramentum*

In Latin this word has two meanings:

It is a legal term which denotes the money of the party who loses a trial and which is dedicated to the deity.

It is the word which denotes the action by which a soldier commits himself by taking an oath to his leader and to the emperor.

It is above all this notion of commitment by oath which makes Tertullian speak of baptism in terms of *sacramentum*.

---

## The mystery in St John Chrysostom

There is mystery when we consider things other than those that we see . . . The non-believer who sees baptism thinks that it is only water; I, not just considering what I see, contemplate the purification of the soul brought about by the Holy Spirit . . .

*Homily 1 on I Corinthians*, PG 61, col. 55

## The sign in St Augustine

The sign is something which, over and above the image whose meaning it nurtures, brings forth from itself something else in thought.

*De doctrina Christiana* II.1

Abelard (1079–1142) distinguished between the *sacramenta majora*, useful to salvation: baptism, eucharist, order, penitence; and the *sacramenta minora*, to increase devotion: blessed water, ashes. The unknown author of the *Summa Sententiarum* (thirteenth century) also adds that to be a sacrament the tangible sign must be efficacious. In this way he comes to mark out six tangible signs which are efficacious and thus sacraments: our six (not including marriage). Finally Peter Lombard, in his *Sentences*, written in 1150, included everything: sign, institution, efficacy. He added that the tangible sign, to be a sacrament, has to be the cause of the grace which it signifies. Starting from there, he examined all the sacred rites (from blessed water to the eucharist), finally decreeing that seven only can be called sacraments: the number seven was established.

The first Council officially to name the seven sacraments was the Fourth Lateran Council in 1215. But it was not until the seventh session of the Council of Trent in 1547 that it was defined as being a matter of faith that there are seven sacraments, no more and no less.

However, between Peter Lombard and the Council of Trent mention has to be made of the work of a tremendous theologian, St Thomas Aquinas (died 1274). He did not add anything to Peter Lombard's seven sacraments, but pushed the analysis of the sacraments as far as a theological synthesis which on a number of points will never be surpassed, despite the literary form and vocabulary characteristic of scholasticism. Some of it is quoted in the box on the opposite page.

### The composition of the sacraments

To take account of the way in which the sacraments are composed, Thomas Aquinas borrows from Aristotle the distinction between matter and form. The basis of each sacrament is a human action which gives material expression to the intervention of Christ by means of the form offered by words.

The sacrament of the eucharist is the taking of bread and wine and saying the words of institution over them. Both are necessary.

Another Aristotelian concept allowed Thomas Aquinas to distinguish in the eucharist between substance and accidents. At consecration the substance of bread gives place to the substance of the body of Christ (hence the idea of 'transsubstantiation'), but the accidents of bread (composition, taste, perishable character) remain.

### The function of the sacraments

In reflecting on the function of the sacraments as signs, Thomas Aquinas ends up with the following definition: 'A sacrament is a sign of some sacred reality for the sanctification of human beings.' His analysis of the relationship between sign and sacrament thus brings out that a sacrament is made up of:

The sign itself (*sacramentum tantum*): that is the tangible rite. In the eucharist, this is taking bread and wine and saying the words of consecration over them.

The sign and the reality signified (*res et sacramentum*): this is the immediate effect of the tangible rite. In the eucharist this is the fact that the body of Christ is present in the consecrated bread (the real presence).

The reality alone (*res tantum*): that is the finality of the sacrament, its grace. In the eucharist this is the unity of the mystical body of Christ.

### The hierarchical organization of the sacraments

Not all the sacraments are equal. They can be considered according to two systems:

*The linear system* (with an anthropological basis). Here baptism has priority because it conditions all the rest, since it is a birth. The others are like the rest of life: growth (confirmation), food (eucharist), social organization (order, marriage), etc.

*The circular system.* Here it is the eucharist which has priority, because it is the only sacrament which directly contains the person of Christ. It is as it were the nucleus around which the other sacraments gravitate and are ordered to it: one is baptized to be 'incorporated', one is 'ordained' to serve the body of Christ, and so on.

## Some features of the doctrine of St Thomas Aquinas on the sacraments

*Summa theologiae III, questions 60–65*

*Question 60, article 2:* The term sacrament is properly applied to that which is a sign of some sacred reality pertaining to human beings.

*Question 60, article 3:* Three factors of our sanctification can be taken into consideration: the actual cause, which is the passion of Christ; the form, which consists in grace and the virtues, and the ultimate end which it is designed to achieve, which is eternal life.

*Question 60, article 6:* Just as in the mystery of the Incarnation the Word of God is united to the flesh which we can perceive with our senses, so too in the sacraments words are applied to sensible materials.

*Question 60, article 7:* In the sacraments the words act as the formal principle while the sensible realities act as the material one.

*Question 65, article 1:* With regard to the direct achieving of a positive further fullness of life this takes place in three ways: first through generation, for it is through this that human beings begin to be and to live, and the factor corresponding to this in the life of the spirit is baptism . . . The second way is through growth, for it is by this that the individual is brought to due fullness in size, weight and strength. And the factor corresponding to this in the life of the spirit is confirmation, for it is in this that the Holy Spirit and strength are conferred . . . The third way of directly achieving some positive further fullness of life at the physical level is through nutrition, for it is by this that life and strength in human beings are maintained. And the factor corresponding to this in the life of the spirit is the eucharist.

*Question 65, article 3:* The sacrament of the eucharist is, in an absolute sense, the greatest of all the sacraments . . . in this sacrament Christ himself is present substantially. All the other sacraments are ordered to this one as to their end.

These extracts from the doctrine of St Thomas on the sacraments must inevitably seem just scholarly (scholastic!) dissection.

In this connection intellectual honesty calls for three remarks, particularly for the reader who knows little of the history of theological thought.

1. The work of St Thomas Aquinas has provided sacramental theology with 'monumental' richness. Its construction no longer corresponds to the architecture that one would use today, but it is a cathedral which the church cannot ignore if it is to understand its history, and particularly the history of its faith. One can even regret that recent centuries have forgotten its existence. If people had always referred to St Thomas Aquinas, they would have never arrived at the fragmented conception which presents the seven sacraments as seven distinct actions separate from one another. Nor would the aim of the eucharist have been thought to be the real presence, but the unity of the mystical body which it realizes in communion.

2. It might appear disturbing that it was necessary to wait until the twelfth century to know that there were seven sacraments and even until the sixteenth for this to be defined *de fide*. That is part of the lovely mystery of the church which is not a monolithic block but a living organism. It reveals to us above all that, in the church, life is superior to reflection. Such a remark does not mean that there is no need for reflection and study (if that were the case, there would be no place for this book), but it does remind us that with or without words and definitions, millions and millions of faithful over time (twenty centuries) and space (the whole world) have not ceased to live out their faith and that it is thanks to them that this faith has been handed down to us and that we experience it in our turn.

3. It is worth recalling that our twentieth century has seen a marked return to Thomistic theology, and that this return clearly had an influence on the preparation and development of the theology of the Second Vatican Council. But before we get to Vatican II we have to say something about the Reformers and the Council of Trent.

## The Reformers

There is something almost offensive in attempting to sum up the position of the Reformers on the sacraments in a few lines. We hope that members of the Reformation churches will forgive us, and note that we are doing the same thing for the whole history of theological thought.

Two preliminary remarks:

We owe it to the truth to point out that the attitude of the Reformers was largely caused by a certain number of abuses for which the church was responsible (the excessive increase in masses for the dead, recourse to doubtful means in the practice of indulgences, and so on).

It also has to be said that from the beginning there were differences between the positions of Luther, Calvin and above all Zwingli, and that differences remain today, particularly over the sacraments, their number and their functions. That having been said, the essential position of the Reformers, which provoked the reaction of the Catholic church, can be presented as two points.

1  In the name of scripture, only those sacraments were retained which were explicitly mentioned in the New Testament, baptism and the eucharist. The Augsburg Confession of 1530 also retained penitence, but specifically stated that confirmation, extreme unction and marriage are only ceremonies. As for the priesthood, there could be no question who is the sole priest in the church of Christ.

2.  In the name of justification by faith alone, the sacrament can only be an external sign. It may provoke faith, but in that case it is faith given by God which justifies, and not the sacrament. Calvin was even more radical than Luther in subjecting the saving action of the sacraments entirely to the preaching of the word. For his part, Luther states that it is not the sacrament but the faith of the sacrament which justifies.

---

## The Council of Trent (The Nineteenth Ecumenical Council)

### Seventh Session (1547)

Canons on the sacraments

1. If anyone says that the sacraments of the new Law were not all instituted by our Lord Jesus Christ; or that there are less or more than seven, namely baptism, confirmation, the eucharist, penitence, extreme unction, order and marriage; or that one of these seven is not truly and strictly speaking a sacrament, let him be anathema.

6. If anyone says that the sacraments of the new law do not contain the grace that they signify or that they do not confer this grace on those who do not put any obstacle in the way, as if they were only external signs of grace or justice received by faith, and marks of Christian profession, which also allow people to distinguish the faithful from the unfaithful, let him be anathema.

### Twenty-first Session (1562)

(NB This extract from the second chapter of this session is a reply to the still very topical question of whether one can or cannot change anything in the administration and celebration of the sacraments.)

The Holy Council declares: in the dispensation of the sacraments, their substance being saved, the church has always had the power to decide or to modify what it judges best fitted to the spiritual utility of those who receive them and in respect of the sacraments themselves, depending on the variety of circumstances, times and places.

## The Council of Trent

The Council of Trent presented its doctrine of the sacraments at the seventh session (1547). It did so not only to condemn the errors of the Reformers but also to correct the abuses which it noted in the church and to enlighten and strengthen the faith of the faithful.

For the first time in the history of the church, then, it was defined as dogma that there are seven sacraments, no more and no less, that they are all instituted by Christ, and that they all confer the grace that they signify (see the box on p. 61).

As we said in the case of St Thomas Aquinas, the literary genre, which here is even legalistic, hardly matches our present-day mentality and may sometimes even seem shocking (the anathemas!). But the Council of Trent must not be judged by today's criteria. The state of the church at the time really called for reorganization, and the crisis provoked by the Reformers was a serious one. The work of the Council of Trent was indispensable, and on closer inspection appears less negative than some of its formulations might suggest.

That having been said, a present-day Christian will always ask why there seems to be such a difference between what the Council of Trent says about the sacraments and the way in which they are talked about by Vatican II.

## Contemporary theology of the sacraments

Precisely four centuries divide the end of the Council of Trent (1563) from the beginning of the Second Vatican Council (1962). It is not surprising that responses to the way to present the doctrine of the church, developments in attitudes and changes of tone are numerous. Among all those which are possible (it would take a whole book to analyse just this question), we shall consider only one: it is not the only one, but it is determinative and positive.

Since roughly the beginning of the twentieth century, the church has benefited from the incredible leap forward made by archaeology, history, and linguistic and literary studies. The discoveries in each of these areas are innumerable, and one cannot criticize our sixteenth-century ancestors for not having benefited from them. Still, particularly in theological work, they have led to a considerable advance in questions of biblical and patristic exegesis. That does not mean that we have more faith than our predecessors, but it does mean that we are in a better position to know about the founding period of the church than they were.

It has to be added that the stimulus of contacts between theology and the secular sciences has been to present-day theology what Aristotle was to Thomas Aquinas. This book would not exist without the great theologians and historians of the sacraments, the exegetes and liturgists of the last fifty years. Nor would the fact that one can no longer imagine the sacraments by themselves, outside the liturgical action by which the church celebrates God, who, through them, offers us life in covenant with him.

# Liturgy and the Presence of Christ

Christ is always present in his Church, especially in her liturgical celebrations. He is present in the Sacrifice of the Mass not only in the person of his minister, 'the same now offering, through the ministry of priests, who formerly offered himself on the cross', but especially in the eucharistic species. By his power he is present in the sacraments so that when anybody baptizes it is really Christ himself who baptizes. He is present in his word since it is he himself who speaks when the holy scriptures are read in the Church. Lastly, he is present when the Church prays and sings, for he has promised, 'where two or three are gathered together in my name there am I in the midst of them' (Matt. 18.20). Christ, indeed, always associates the Church with himself in this great work in which God is perfectly glorified and men are sanctified. The Church is his beloved Bride who calls to her Lord, and through him offers worship to the eternal Father.

Vatican II, *Constitution on the Sacred Liturgy* 7

# 8

# The Sacraments as Actions of the Church

Liturgical services are not private functions but are celebrations of the Church which is 'the sacrament of unity', namely, the holy people united and arranged under their bishops.

Therefore, liturgical services pertain to the whole Body of the Church. They manifest it, and have effects upon it. But they also touch individual members of the Church in different ways, depending on their orders, their role in the liturgical services, and their actual participation in them.

*The Constitution on the Sacred Liturgy*, 26

Mother Church earnestly desires that all the faithful should be led to that full, conscious, and active participation in liturgical celebrations, which is demanded by the very nature of the liturgy, and to which the Christian people, 'a chosen race, a royal priesthood, a holy nation, a redeemed people' (I Peter 2.9) have a right and obligation by reason of their baptism.

In the restoration and promotion of the sacred liturgy the full and active participation by all the people is the aim to be considered before all else, for it is the primary and indispensable source from which the faithful are to derive the true Christian spirit.

*The Constitution on the Sacred Liturgy*, 14 chs 6 & 7

A generation ago, for many Christians sacramental celebrations were above all acts of personal piety. Of course taking communion, making confession and receiving the last rites nourished faith, but they were not seen as something involving the whole community. It was a matter between God and the believer, albeit through the intermediary of a priest.

That was particularly true in the large towns, which favoured anonymity. In rural areas domestic happenings affect the neighbourhood. It is quite otherwise in the fabric of city life. We can all remember infant baptisms carried out in obscure baptismal fonts in remote corners of the church, at a time when none of the community was present! Adult baptisms were supposedly done discreetly, that is to say, in private chapels where one could be hidden. Sick communion and the last rites were received almost in secret! It was difficult to see in them the actions of a church acting as community.

And yet the Second Vatican Council strongly affirmed: 'Liturgical services are not private functions but are celebrations of the church.' And it went on to say: 'They pertain to the whole Body of the church. They manifest it, and have effects upon it.' What can we do to recover the church-centred nature of these celebrations?

One might humorously adopt as a slogan to the undertaking this simple phrase: 'The priest and the subject must be taken out of their isolation.' 'The priest's isolation', when he finds himself the only active participant during a celebration when those present seem to be only there as spectators; 'the subject's isolation', when last rites are given hurriedly, baptisms are given 'in strict privacy', communions take place outside the context of the mass. And yet the priest is present in the name of the church and the Christian belongs to a community. It is important for that to be seen.

For a better understanding of the effort to be made and above all in order to act with integrity, we must begin by examining the church with the aim of finding out the relationship which ought to exist between the whole community and those who have the responsibility of the priestly ministry. The church is not a body of indistinguishable people. All ought to be able to act together, but each person has his or her own role.

## A holy people

It is often said that the Second Vatican Council brought back into favour the idea of the church as the 'People of God'. What are we to understand by that? The word 'church' does not only indicate the members of a hierarchy – priests and bishops – but all Christians together as an organized community, as the Body of Christ.

The Council's deliberations were based on a text from I Peter: 'But you are a chosen race, a royal priesthood, a holy nation, God's own people, that you may declare the wonderful deeds of him who called you out of darkness into his marvellous light' (I Peter 2.9).

A priestly nation, a priestly people – what does that actually mean? The expression might seem novel. In common parlance the adjective 'priestly' is reserved for the clergy. And here we are using it when speaking of the whole gathering of church members.

The Council explained this in the Constitution on the church entitled *Lumen Gentium*:

Christ the Lord, high priest taken from among men, made the new people 'a kingdom of priests to God, his Father' (Rev. 1.6; cf. 5.9–10). The baptized, by regeneration and the anointing of the Holy Spirit, are consecrated to be a spiritual house and a holy priesthood . . .

Though they differ essentially and not only in degree, the common priesthood of the faithful and the ministerial or hierarchical priesthood are none the less ordered one to another; each in its own proper way shares in the one priesthood of Christ (*Lumen Gentium*, 10).

---

### A holy people

To him who loves us
and has freed us from our sins
by his blood
and made us a kingdom,
priests to his God and Father,
to him be glory and dominion
for ever and ever. Amen.                    Rev. 1.5–6

For you were slain and by your blood
    you ransomed people for God
from every tribe and tongue and people
    and nation,
and have made them a kingdom and
    priests to our God,
and they shall reign on earth.             Rev. 5.9–10

Like living stones be yourselves built
into a spiritual house,
to be a holy priesthood,
to offer spiritual sacrifices
acceptable to God through Jesus Christ.   I Peter 2.5

But you are a chosen race,
a royal priestly community,
a holy nation,
God's own people,
that you may declare the wonderful deeds
of him who called you out of darkness
into his marvellous light.                I Peter 2.9

By his or her baptism, every Christian becomes a member of the Body of Christ and a participant in its priesthood. That is called the 'priesthood of all the baptized'. There is no difference of 'degree' in the priesthood between priests and laity, as if they were all priests, but more or less priests, depending on the case. These are two different functions, but they are both called priestly, because both stem from the unique priesthood of Christ. We shall develop a better understanding of the difference during the course of this chapter.

The Constitution on the Liturgy emphasizes the consequences of this affirmation when it states, in the text in the box, that liturgical acts are not private acts but belong to the whole Body. And in the letter which he wrote to the Latin-American Episcopal Conference (CELAM), Cardinal Villot, Secretary of State, made it clear that:

> In order to arrive at this deep perception of the mystery and even transform it into a source of internal renewal of liturgical reform itself requires an effort which encourages the participating community to understand the different signs proper to the celebration.

> In the first place, to understand the value of the assembly, of the meeting of the people of God in the celebration, as a symbolic expression, as an act of faith on the part of the church. Through this meeting, the church reveals itself to the world, bears witness to its presence as a royal people, prophetic and priestly, focussed on the worship of God and the renewal of the world . . .

> To understand the value of the sacrament as an ecclesial act which extends the contact of present-day people with the saving humanity of Christ, with his mystery made present through faith, invocation, the action of the Church guided and sustained by the Spirit.

So as to have a better understanding of the value of the sacrament as a ecclesial act we shall approach it from two perspectives:

First we shall look at the church, the Christian community, made up of priests and lay people, as it is active in the celebration. *It is the church which acts in the sacrament.* We shall then have to define exactly how each of the participants, priest and congregation, acts in the appropriate way.

Secondly, we shall see the church being entirely brought to life by the sacrament, being nourished and built up by it. *It is the church which lives the sacrament.* We shall also discover why the Council expressed the preference that a celebration should be communal, whenever possible.

## It is the church which enacts the sacrament

### 'Taking the priest out of his isolation'

It is a figure of speech, yet it expresses a great truth. In most of the celebrations, the members of the 'audience' watch the priest doing what he has to do without appearing to suspect that they are called upon to take part in his actions. The very vocabulary leads us to believe this. We say that we are going to a baptism, but we ought to say that we are going to take part in it. There are celebrations when the priest deeply resents his isolation. It is understandable why the Second Vatican Council's Constitution on the Liturgy returns to this question many times and demands from Christians a 'full, conscious and active participation in liturgical celebrations'.

In every liturgical celebration there are several roles, several functions, several ministries which are carried out by different members of the community. It is very important to be absolutely certain of the place of each one – that of the president, bishop, priest or deacon, and that of all the other members of the community who celebrate with him. In order to make this easier, we shall speak of the role of the priestly minister, or the role of the priest, because it is he who usually presides.

### Rediscovering the church as an 'actant'

When we analyse an action we ask ourselves who is acting, what action is being performed, and upon what or whom it is being performed. We could ask the same question in respect of the sacraments. Who does what? Who acts in the sacrament? The answer is clear: it is Christ, the one and only priest, who acts through his Spirit. His priesthood is exclusive, as the letter to the Hebrews says.

It is right to affirm that it is Christ who presides at our eucharist. In the strict sense of the term, it is he, by the Spirit, who consecrates the bread and wine.

But who is Christ today? Who makes his action visible? The church, the body of Christ – the whole church and not just the priest! And so it is the church which forgives sins, the church which baptizes, the church which consecrates. The church is a holy people, and as such carries out its function in all its liturgical actions.

When we speak of the church, the body of Christ, we must remember that it is an entity with its own organization and hierarchy. There is no church in the strict sense unless it has at its centre an ordained ministry. That is where the role of priest, president of the assembly, comes in. The assembly is not fully the church without him as its president; however, he cannot act in isolation, but only when surrounded by the assembly.

To affirm that the assembly is the true agent in the celebration is not to remove or even diminish the role and importance of the one who is presiding. The church exists only in the interaction of the two.

---

## Jesus Christ, the only priest

The first Christians thought of themselves as being very different from all the other religious groups around them. When they started up their communities they had no temples, like the others, but met in houses. They did not make sacrifices of animals or fruits of the earth. They had no clergy, but they strongly affirmed: There is only one priest, Jesus Christ. He always lives to make intercession to God. His priesthood is exclusive (Heb. 7.23–27).

It is not easy for us to understand what they were trying to say, because our Christian communities today have at their heads people whom we call priests. For a better understanding, we need to explain our vocabulary. English has in fact only one word to denote what were originally two distinct functions.

*Elders* or presbyters: When the first Christian communities became organized, they were presided over by a college of elders (Acts 14.23; 15.2 etc.). They were called after the Greek word *presbyteros*, which means 'older person'. At the beginning these elders corresponded to the priests of our communities.

*Sacerdos* (a Latin word) or pontiff, the equivalent of the Greek *hiereus*. This was used of the person who carried out the sacred duties, who presented the offering of the faithful to God and acted as intermediary between God and human beings. In English the word is translated by 'priest', which makes for confusion with the word above.

For Christians, there is only one true priest (*sacerdos*), who is Jesus Christ. But each Christian community is presided over by men who share in the priesthood of Christ and who are the successors of the elders of the early church.

---

## Epiclesis

A prayer called the *epiclesis* is to be found in almost all sacramental celebrations. It is an invocation to the Holy Spirit, a request for the Spirit to be given, and that he should accomplish his work of sanctification. In the eucharistic prayer there is often an epiclesis just before the account of the institution. It is at this moment that the celebrant stretches out his hands over the bread and the wine. For our brothers in the Eastern churches, this is the prayer of consecration, by which the bread and wine become the Body and Blood of Christ. But there is also another epiclesis after the words of institution, a prayer offered over the assembled community asking that, by the power of the Spirit, it may become the living Body of the Lord.

This prayer is important. It demonstrates that God's power is involved, not the power of the priest. There is an epiclesis in the celebration of baptism, when the water is blessed, and when the oil and holy chrism are consecrated for the anointing of the sick.

In some circumstances the priest may find himself alone – as sometimes when giving the sacrament to the sick. He must then remember that he represents more than himself. He gathers together, at least in thought, all the members of the community. A lone priest is *waiting for* the assembly, just as an assembly without a priest is *waiting for* an ordained minister.

### A new plan

Take a look at the diagram. The section on the left represents the thought-pattern of most people. The priest appears as the intermediary between God and the believer. There is no reason to be surprised by this, because this is the case in most non-Christian religions.

It is not the same in Christianity. Jesus Christ is the 'only priest', the one who is the intermediary between God and humankind. He exercises this priestly role today through the church, which is his body. The priest is at the centre of the community.

He is at its service so that it may be the body of Christ. One could say that the priest allows the church to be itself; he allows it to act *in nomine Christi*, in the very name of Christ. We see this in the right-hand section of the diagram.

A Christian community is never a democracy in the sense that we understand the term in the political sphere. The one who presides over the assembly does not do so as a delegate of the other members. He is the sign of the presence of the Lord; he is the sacrament of Christ, who is head of his church. At certain times and in certain countries, Christian communities have chosen by election or acclamation the one who was to become priest or even bishop. Yet it is not because he is so chosen that he performs his role, but because he receives *ordination* by the laying on of hands of the other bishops.

We have a good example of this in the Acts of the Apostles. A need arose in the community in Jerusalem that no one should be 'neglected in the daily distribution'.

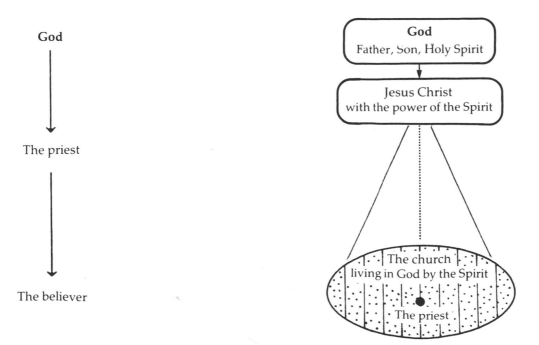

69

The Twelve summoned the body of the disciples and said: '. . . Therefore, brethren, pick out from among you seven men of good repute, full of the Spirit and of wisdom, whom we may appoint to this duty.' . . . And what they said pleased the whole multitude, and they chose Stephen . . . and Philip . . . these they set before the apostles, and they prayed and laid their hands upon them (Acts 6.2–6).

The choice is made by the community, the commissioning is done by the apostles. This procedure is very significant.

All the 'services' in the community have a similar way of working. No one claims a function for himself; he has to be called to it, as the Epistle to the Hebrews says (Heb. 5.4).

In the new rite for blessings which appeared in 1988, there is a special prayer for sending catechists out on missionary work. Supporting the catechetical instruction of children or adults is in fact a service of the community. Those who take it on come to make an offering of their own free will or in response to someone's request. Once chosen, they receive as it were a delegation. This is the way in which children experience things. They do not think that the words of their catechist are her own personal words, but they accept them as the teaching of the community in whose name she speaks.

## How did we arrive at this situation of the priest's isolation?

Let's look at the usual arrangements for liturgical celebrations. A priest stands alone in the choir, with the faithful facing him in the nave. In these circumstances, it is difficult to show the unity of action between the two. How have we got to this state?

P. Jounel, the liturgical historian, explains.

The fourth century saw the development of the liturgy in buildings of the basilica type, adapted to Christian worship. The fifth and sixth centuries saw the first surge of Barbarians and in the ninth and tenth centuries the second wave of invasions succeeded in breaking up the framework of culture within which the Roman liturgy had been born. From the eighth century onwards, the common people no longer understood Latin. Moreover, in the face of the church's inability to work out a practice of penance compatible with daily life, it was not long before the faithful had given up communicating except at the three or four major festivals of the year. For these two reasons the celebration of the eucharist became a clerical act, the people providing no more than a passive presence. In the Middle Ages the choir was rearranged for the celebration of the liturgy by the clergy. It was only in the period following the Council of Trent (1545–1563), with Catholic reform, that a concern for 'liturgical pastoral care' showed itself in the arrangement of the churches.

The choir, where the liturgical action took place, was only inhabited by clergy, by monks and, later on, by 'little monks' who were also called 'altar boys'. Remember the rood-screens, which completely closed off the space where the celebration took place! These were not done away with until the eighteenth century.

But in the last few centuries, the church's pastoral effort has been in giving substance back to the liturgical assembly. As we used to say, the 'audience' became increasingly large. The rood screen, that real separating wall, gave place to a grille in front of the choir. The assembly was associated with the responses by the servers in so-called dialogue masses. Then the Council completed these improvements by asking for true liturgical ministries entrusted to the laity to be revived. And so the community once again became active in the celebration. The community acts with the priest and not opposite him. Everyone celebrates, but the priest is given the office of president.

## Complementarity

The church is the body of Christ. Raised from the dead, he is still the only head today. We need to remind ourselves of this, and to live it out. That is the reason why, in all of our liturgical acts, the function of the one who presides over the assembly is to be the sacrament of Christ the head.

We shall define the role more precisely in Chapter 10, when we deal with priestly ordination. For the moment we need to note it in order to see how it is the priest's task to show the working of God in all sacramental action. He is also charged with furthering unity and communion between members of the community, and communion between the assembly over which he presides and the church universal. At the head of the assembly, he demonstrates that the action performed in unity by all the members is really that of the one head. That is the reason why, at the heart of the celebration, he is the one who pronounces the sacramental words in the name of Christ, and in the Holy Spirit.

Emphasizing the irreplacable role of the priestly ministry ought not to result in our neglecting to encourage the participation of the laity. The whole community ought already to be playing a part during the preparation and all along the sacramental way. The ministries which become apparent at the time of the liturgy ought to have taken root during the time which preceded it. The ministry of the catechist or of godfather or godmother are of this kind. And in the same way it is important to make sure that the members of the laity who have worked at the preparation are present during the celebration. The new rites published by the Council demonstrate this interaction fully (see the box).

## It is the church which lives the sacrament

While it is true to say that the 'church makes the sacraments', it is also true to maintain that the 'sacraments make the church'. The church is built up on the sacraments. Christians do not come to church to *be present* at a celebration. They are the actors in it, each one according to his or her role, but at the same time they and the whole community are

### Power and significance

The distinction between priest and laity is often spoken of in terms of power. Only the priest has the power to hear confession; only he has the power to preside at the eucharist or give the sacrament to the sick. This way of looking at things is not wrong, but we ought also to be able to speak in another language and look for the significance of the role assumed by the priestly ministry.

The church assures us of the visible presence of the Risen Lord today. The church stands in the midst of men and women as a 'sign of salvation'; it is a sacrament. Its existence and its manner of working follow from this vocation of being a sign. In it, all the functions converge in the fullness of the sign. The priest's task is not only to hold power, but to work towards establishing in its integrity the sign of the Body of Christ made up of the different members and united by the Head.

given life by this sacrament and are enriched by it.

In a sacramental celebration, Christians are never just alone before the priest. Individuals have to be looked upon as members of a community which is involved with them. That is what we mean by saying 'Take the subject out of his or her isolation.'

## The sacrament, the saving event of the community

Let us consider adult baptism. What riches this has brought to parishes since we started celebrating it again on Easter Eve! One can even say that, in some of its members, it is the assembly which is baptized and which lives out the Lord's Pasch. The liturgy expresses this well, in that it provides for the renewal of baptismal promises on the part of all the participants and for sprinkling the water of baptism over each one immediately after the pouring of water over the newly baptized.

When one of our brothers or sisters is ill, for us he or she is a sacrament of the suffering Christ, and we are for them a sacrament of the compassionate Lord. Jesus was in fact the brotherly companion of

# The presentation of the sacraments

## The rites

The official book which contains all the necessary elements for the celebration of a sacrament is called the *Ritual*. It includes instructions on how to perform the liturgy (*rubrics*) and the texts of the various prayers. In a 'General Introduction' it explains the church's thinking and gives the necessary pastoral guidance for a good understanding of the sacrament.

If we make a careful study of the new rites arising from the liturgical reform following the Second Vatican Council, we shall find that their presentation is arranged in a slightly different way from that of the rites which came out of the Council of Trent.

The Council of Trent had a more legal approach; Vatican II adopted a more pastoral one.

## A more legal approach: minister, subject, substance

For each sacrament the material is arranged in three parts:
– Who is the minister of the sacrament? The person who administers it.
– Who is its subject? The one who receives it.
– What is the matter of the sacrament? That with which it is performed.

This systematic presentation is certainly practical from a legal point of view, but very much less so pastorally. It has the advantage of being clear, and the disadvantage of being too simplistic. Thus it is useful to know that a priest is the usual minister of the eucharist, that the subjects are all baptized Christians who have attained the age of reason, and that the matter is the consecrated bread and wine. But that gives little scope for helping Christians to share in the liturgy. It says nothing about the place of the eucharist in the life of the community, in the sense of gathering together on a Sunday.

We know that extreme unction is given to a sick person by a priest with oil. But what is the community's role on this occasion? Here is another example. In such a perspective how ought we to regard the place of godparents at a baptism? What is the role of catechists? Are they to be counted as those who give or as those who receive the sacrament? Moreover, it is customary, in the case of the baptism of small children, to think of godparents as standing in place of the child; they respond on his or her behalf. In fact we know that they represent not the one who is being baptized but the Christian community.

Such a presentation is very clear in making sure that the celebrations are valid, but it does not encourage the priest to develop an appropriate pastoral approach and to discover, from amongst the members of the community, Christians to play their part in the celebration.

## A more pastoral approach

The new rites implemented after Vatican II use a new method of presentation which is also in three parts.

---

all those who were brought to him to be cured, before he himself became the *man of sorrows*. We all have to discover and to travel the way of God present in human suffering. And this happening which concerns us all is the place where the struggle of faith is carried out. In the Spirit, it becomes the receiving of the Word of God. Together we celebrate its sacrament.

When young children make their first communion, this sacrament is our concern. The way we look at them ought to be changed. We are called to think of them no longer as little ones to be spared our problems, but as those who have become old enough to share with us in our most precious riches, the body of Christ. It is important to remember this when meeting with parents before

## (a) The significance of the sacrament for the church

Each sacrament is in fact linked to the proclamation of the gospel. It contributes towards giving a face to the church, and by the same token it is a kind of message proclaimed openly to the world.

And so when the community celebrates confirmation it proclaims the work of the Spirit. When the church celebrates extreme unction, it demonstrates that those who suffer are part of the community. It emphasizes the importance of all those who work in the world of healing and reminds the world that the Christ of the cross, the suffering Lord, reveals to us a mysterious face of God.

If we want to understand properly the importance of the liturgical action, it is useful to ask ourselves each time, 'What is the church saying when it celebrates such and such a sacrament?' And so in 1981 the eucharistic congress at Lourdes proclaimed: 'Jesus Christ, bread broken for a new world!' Is not an important part of the gospel message brought out in this way? In the same way the introduction to each rite deals first of all with the problem of significance.

## (b) The ministers and their functions in the celebrations

In the performing of a sacrament, not only the priest has a role to play. A number of Christians have their part in the preparation, in what goes on in the celebration. Each one performs a ministry or a function.

Suppose we just reflect on the catechumenate.

Certain people, in the name of the church, welcome those who are asking for baptism. Others have the task of teaching them catechesis. There are godfathers and godmothers. There are also all the Christians who know those who are to be baptized and who each have a share in the responsibility. There is the whole community which has to open itself to the arrival of the new members.

For a first communion, the parents have their own place, but also all those who take part in the catechetical instruction, the child's friends, and all the friends and relatives who have travelled from elsewhere for the ceremony. Every one of these is a member of the church and ought to be aware that in this way they are carrying out part of its mission, that they have a set role.

## (c) The one for whom the celebration is held

The one who is called the *subject* of the sacrament is the one who is the cause of that particular celebration: a child who comes to be baptized, two young people who come to be married, a priest who comes to be ordained, a Christian assembly which shares in the eucharist, etc. Their role is important. It is not a purely passive role; they have their part in the action. They bring alive to the community this sacrament which concerns them in the first place, but which also waits on and enlivens the whole community. 'Liturgical services pertain to the whole body of the church. They manifest it and have effects upon it,' says the Constitution on the Liturgy. We have seen that this particular role is very like that of a prophet.

---

the festival day, and to say it to the whole parish as well.

Why is it that the time of confirmation is not put to use to rediscover the place of the Holy Spirit in the life of the church? Every parish ought at regular intervals to have a vigil of prayer when the Holy Spirit is invoked upon the community. During the evening, prayers would be offered for those about to be confirmed that they might live out the sacrament.

A community which no longer celebrates in some visible way within itself baptisms, first communions and even the sacrament of the sick is in the process of impoverishing itself. The sacraments are the events by which the community experiences salvation. Their celebration ought to take place quite normally within the daily life of the parish. And the way the celebration is organized ought to take account of this active participation of everyone. In this way the liturgy will truly become the mainspring and achievement of the life of the church.

The council has marked out the path towards a rediscovery of the ecclesial aspect of the sacraments, in the following three ways:

### (a) Preference for a communal celebration

It must be emphasized that rites which are meant to be celebrated in common, with the faithful present and actively participating, should as far as possible be celebrated in that way rather than by an individual and quasi-privately. This applies with special force to the celebration of Mass and to the administration of the sacraments (*On the Sacred Liturgy*, 27).

We have now understood that the purpose of this communal celebration is not to provide companions for those who are presenting themselves for the sacrament. It has an important part to play in making the life of the community complete.

This requirement of the Council seems quite natural and easy to achieve in the case of the eucharist. With the other sacraments, it has led to some rethinking. This has given rise to communal celebrations of the sacrament of reconciliation which, according to the Council, ought to be given preference over an individual celebration. The same thing has happened with infant baptisms, which are held together on one Sunday in the month, or those which are celebrated during the Parish Mass.

It was a real discovery when communal celebrations of the sacrament of the sick were begun. It was at Lourdes in 1968 that such a liturgy took place during the pilgrimage of the Rosary and Cardinal Feltin received the sacrament on this occasion. Ever since that time, a similar celebration has been organized each year in certain parishes, preceded by a short remembrance service. Because of this the

anointing of the sick no longer appears as something that is done only when a person is at the point of death. It has a part to play when the course of someone's life is changed by a serious illness; and it is also appropriate for those handicapped by old age.

### (b) The active participation of the assembly

To promote active participation, the people should be encouraged to take part by means of acclamations, responses, psalms, antiphons, hymns, as well as by actions, gestures and bodily attitudes. And at the proper time a reverent silence should be observed (*Constitution on the Sacred Liturgy*, 30).

Singing is undoubtedly one of the best examples of the assembly's participation. It builds up a communal identity, a common action. It is easy to find chants, hymns or even songs for processions, for meditating, for entering, for communion and for leaving, for thanksgiving. We are often not so successful in finding sung music which provides for a true participation in the sacramental act. We need to show the community's unity with the celebrant during the most important moments.

Thus during a baptism the whole assembly could invoke the Holy Spirit briefly, the celebrant linking the action with the words 'I baptize you in the name of the Father, and of the Son and of the Holy Spirit', and the assembly repeating its invocation. That would show a unity of all the participants at the very heart of the sacramental action.

In the same way, some singing by the assembly could be introduced into the eucharistic prayers during children's mass. That would avoid too long a monologue from the president, which almost always results in people's attention wandering at the vital moment of the eucharistic action.

It is noteworthy that the Constitution on the Sacred Liturgy calls for a 'reverent silence', as a means by which all may participate. To perform this function, it must be prepared for, be expected, and be meaningful. In this way it can truly be a time of great intensity. Otherwise it is just empty.

Servers, readers, commentators, and members of the choir also exercise a genuine liturgical function (*Constitution on the Sacred Liturgy*, 29).

The increase in liturgical ministers has a double effect. They show that the community is taking part in the action, but also allow it to live out the acceptance of God's gift with more intensity.

When it is lived out with the full participation of the whole assembly, the sacrament takes on the role of being the community's profession of faith. Let's think again of the story of the disciples on the way to Emmaus. After recognizing the Lord on the road, they returned to Jerusalem. 'They found the eleven gathered together and those who were with them, who said, "The Lord is risen indeed, and has appeared to Simon!" Then they told what had happened on the road, and how he was known to them in the breaking of the bread.'

This is what happens in every liturgical celebration. The one who comes to bring the sacrament to life meets the community and everyone together confesses their faith in Jesus Christ raised from the dead and present in the world. And so it is constantly happening afresh: 'Jesus was there in the midst of them, and said to them: "Peace be unto you".'

---

## The faith of the church

The expression 'the faith of the church' can have two meanings:

1. It indicates the content of the faith, all the articles of the creed, or, in a more vivid sense, the message of the gospel. So a non-believer sometimes wants to know what the faith of the *church* is; in that case we try to explain what the church has believed and taught from the time of the apostles to the present day. It is not up to each person to give his or her own content to the faith; this has been handed down by a tradition stretching from Christ to the present day.

2. It also indicates the loyalty which the ecclesial body shows to the gospel, the internal attitude which is a gift of the self to the person of Christ. In this sense we can say that the faith of each Christian meets up with the faith of the church. At the same time, the faith of the church confirms the personal faith of each believer, encompasses it and goes beyond it.

The word 'faith' can therefore indicate either a content (the object of faith) or an attitude (the act of faith).

The Second Vatican Council, with the whole of Christian tradition, affirms that the sacraments are sacraments of faith. But how are we to understand them? In two senses:

1. The sacraments are part of the gift of faith. It is not up to anyone to invent their meaning. They are handed on by the Christian tradition which the church bears through time and space.

2. The sacraments cannot be lived out except within the faith. That is acceptance of the gift of God, the Holy Spirit. But the faith within which the sacrament is lived is the faith of the church.

At its baptism, an infant is not yet living in the faith, but the godparents, together with some of the assembly, are invited to make the confession of faith. And the pastoral decision about whether the child is to be baptized is not dependent primarily upon the faith of the parents but upon their willingness to allow their child to have contact with the faith of the Christian community when he or she is growing up.

Young people who marry are often not very clear about what their faith is, and yet, in coming to the church, they associate themselves with the faith of the church.

The faith of each one of us is always wanting in some way, but we want to join with the faith of the community with which we celebrate the eucharist.

The celebration of the sacraments is an important moment when the community lives out its faith. We can say that the sacraments express and nourish the faith of the church.

The church is not a permanent community. Christians live scattered about in the world. This communal confession of faith builds up a *communion* between them.

Although scattered, they come together at regular intervals because they believe in 'one baptism for the remission of sins'; they believe in forgiveness, and they demonstrate and believe that a man and a woman can make a 'covenant'. They need to rediscover the lodging place at Emmaus where the Lord waits for them because he has prepared the table for them. So the church builds itself up by means of all the events throughout history, in all times and in all places where believers meet together to commemorate Jesus Christ.

And their meeting together becomes a thanksgiving. We have to give back to God the gifts he has given us, we have to praise him and give him thanks. That is why many sacramental celebrations finish with a eucharist. The church is the people of the New Covenant who lift up to God the praise of the New World.

## The role of the prophet in the sacraments

In thus emphasizing the role of the whole community in this way in the celebration of the sacraments, we are in danger of forgetting the importance of the principal actors. In our presentation, what place is to be accorded to the child who is baptized, the catechumen, the young couple who are being married, the sick person who is anointed?

They are at the centre of everything. It is their confession of faith which links everything up and nourishes everyone else. They first receive the Spirit, to live through it.

They are the prophets of the sacrament. The prophet is the person who uncovers and reveals the depths of things and events. He is also the one who announces the living word of God to his brothers and sisters. The catechumen who receives baptism tells us of the reality of Easter today. The couple who marry show us the greatness of the God of the covenant. The child making his or her first communion reminds us that human beings do not live by bread alone but by every word that comes from the mouth of God.

In our lives, when we are so often preoccupied with our jobs, we need prophets to open our eyes and make us discover the kingdom which is the work of the Spirit. Each of us in turn takes on this role of prophet to the rest of the community.

# PART THREE

# *Living out the Pasch Today*

There are seven sacraments.

Seven, like the days of the week.

Seven, like the gifts of the Spirit.

Seven is a highly symbolic figure. By itself it hints that all life becomes sacramental when it is lived under the guidance of the Spirit and in the light of the Word of God.

There are seven sacraments, but we cannot line them up side by side as if they were all the same. We have already pointed this out in Chapter 2.

At the centre is the eucharist, the sacrament of the Pasch, the sacrament of the body of Christ, the sacrament of the church.

The sacrament of order is the service of the body of Christ and of its mission. It is the sign of Christ, the head of his church.

Baptism, confirmation and first communion are called sacraments of Christian initiation. They are as it were the way which leads to full participation in the eucharist, to participation in the life of the church. Through baptism and the eucharist the whole life of the Christian is conformed to the Lord's death and resurrection. Baptism is like the foundation, the eucharist is like the pinnacle. But we must live out the Pasch among all the realities of daily life. In this sense we can say that through baptism and the eucharist the whole life of the

believer becomes sacramental.

The sacraments of reconciliation, marriage and the sick enable us to live out the Lord's Pasch, his death and resurrection, in the most important situations of our lives. We could go on and on discussing why it is these particular three which have been retained. It is more as a result of the history and the life of the community than of a pre-established theory.

There is no human life without conflict. To live out the Pasch is therefore to work towards reconciliation, because God is forgiveness.

There is no human life without tension between solitude and relationship with others. To live out the Pasch is therefore to welcome those others into a covenant, a reflection of the one made between God and humankind.

There is no human life without confrontation with sickness, suffering and death. To live out the Pasch is therefore to discover that human life is still greater than the one we have already been given to live.

In the third part of this book, we shall study each sacrament in turn. For each one, we shall first of all work out what has been its own particular significance since the beginnings of the church, and the place which it occupies within the mission of the whole body.

The way in which this sacrament has been lived out may have varied over the centuries. For this reason, we shall then give a brief historical résumé of each one.

We shall then be in a position to look at the present situation, the difficulties we are up against, and the guidelines we have been given since Vatican II for the life of Christian communities.

Jesus Christ died and was raised to life again so that the world might have life. Those who are willing to put their lives under the sign of the Lord's Pasch become members of this body of which he is the head. Together, through and within the sacramental celebrations, they receive the gift of the Spirit by which they proclaim to the world this new kingdom built by the presence of God in the midst of humankind.

## The beginning of the sacraments

In our Christian faith we affirm that 'the sacraments were instituted by Jesus Christ'. This indicates that there was no sacrament before him and that the sacraments derive their meaning and power from Jesus, who chose them as the means of grace.

But the fact that Jesus Christ instituted the sacraments does not mean that he invented the gestures and the actions of the rites, which are their human supports. Christian baptism is not the same as John the Baptist's, and the existence of this baptism clearly shows us that Jesus made use of a rite which existed before him.

The Christian sacraments have their roots in biblical events (such as the crossing of the Red Sea in the case of baptism; the covenant on Sinai for the eucharist, etc.) and in the practices of the Jewish religion prior to Christianity:

- baths of purity (with the Essenes and John the Baptist), the baptism of incorporation (the baptism of proselytes, those pagans who converted to Judaism);
- anointings for consecration (Saul and David: I Sam. 10; 16) or of healing (Tobit 11);
- thanksgiving sacrifices in the Temple, followed by the sacrificial meal at home in the case of the paschal meal;
- penitential ceremonies and practices (Yom Kippur, or the Day of Atonement, see p. 124);
- weddings (Tobit 7; Cana);

None of these practices is a sacrament, but all of them through their ritual approach and their relationship to the covenant prefigure the sacraments of the new covenant.

# 9

# The Eucharist, the Sacrament of the Pasch

*For I received from the Lord what I also delivered to you, that the Lord Jesus on the night when he was betrayed took bread, and when he had given thanks, he broke it, and said, 'This is my body which is for you. Do this in remembrance of me.' In the same way also the cup, after supper, saying, 'This cup is the new covenant in my blood. Do this, as often as you drink it, in remembrance of me.' For as often as you eat this bread and drink the cup, you proclaim the Lord's death until he comes.*

I Cor. 11.23–26

Let's open the Acts of the Apostles. The first description of the Christian community is given immediately after the account of Pentecost: 'And they devoted themselves to the apostles' teaching and fellowship, to the breaking of bread and the prayers' (Acts 2.42). As we have already noted in Chapter 3, the term 'breaking of bread' was, with 'the Lord's supper', one of the first names used for the eucharist. From the very beginning, it was this that was at the heart of the life of the Christian community in Jerusalem.

Today, it is still at the heart of the life of the church; it is the heart of its life, and also the expression of its being. Since the Second Vatican Council, people have liked to call it 'the source and the climax of the whole life of the church'. It is not therefore one sacrament among the others, as if it were on a par with them. We could call it the 'primordial sacrament', the one from which all the others come, the one towards which they all converge. That is why it occupies first place in the survey which we are about to make in this third part.

The richness of Christian thought on the eucharist is such that it is difficult to do justice to in the confines of a single chapter. We shall have to be content with emphasizing the main points:

It is the sacrament of the body of Christ.

It is the sacrament of the Lord's Pasch.

It is the Pasch of the universe, the sacrifice of praise.

It is the sign of the kingdom which is coming.

## The body of Christ

On the night before his passion, while taking the bread to give to his apostles, Jesus said: 'This is my body, which is for you'; so says the apostle Paul in his first letter to the Corinthians. There we have the oldest Christian text on the eucharist. It was written thirty years after Jesus' death. In this same letter, just before speaking of the Lord's Supper, the apostle had recalled: 'The bread which we break, is it not a participation in the body of Christ? Because

79

there is one bread, we who are many are one body, for we all partake of the one bread' (10.16–17). A little further on in the same letter, he develops the image of the various limbs of the human body. He then invites Christians to feel solidarity one with another, each one taking his or her place in the community as a whole. He adds: 'Now you are the body of Christ and individually members of it' (12.27).

Paul's terminology is not just an attractive figure of speech. He takes it up again in the letter to the Romans: 'So we, though many, are one body in Christ, and individually members one of another' (12.5). It is to be found three times in the letter to the Ephesians, where it is clearly stated that God has given Christ to be head of his church, which is his body.

How can we ignore this comparison drawn by St Paul? With the same realism and the same solemnity he affirms at the same time that Jesus gives us his body and that we ourselves become the Body of Christ! We can understand why St Augustine instructed his Christians to make the heartfelt response 'Amen' when they receive the eucharistic bread in their hands. 'Amen' is a cementing, it is the approval and commitment of our faith. 'Amen', in its primary sense, means 'that's true, that's certain, that's sure'. Augustine was in fact saying: 'We receive what we are, we become what we receive.'

---

The words and acts of Christ at the institution of the eucharist stand at the heart of the celebration: the eucharistic meal is the sacrament of the body and blood of Christ, the sacrament of his real presence. Christ fulfils in a variety of ways his promise to be always with his own even to the end of the world. But Christ's mode of presence in the eucharist is unique. Jesus said over the bread and wine of the eucharist: 'This is my body . . . this is my blood . . .' What Christ declared is true, and this truth is fulfilled every time the eucharist is celebrated. The Church confesses Christ's real, living and active presence in the eucharist.

*Baptism, Eucharist and Ministry*, Eucharist 13

---

And that is the work of the Spirit. He is the power of God in our world. He is the force for unity, the link which binds us, the communion which holds us together: 'For by one Spirit we were all baptized into one body – Jews or Greeks, slaves or free – and all were made to drink of one Spirit' (I Cor. 12.13). In the great eucharistic prayers of the Christian tradition we find two solemn invocations to ask for the coming of the Spirit (they are called *epicleses*, see p. 68). The first is over the bread and the wine that they may become the body and blood of Christ; the second is over the community, that all who partake of this meal may become members of one body.

*Presence*

The eucharist is certainly the sacrament of the body of Christ. A body is the manifestation of a presence. By means of our bodies we are there in the world, at a particular time and place. We become capable of entering into relationships with others; we are enriched by their presence and they are by ours. To speak of the body of Christ is therefore to affirm the presence of the Risen Lord, his presence in his church, and his presence in the world through his church.

Let us recall how that began on the evening of the first day, when two disciples were on the way to Emmaus. The Lord joined them, but their eyes were prevented from recognizing him. 'When he was at table with them, he took the bread and blessed, and broke it, and gave it to them. And their eyes were opened and they recognized him . . .' Faith in the 'real presence' is not the result of theological or philosophical speculations. It is born out of experience; it is the fruit of the life of the first witnesses of the resurrection.

The promise made by Jesus becomes reality: 'Lo, I am with you always, to the close of the age.'

This presence does not show itself in a tangible way. It was only at the end of a long road that the disciples recognized him (see Chapter 4). This presence is not a spectacle that we can look on: 'Yet a little while and the world will see me no more, but you will see me; because I live, you will live also'

(John 14.19). It is the source of life: 'He who eats me will live because of me' (John 6.57); it is where God dwells: 'He who eats my flesh and drinks my blood abides in me, and I in him' (John 6.56).

---

## Abiding

'He who eats my flesh and drinks my blood abides in me, and I in him.' This is how Jesus expresses himself in the great eucharistic discourse which we find in John's Gospel (John 6.56). 'Abides in' is an expression which often recurs in the writings of John. It is to be found about thirty times. It stands for a union of such depth that it takes on a permanent and stable character. 'Abide in my love' (John 15.9) . . .' Abide in my word' (John 8.31) said Jesus to his disciples. But this usually means an interior union which reflects the relationship between God the Father and Son: 'Even as you, Father, are in me, and I in you, that they also may be in us' (John 17.21).

This is a curious expression because it is put in reciprocal terms. We abide in God, but he abides in us (I John 3.24). John alone uses this expression. It reveals to us the achievement of the new relationship which God wills to have with humankind by the coming of his Son, a relationship which is lived out at its most supreme moment in the celebration of the eucharist.

'Abide' signifies a length of time, but also an intimacy. The word takes us back to the time of the Exodus. The people of God is a nomadic people, without a permanent home. But God has chosen to pitch his tent in the midst of his people, and accompany them step by step. This 'tent' of God (the Latin word is *tabernaculum*, from which our word tabernacle comes) is also called his 'house', and the word is also used later of the Temple in Jerusalem. 'To abide' with is to share in the life of a group, to set up camp with it and to move on at the same time as it. And so St John says in his Prologue that the Word was made flesh and pitched his tent among us (John 1.14). So that he could abide in the midst of his own people, Jesus made himself eucharist.

'Destroy this temple, and in three days I will raise it up', said Jesus during a discussion at Jerusalem (John 2.19), and John adds: 'But he spoke of the temple of his body'. Today, Christians have become members of this Body, which is why Paul said to them: 'You are fellow citizens with the saints and members of the household of God, built upon the foundation of the apostles and prophets, Christ Jesus himself being the cornerstone, in whom the whole structure is joined together and grows into a holy temple in the Lord; in whom you also are built into it for a dwelling place of God in the Spirit' (Eph. 2.19–22). The community of believers is truly the people of a presence, the people who have to show this presence of God in the midst of humankind to the world.

---

*He who eats my flesh and drinks my blood*
*abides in me,*
*and I in him.*
*As the living Father sent me,*
*and I live because of the Father,*
*so he who eats me*
*will live because of me.*

John 6.56–57

---

### Unity

Members of one body and fed by the same bread, Christians are called to live in unity. The eucharist is the sacrament of this unity. But we are well aware that unity always lies before us; we always have to build it up and mend it again in spite of all the causes of division and all the ruptures which have happened throughout history.

It is to the credit of the ecumenical movement that it has taken seriously Jesus' prayer to his Father: 'That they may all be one; even as you, Father, are in me, and I in you, that they also may be in us, so that the world may believe that you have sent me' (John 17.21). We need to remind ourselves that the prayer which comes just before communion, during the Mass, is to Jesus Christ to ask him to lead his church towards perfect unity.

But this progress towards unity does not merely have as its goal unity between all Christians, nor even between all believers; it directs them towards the huge task of uniting all the human family. Is not that God's great plan? 'For he has made known to us in all wisdom and insight the mystery of his will, according to his purpose which he set forth in Christ as a plan for the fullness of time, to unite all things in him, things in heaven and things on earth' (Eph. 1.10).

### The people of the brotherhood

The church is a communion. That's a good name; the first Christians were fond of it. It even became the name of their community. That is why the Acts of the Apostles states that the newly baptized were faithful to the brotherly communion.

Much later the word communion was used to denote the action by which Christians share in the eucharistic meal. And so we 'make our communion'. This is only a meaning derived from the first one, yet it expresses very well what it conveys that to receive the Body of Christ is to agree to live in communion with one's brothers and sisters; it is to live already in communion with them, in the faith of the same Lord.

We also speak of the 'communion of saints', and by that we mean the community which, throughout all time and all places, makes up the great host of those who have put their faith in Jesus Christ. Members of the same body, it is certainly true to say that they hold all their wealth in common, so that each one of them in his or her turn shares in the riches of a Francis of Assisi or of a Teresa of Avila.

## The Lord's Pasch

'For as often as you eat this bread and drink the cup, you proclaim the Lord's death until he comes' (I Cor. 11.26). This solemn warning was given by Paul to the Corinthians, who seemed not to have fully understood the dignity of the Lord's meal.

We need hardly be surprised at this. Ritual meals were customary among religious groups in the Hellenistic world. We do not know whether they existed in Palestinian Judaism at the time of Jesus, but the custom was already well established in the Jewish community in Rome, and the Essene sect also practised it at Qumran, at the edge of the Dead Sea. A generation later, after the fall of Jerusalem in AD 70, it came into use in Pharisaic circles.

So there was nothing out of the ordinary in this custom which the new communities, formed by the disciples of Jesus of Nazareth, had of meeting around a table when they came together for their weekly reunion on the first day of the week. And yet it was important that the new converts did not confuse their Christian communal meal with those which they had eaten within their old religion.

Paul certainly reproached them for a lack of mutual love, because they sat down at table without attending to one another's needs, or noticing that one remained hungry while another had too much to drink! 'It is not the Lord's supper that you eat', said the apostle (I Cor. 11.20). But the reproach went further than this lack of solidarity. And Paul had no hesitation in saying: 'For any one who eats and drinks without discerning the body eats and drinks judgment upon himself' (I Cor. 11.29).

For this body is 'the body which is given for you' (Luke 22.19), and this blood is 'my blood of the covenant, which is poured out for many' (Mark 14.24). To eat and drink in memory of the Lord is to live his Pasch. In order to 'become what we receive', to quote St Augustine's happy expression, it is not enough to reply 'Amen' and to live in communion with one's brothers and sisters; it is also necessary to become in some way 'the body given' and 'the blood poured'. To forget this is to forget that we proclaim the Lord'a death until he comes.

Christ's Pasch is not only his death. Already in the Old Covenant, Passover was deliverance, the land's freedom from bondage, the escape from slavery. Passover is the birth of a people marching towards the fulfilment of a promise. Life is their horizon.

John is the evangelist who has best emphasized the relationship between the Lord's passion and the

Jewish Passover. For him, Jesus died at the hour the lambs were sacrificed (John 19.14). Luke also has Jesus say: 'I have earnestly desired to eat this passover with you before I suffer' (Luke 22.15). And Paul affirms. 'Christ, our paschal lamb, has been sacrificed' (I Cor. 5.7). Jesus' Pasch is his passing from this world to his Father (John 13.1) – not just his death, but still more his resurrection.

On the evening of Maundy Thursday, when Jesus gave himself to his disciples and said to them, 'Do this in remembrance of me', he was already announcing his resurrection. He was giving them not only a memory of something that had happened in the past, but the presence of someone who was alive.

This is the reason why the Lord's supper is always celebrated on the first day of the week. If it was only the commemoration of the Last Supper, the meal would have been held on Thursday evening; if it was to recall Jesus' death, one would celebrate it on Friday. But it is his resurrection that is being acknowledged, and so it is celebrated on the first day of the week. And this day, stamped by this meal, became known as the Lord's Day.

### Resurrection and hope

The presence of the Risen Lord in the midst of his people caused hope to spring up. The apostles were shut up in the Upper Room, terrified, all doors closed for fear of the Jews. But Jesus came and stood in the midst of them and their fear turned into joy. On the road to Emmaus, the two friends were walking along sad and downhearted, but their mysterious companion explained the scriptures to them and their hearts burned within them. When they recognized him in the breaking of bread, they changed direction and returned joyfully to Jerusalem to find the other disciples. They had just lived out a Pasch, a passage from darkness to light, from despair to hope.

It is in this way, over the centuries, that Christians have understood the eucharist. They have never celebrated it as a simple recalling of a past event. Jesus is not remembered as a beloved person who has been taken away too soon; he is someone who is welcomed. He is alive, he is here now.

The Lord's Pasch did not just happen in the past; it is realized today and for ever. In Jesus, the whole of humanity makes its 'passage' to God. In him and in all times, humankind dies to the old world in order to rise again to the new life. This is what God accomplishes in humankind through his Son Jesus Christ, whom he gives to us. This is the true meaning of the memorial which the Lord invites us to celebrate.

### The people of hope

Christians are neither naive nor complacent. They do not believe that everything happens for the best in the best of all possible worlds. The paschal mystery is a mystery of death and life. In us and in the world, the forces of death are constantly at work, but the Lord's resurrection proclaims that life triumphs over death.

Very often in our daily life we experience difficulties, suffering, pain. We cannot fail to see the drama being played out again and again in so many of our fellow men and women, and yet we keep hold of our expectation (and not just hope) in the power of God which is shown in Jesus Christ.

If the world were not a tragic place, it would have no need of hope. 'In hope, believing against hope', is the way St Paul puts it (Rom. 4.18). This is valid because of Christ's resurrection, and for that reason only. We can understand why the apostle says: 'If Christ has not been raised, then your preaching is vain and your faith is in vain' (I Cor. 15.13).

From this time on we can claim that the forces of 'yes' are greater than the forces of 'no'; love is stronger than hate; the light cannot be quenched by the shadows; life can always triumph over death.

And so Christian faith becomes a gospel, good news. The people of the eucharist, the people of the new covenant, are called to be, above everything else and for all time, the people of hope.

# The Pasch of the universe

Jesus is the first-born of all creation. We might say that he is the centre-point. He recapitulates within himself the whole of that great effort of the universe from which life comes. His Pasch is not just a personal event. It is the whole creation which causes him to return to his Father.

On the evening of Maundy Thursday Jesus took the bread and the wine and, after giving thanks, gave it to his disciples, saying, 'This is my body, this is my blood'. In the words of the liturgy, are not the bread and the wine 'the fruits of the earth and the work of human hands'? So in this way the creation is associated with the work of Christ.

Bread is the daily bread of men and women working in the world where we have been put. Bread is our day-by-day communion with all that surrounds us and that we must make fruitful. Bread is also something that is easiest to share amongst people. Bread is our everyday hunger and our need to be satisfied. Bread is our poverty turned into riches as we affirm that 'man does not live by bread alone'.

Wine is the joyfulness of the feast. How can we celebrate a marriage when 'there is no more wine left?' But it is also the crushed grape and the blood of the vine. It is the cup which must be drunk, and which Jesus himself wished to see depart from him.

The bread and the wine are to remind us at each eucharist that we must bring all things together and raise them up to God in a single act of offering to the one who is the source of all that is good.

### Jesus took bread and made eucharist

Taking the bread and the wine, Jesus 'made eucharist'. This is the literal translation of the term used by Luke and Paul. We more usually say, 'He gave thanks'.

With Jesus our offering becomes eucharist. It becomes a song of praise, a thanksgiving, joyfulness before God. Offering and giving thanks is performed in a single movement, a single thrust. Each of us, all together, and the whole creation, are

The eucharist is the great sacrifice of praise by which the church speaks on behalf of the whole creation. For the world which God has reconciled is present at every eucharist: in the bread and wine, in the persons of the faithful, and in the prayers they offer for themselves and for all people. Christ unites the faithful with himself and includes their prayers within his own intercession so that the faithful are transfigured and their prayers accepted. This sacrifice of praise is possible only through Christ, with him and in him. The bread and wine, fruits of the earth and of human labour, are presented to the Father in faith and thanksgiving. The eucharist thus signifies what the world is to become: an offering and hymn of praise to the Creator, a universal communion in the body of Christ, a kingdom of justice, love and peace in the Holy Spirit.

*Baptism, Eucharist and Ministry*, Eucharist 4

gathered up into the offering by which Christ himself gives thanks to the Father.

Only the power of the Spirit, at work in the resurrection of Christ, makes such a eucharist possible. On the evening of Maundy Thursday Jesus did not give thanks for the life he had just lived. He was not looking back to the past; he was wholly occupied in looking to the future. And so during that night, when his betrayal had already begun, when his agony in Gethsemane and his abandonment by his friends was near, in the last moments of his freedom when his hands were not yet bound, he took his life and in the same gesture offered it to his Father and gave it to his friends. 'This is my body which is given for you. This cup which is poured out for you is the new covenant in my blood' (Luke 22.19–20). 'No one takes my life, but it is I who give it.'

On the evening of Maundy Thursday, Jesus was already committing his life to this 'passage' towards his Father which is the true Pasch. In this way he celebrates his death and his resurrection. If Jesus had done nothing except die to bear witness to the truth, he would certainly have been a worthy example, as numerous witnesses throughout human history have been; but he would not have opened the gate of life for us.

Christ's sacrifice does not lie in his death but in his passing, his Pasch. There is meaning only in the resurrection. Sacrifice, the pagan word, denotes only deprivation. But the true sacrifice is not deprivation but gift. 'Whoever saves his life will lose it, who gives his life will find it.'

Sacred and sacrifice are two related words; one derives from the other. The sacred crushes human beings and the sacred liberates them. And by his sacrifice Christ initiates us into this sacred which frees us from fear to show us a Father God, a God who becomes incarnate in the history of human beings to save them, make them grow, raise them up and so make them enter into communion with him. Then the work of human beings from the creation of the world right up to the smallest gestures of solidarity takes on a sacred worth.

For the whole of life is a sacrifice. Obsessed with the images which derive from the old pagan religious depths of humanity, too many Christians still think that the sacrifice of Jesus took place through his bloody death. Yet the Lord's very life already had a full sacrificial value. That was the case from the very beginning, as the author of the letter to the Hebrews maintained: 'When Christ came into the world, he said, "Sacrifices and offerings you have not desired, but you have prepared a body for me; in burnt offerings and sin offerings you have taken no pleasure." Then I said, "Lo, I have come to do your will, O God"' (10.5–7). Christ's whole life was

---

## Eucharist

Eucharist is the name we give to the Lord's Supper. The church meets together and celebrates the eucharist.

The word comes from the Greek *eucharistein*, and is still in common use today. It quite simply means 'thank you'. But it has a lovely etymology. *Eu* means 'well', 'good', as in euphony, euphoria, etc., and *charis* means gift. To say the word 'eucharist' is therefore to proclaim, 'the gift which you have given me is good!'

But the use of the word comes to us from the liturgy of the Temple in Jerusalem. In the time before Christ it denoted the most important of sacrifices, the one which was at it were the climax, the 'sacrifice of praise'.

For a long time the prophets had been seeking to discover a more spiritual dimension to sacrifice than the burning of oxen or sheep. 'For I seek steadfast love and not sacrifice,' says God, 'the knowledge of God, rather than burnt offerings' (Hosea 6.6; cf. Matt. 9.13, 12.7).

On the return from Exile, perhaps under the influence of the highly spiritual Persian religion, a custom was introduced to the Temple at Jerusalem of accompanying the act of offering a communion sacrifice (also called a full sacrifice or a peace offering (cf. Lev. 3.1) with an act of thanksgiving. Thus the thanksgiving became a ritual action consisting in a proclamation of the work of salvation accomplished by God. It was a memorial, an acknowledgment of God's action. In due course this thanksgiving came to be thought of as the most important event in the sacrificial process. It was more vital than the animal or vegetable offering. In Hebrew it was called *todah*, and the Greek Bible translated this word *eucharistia*. So when the Gospel says that Jesus 'gave thanks', it clearly means that this last supper of the Lord is the true sacrifice of praise.

When Christians today rediscover the meaning of thanksgiving, let's not imagine that they forget the value of the sacrifice. On the contrary, they are faithful to the great biblical tradition which finds an echo in the Psalms: 'He who brings thanksgiving as his sacrifice honours me; to him who orders his way aright I will show the salvation of God!' (Ps. 50.23).

This is how the author of the letter to the Hebrews understood it: 'Through him then let us continually offer up a sacrifice of praise to God, that is, the fruit of lips that acknowledge his name' (Heb. 13.15).

one long movement of freedom at the heart of humanity. And this is the work of the Holy Spirit. It is he who makes it possible to live in communion with the Father.

The drama of the passion is only the logical crowning of the whole of a life. 'When Jesus knew that his hour had come to depart out of this world to the Father, having loved his own who were in the world, he loved them to the end' (John 13.1).

And within the drama of the passion, this liturgical time of the last supper is when he makes us understand that the sacrifice only attains its full meaning when it culminates in a eucharist.

## *The people of praise*

Without a doubt, the finest name one could give the people of the new covenant is to call them 'the people of praise'. Their vocation is to raise the whole of creation towards God in a thanksgiving. The life of the whole universe becomes one of praise to the Lord of Life.

That is the full role of human beings. We are the self-awareness of the cosmos. We are not just passive, within the world in which we happen to find ourselves. It is up to us to put the finishing touches to creation, to order it, and to make it serve life. It is up to us to fight against the heaviness which leads to death. We have to give a spiritual dimension to the whole world, to transform it into the kingdom and to offer it all to God through Christ in a true eucharist.

> Truly, truly, I say to you,
> he who believes has eternal life.
> I am the bread of life.
> Your fathers ate the manna in the wilderness,
> and they died.
> This is the bread which comes down from heaven,
> that a man may eat of it and not die.
> I am the living bread which came down from heaven;
> if anyone eats of this bread,
> he will live for ever;
> and the bread which I shall give for the life of the world
> is my flesh.
>
> John 6.47–51

## The coming kingdom

Christ's resurrection brings in a new world. The joyful affirmation of the resurrection is celebrated on the first day of the week. But the first Christians liked to speak of it as the eighth day to indicate clearly that it was a new beginning (just as, after the concentration camps, people spoke of the twenty-fifth hour to indicate the time of horror that was beyond time). 'This day which is the first will be the eighth,' said St Augustine, 'in that the first life is not raised, but made eternal (*Comm on Ps.* 55.17).

The eucharist becomes a prophetic act. The kingdom is proclaimed by Jesus Christ, it is even inaugurated by him, and yet it is up to us to complete it. The church is not the Christ, nor is it the kingdom, it is only the sacrament.

Certainly every prophetic word unveils what is already there, but at the same time it bursts through reality instead of imprisoning us in it. It inserts the life we are in the process of living into a reality which is even greater.

It is true that all communion between human beings is a sign of the kingdom. But unless we rest in this communion which has already been realized, we see it as a proclamation of a still more perfect and deeper communion, and we are drawn towards its full realization. Human beings are still waiting, in other words still on the way.

This is not to relativize human efforts to build a truer world, or to do away with the part we play. But all human efforts are as it were the threshold to a reality which always exceed the results we achieve. That reality takes form in and through us because it is given to us by Another. And while we work to bring it into existence, we wait for it in hope.

In this way, within a world which is in the process of forming itself and integrating itself into the human enterprise which is the achievement of freedom together with brotherly and sisterly communion, the resurrection of Christ opens up a vision of a future which is in our hands, but which is a gift which has come from God.

We have to proclaim this to the world, but in order to do that we must accept it completely ourselves, let it resound in our lives, let it envelop us and take shape in us; and so our individual small efforts will be signs of what is being proclaimed. 'Therefore, if anyone is in Christ, there is a new creation; the old one has passed away, behold, the new has come. All this is from God, who through Christ reconciled us to himself and gave us the ministry of reconciliation' (II Cor. 5.17f.).

The church recognizes the proper worth of the human enterprise, because the kingdom of God has to be present in the world. The Creator's plan can only be realized in the world. It goes through the development of humanity, but is not reduced to that. That is why the church must not act as a substitute for those responsible for this enterprise. When it celebrates the eucharist, when it proclaims the word of God, it puts itself at the service of humankind in order to carry out the work of its Lord, who said, 'I came that they may have life, and have it abundantly' (John 10.10).

*The people of the new age*

Is the church a utopia? Without a doubt, in the sense that it never attains its full potential. It is in tension with a world which is on the way. As the apostle Paul said, we have to 'grow up in every way into him who is the head, into Christ' to attain 'the measure of the stature of the fullness of Christ' (Eph. 4.13).

The eucharist stands at the heart of the Christian life as a call for an everlasting 'going beyond'. If the Passover of the old covenant marked the Exodus from the land of slavery and the beginning of the long journey towards the Promised Land, the new covenant, too, draws us towards a new country and towards that future of the world which is augurated at the resurrection.

> The eucharistic church, in making itself open to God's gift, forms a people who are brothers and sisters, members one of another and in solidarity with the whole human race . . . It is not enough for us to be united among ourselves. Christ requires that we give tangible form around us to what he has given us in the eucharist. The bread which is shared makes us into sharing people. In this way the eucharistic community becomes a force for change in the world, just as the yeast works in raising the bread. It is not possible to be united with Christ and keep our distance from the hungry and thirsty, the strangers, the imprisoned, the sick, and the men and women helpless in the face of those who exploit them. For Christ identifies himself with these people . . . Liberated and forgiven by God, how can we not fight together so that men and women live free and forgiven? It is in the actual and concrete involvement of day-to-day life that the eucharistic practice is borne out.
>
> *Jesus Christ, Bread Broken for a New World,*
> Eucharistic Congress, Lourdes 1981

---

## A history of the sacrament of the eucharist

### The beginnings

*The Lord Jesus, on the night when he was betrayed took bread, and when he had given thanks, he broke it (and gave it to them) and said, 'This is my body which is for you. Do this in remembrance of me.' In the same way also the cup, after supper . . .*

I Cor. 11.23–26; cf. Luke 22.19

That is how the oldest text refers to the eucharist (see p. 79). It takes us back to the church of Corinth in 55, twenty years or so after the death of Christ. The words which describe this action have varied – the Lord's

87

Supper (I Cor. 11.20); the breaking of bread (Acts 2.42); Mass (end of the fourth century); eucharistic celebration (after Vatican II), but it is always 'this' which the church does, right up to the present day, with an astonishing and admirable faithfulness.

And yet this faithfulness has not prevented each period in history from giving its own special emphasis to the eucharist, 'the substance being saved' (cf. the Council of Trent cited on p. 61). It is these emphases that we are going to look at, rather than at all the stages of the development of the mass, since it is impossible to trace its history fully here.

## The first centuries: the *ecclesia* meets together

The first emphases which make themselves felt in the New Testament and in the first Christian writings stress the very strong link which exists between the eucharist and the assembly (Greek = *ecclesia*). 'When you assemble as a church,' said Paul to the Corinthians (I Cor. 11.18); 'they broke bread in their homes' said Luke of the first Christian community (Acts 2.46), and further on (Acts 20.7), of the community at Troas: 'On the first day of the week, when we were gathered together to break bread . . .'

'On the Lord's day, meet together to break bread' says the *Didache*, the first non-biblical Christian document, around the year 100.

'Christians are in the habit of gathering together on a particular day before dawn', said Pliny the Younger in a letter dated 112. It is the first non-Christian writing to speak of Christians.

'On the day which is called Sunday, all the Christians living in the town or the country gather together in the same place,' said St Justin in his first *Apology*, around 150. He then gives the first description that we have of the eucharistic celebration.

'Let no one diminish the *ecclesia* by his absence, that the Body of Christ may not be diminished by one member. Do not tear apart the Body of Christ!' says the *Didascalia Apostolorum* in the third century.

This word *ecclesia* is so powerful in the life of the communities that it ends up by becoming the name of the group itself; it is the assembly, the church which is in a particular town (e.g. I Cor. 1.2).

So the assembly meets together to break bread. It does not yet have a church building, or a missal. It meets at the house of one of its members (Acts 2.46; Rom. 16.23), and for its celebration it takes its inspiration from the Jewish liturgical models (synagogue, paschal meal, temple) which were well known to those converted Jews who were the first Christians. When the apostles were no longer there to preside in person, their writings were circulated and read, copied and commented on. Fixed patterns of prayer evolved on which the presidents improvised. At the very beginning the eucharist took place during the course of a communal meal (I Cor. 11), but very quickly became dissociated from it. In 150, St Justin described the celebration without mentioning a meal other than 'the distribution and sharing of the consecrated elements to each person', that is to say, the communion of the Body and Blood of Christ.

Finally, it was the act of faith itself which had to be shared rather than these external details. Because of some of Jesus' words, such as 'This generation will not pass away before all these things take place' (Mark 13.30) the first Christians were firmly convinced that the Lord's return was imminent. The eucharist took on a very eschatological tone from this. It was the Lord's Supper in which the community gathered together in the expectation of the Lord's appearance. St Paul expresses it in this way: 'For as often as you eat this bread and drink the cup, you proclaim the Lord's death until he comes' (I Cor. 11.26). As these first Christians realized that the Lord was not coming back, their ardent expectation waned, but the eucharist retained its initial character as an eschatological meal, as being inherent in its meaning (hence the acclamation in the *anamnesis*, 'Come Lord Jesus!').

## Organization and creation: from the fourth to the eighth centuries

The peace which the emperor Constantine offered the church in 313 was to have a whole series of consequences:
- First of all, freedom from the risk of persecution and the emperor's favourable view of Christianity resulted in a significant increase in the number of Christians.
- The assemblies became too big to be held in people's homes. The imperial buildings (basilicas) were used, then special buildings were put up dedicated to the meeting of Christians: these were 'church buildings'.
- Because there were more faithful, there was need of more ministers. Not all were educated and trained. The need for liturgical books (the Order of Mass, sacramentaries containing prayers, lectionaries) made itself felt, but was met in a great variety of ways depending on region and culture (East, West, Rome, Milan, Gaul, Spain, etc.).
- This series of new situations meant that the liturgy became increasingly official, but this did not hinder the participation of the faithful, which was always full and warm.

## Uniformity and privatization: from the eighth to the sixteenth centuries

For reasons which are both religious (dispersion and the variety of usages, the ignorance of the clergy) and political (a desire to unite the empire), the Carolingian dynasty (with Pepin the Short and Charlemagne) was to have a positive influence on the development of the liturgy, especially on the Mass.
- The Roman formularies were imposed on Gaul, then on Spain. They did not do away with local variations, but brought them a common basis.
- Roman liturgical chant (*cantilena romana*) was introduced into Gaul. Under the impetus of the Bishop of Metz, in particular, the Roman melodies were developed and decorated to become 'Gregorian chant'.
- In 794, in order to combat the 'adoptianist' heresy, Charlemagne made the recitation of the Nicene Creed compulsory after the gospel.

The combined effect of these measures was to consolidate the liturgy a little more and gradually to transform the eucharist of the assembly into the official worship of the empire. The development of the chant, the work of specialists, which had to be performed by them (*schola*, i.e. monks), considerably reduced the active participation of the people, made the action increasingly remote and led to the composition of great numbers of private prayers which only the celebrant recited, as well as the privatization of public prayers. In this way the *canon* (the eucharistic prayer) began to be recited in an undertone, while the choir chanted the *Sanctus* and then the *Benedictus*.

Because of the progressive distancing of the people from the liturgical action and because of a trend to a piety which emphasized unworthiness and a fear of sin, the people communicated less and less. In addition, there were practical and hygienic reasons. The communion rite was considerably changed from the ninth century onwards:
- only unleavened bread was used, which was easier to keep;
- there was no longer communion from the chalice;
- communion was taken on the tongue, and no longer in the hands;
- in order to do this more easily, the custom grew up of kneeling to receive communion.

The thirteenth century was marked by two reactions:
- In 1215, the Fourth Lateran Council was obliged to stipulate that all the faithful had to communicate 'at least once a year', after making confession 'of all their sins', at Easter.
- Through a kind of deeply held popular feeling that a Christian could not be completely separated from the eucharist, the cult of the 'blessed sacrament' grew up and was continually expanded. Evidence of this is

the custom which evolved, and was then prescribed, of elevating the host after the consecration: the elevation of the chalice only came towards the end of the thirteenth century.

Here are some other important points relating to this period:

- The new art known as *Gothic* allowed the construction of much bigger religious buildings (cathedrals). Admirable though the art was, the liturgical consequences were unfortunate: the faithful were placed further and further away from the sanctuary, that is, from the centre of the action. The custom which was soon to grow up of enclosing the sanctuary with grilles did nothing to help.

  'All this resulted in making the laity such passive members that the liturgical books no longer even mentioned their presence' (*The Church at Prayer*, II). The faithful no longer took part in the Mass except indirectly, while at the same time, for their own personal sanctification, they multiplied acts of devotion which had no real relation to the liturgical action (such as, later on, saying the rosary during Mass).

- In the end, the combination of these tendencies and devotions was to result in a change in the way of thinking about and celebrating the Mass: more and more, first of all in the country, then in the monasteries and then generally, priests came to celebrate Mass almost privately with a very greatly reduced number of the faithful, perhaps even with a single server. The 'complete Missals', which contained all the prayers, chants and readings, made this possibility easier, and the increase in Masses said for the dead increased the number of occasions on which this happened.

## The Council of Trent: the sixteenth century

We must rid ourselves of the idea that the Council of Trent did nothing but hurl anathemas around! It did do this, to be sure, in the spirit and the style of the time, in order to preserve and restate the Catholic faith, particularly in respect of the sacrament of the eucharist, but it also showed its ability in a truly pastoral sense to put right the abuses and correct the imbalances which were current in the Catholic church itself, to the point where one could say, after examining some of its insights and requests, that we had to wait for Vatican II before Trent could be put into action.

On the subject of the Mass, the bishops wanted a unified way of celebrating it which would remedy the grave situation of the liturgy and the danger that this was posing to the eucharist.
There were
- exorbitant taxes on liturgical acts;
- priest whose only function was to say Masses for the dead;
- uneducated clergy, because there were still no seminaries;
- a proliferation of devotional excrescences surrounding the rites (the development of private prayers, making signs of the cross, kissing devotional objects);
- allegories which deflected the meaning of the eucharistic liturgy (the laying on of hands before the consecration was no longer a sign of invoking the Holy Spirit, but of laying upon Christ the sins of the world);
- the proliferation of ancillary liturgical acts (the showing of relics, processions);
- increasing separation between what the clergy were doing in the sanctuary and what the laity were doing in the nave;
- a change of understanding in the eucharist towards seeing and understanding it to the detriment of participating in the eucharistic mystery, to such a degree that some bishops were already suggesting that the Mass should be celebrated in the vernacular, and Cardinal de Cusa already said in the fourteenth century: 'The Holy Sacrament was not inaugurated as something to look at, but as a food';
- the suppression of Sunday as the celebration of the risen Christ under the flood of saints' days.

The Council of Trent, like Vatican II, did not go as far as a detailed revision of the Order of Mass, but charged Pope Pius IV with setting the work of reform in motion. When he died, Pius V carried on his work. Unfortunately, for lack of time, historical knowledge and expert advice, in the end it was the missal of the Roman Curia which Pius V promulgated on 14 July 1570. And this missal had been drawn up for the celebration of private masses: it was a missal of a Mass without people!

The use of this missal was gradually to extend throughout the West, but, following the principles of the Council itself, dioceses were allowed the opportunity to continue to perform their local liturgy with its special customs, if these were more than two hundred years old. And so Milan, Lyons and the Dominican Order kept their own rite and in 1830 the Archbishop of Paris, Mgr de Quelen, was still publishing the Parisian Missal and not the Roman one.

## From the Council of Trent to Vatican II

For four centuries, Mass was celebrated silently by the priest, usually in the presence of the faithful. The obligation of having a 'server at Mass' was the only remaining witness to the importance of the assembly.

However, there were developments, some of which widened still further the division between priest and assembly:
– the custom of reciting the rosary during Mass was encouraged;
– Benediction of the blessed sacrament was solemnized and encouraged to the point of often being preferred (except on Sundays) to the ordinary Mass to indicate significant times: the month of the Rosary, the month of Mary, the first Friday in the month, etc.

Others tried constantly to restore a fairer participation in the liturgy to the faithful:
– from the seventeenth century, there were translations of the missal for the use of the faithful;
– at the instigation of the Oratorians, a popular plainsong was created (the Mass of the Angels, Dumont's Royal Mass, etc.)
– there were commentaries on the liturgy with an authentic concern in the translation to fight deviant allegories (Dom Gueranger's *Liturgical Year* came in the middle of the nineteenth century).
– above all, there was the restoration by Pius X of frequent communion in 1905 and of communion at an early age in 1907. The same pope called for 'the active participation of the faithful in the liturgy'.
– Finally, as a prelude to Vatican II, there was the liturgical work of Pius XII:
    the encyclical *Mediator Dei* in 1947,
    the restoration of the Easter vigil in 1951 and of Holy Week in 1956,
    the restoration of evening masses and the relaxing of the eucharistic fast in 1953.

We should note that this movement towards liturgical renewal, which culminated in Vatican II's Constitution on the Sacred Liturgy and its reform, would not have come into existence without the biblical, patristic and historic renewal which began at the beginning of the nineteenth century. It is also due to the unflagging work of returning to sources which was particularly evident in Germany (the abbey of Beuron), Belgium (the abbeys of Maredsous and of Mont-Cesar) and France (founding of the Pastoral Liturgical Centre which after the Council became a national centre).

## The reform of Vatican II

This reform is the source of the present liturgy. Here are the principal rules which guided the work of the Fathers and the experts of the Council. Far from being a series of innovations, even on the points which caused most surprise (the priest facing the people, the use of the vernacular, communion in the hand, etc),

the reform was a return to the sources and especially to the way of celebrating and praying which the church used in the first centuries, in particular in the following points:
- a simplification of the way in which the celebration unfolds;
- the most practical placing of objects (the celebrant's chair, the ambo, the altar facing the people) so as to allow the maximum communication;
- the reestablishment of concelebration and the end of parallel and simultaneous masses;
- priority given to celebration on Sunday, the Lord's Day, over saints' days and 'votive masses';
- first place accorded to a mass with people present, and their participation in the liturgical action;
- the use of the language spoken by the participants for the language of the liturgy;
- importance restored to the Word of God, including the Old Testament and the Psalms;
- a return to the eucharistic prayer proclaimed in an audible voice;
- a reintroduction of the General Intercession, of communion in the hand and even, on certain occasions, in both kinds.

These points of reform, among many others, turned the Mass of Vatican II, according to the *Ordo missae* of Paul VI, promulgated on 3 April 1969, into a celebration more in keeping with that of the first centuries of the church, and so closer to the Lord's Supper.

---

## Today

Liturgical reform began well before the Second Vatican Council. That brought together efforts made over a long period. In the Introduction to the Roman Missal, Pope Paul VI spoke of four centuries of progress in the liturgical sciences. The Council of Trent, which finished in 1563, called for a return to the riches to which the ancient traditions bore witness. The work was begun even then, and followed through during the seventeenth and eighteenth centuries, thanks to the work of the Benedictine abbeys. For the more recent period, we can cite the names of Dom Guéranger (1840) and Dom Lefevre (1920).

In 1948, Pope Pius XII set up a Commission for Liturgical Reform, and began with the restoration of the Easter Vigil.

In taking note of the work achieved and of the directives suggested by previous popes, Vatican II brought into the everyday lives of the faithful what was still only the privilege of a restricted group of people. It wanted the eucharist to become 'the source and the climax of the life of the church'.

We can list the four most important points on which the changes hinged: the rediscovery of the assembly, of the place of the Word, of the importance of thanksgiving, and of the prayer of the faithful.

### The body of Christ

The most spectacular changes concern the way the celebration is arranged. There is no longer a celebrant with other people present. The whole assembly is invited to celebrate while associating itself with the prayers of the priest who presides. We have forgotten that we used to speak of low masses!

There has been a tendency towards creating real liturgical ministries, such as those of chant leader, reader, or auxiliary ministers of communion. We have forgotten the time when the priest had to be a one-man band.

The use of the vernacular has deeply affected the attitude of those taking part. It is understandable that some people regret that this has meant a shelving of part of the musical inheritance built up by tradition. Pope Paul VI said about this: 'A real sacrifice is being made there. And for what? . . . An understanding of prayer is more precious than the ancient silken vestments in which it was regally arrayed. The participation of the people is more precious, the people of today, who want us to speak clearly and in a way they can understand and translate into their everyday tongue.'

There is a simple reason for all these changes: all liturgical action is the work of Christ the High Priest and of his body which is the church. In accordance with the words often repeated by the Council, all the members of the Body of Christ ought 'to play a full, intelligent and active part in the liturgy'.

### The two tables

'Man does not live by bread alone, but by every word that proceeds from the mouth of God' (Deut. 8.3; Matt. 4.4). The old tradition of the church liked to emphasize that the liturgy puts us in touch with two basic foods: the bread of the Word and the bread of the eucharist.

Readings of the Word of God have been considerably increased. They are divided up into a three-year cycle for Sundays, and a two-year one for weekdays. Gradually, the people of God is rediscovering this taste for the holy scriptures, which diminished at the time of the struggle between the Catholic church and the Protestant Reformation.

The homily has regained its rightful place in the liturgy of the Word. It shows the relationship between the Word which has just been proclaimed and the life of those taking part. It is an introduction to the thanksgiving. From now on, the proclamation of the Word of God will not seem to be mere teaching, but the source from which our eucharistic praise bursts forth.

Running parallel to liturgical reform, we have seen the creation of a number of Bible groups, and scripture studies have found a principal place again in the training of clergy and in Catholic universities.

### The thanksgiving

Whereas we used to say 'go to Mass', 'attend Mass', today we more readily say 'take part in the euchar-

ist', 'celebrate the eucharist'. The shift in vocabulary is important.

As we have seen, the eucharist is the true sacrifice of thanksgiving. This aspect of praise comes more to the forefront in the revised liturgy.

The missal has been enriched by numerous prefaces; they number eighty-eight in the official edition of the missal! Eucharistic prayers which lead the praise of the whole community have found a place beside the Roman canon. There are nine of them in the missal, some of them recalling the prayers of the liturgy of the first centuries.

The number of prayer groups which have sprung up in the last twenty years or so have been as a result of the rediscovery of the prayer of thanksgiving.

### The prayer of the faithful

This was the great tradition of the first centuries of the church. Each Christian had to be associated with the prayer of Christ for the world. In this way he or she demonstrated what their baptism has made them a part of – the unique priesthood of Christ. Gradually this prayer fell into disuse and was sometimes replaced by the 'prayers of the prone', in which the dead of the parish were particularly mentioned. In restoring the 'prayer of the faithful', also called the General Intercession, the Council asks us to intercede in our worship for the whole church, the world, for the underprivileged and for our community.

In this way, the community tries to avoid being self-centred. The prayer can become less timeless and the echo of people's daily lives can be voiced in the assemblies.

In many countries of the world, and especially in the young churches, the eucharist has truly recovered its central place in the life of the community. Week by week throughout the year Christ's disciples meet together, and in a way that goes beyond words and is better than all explanations, they discover the true face of their church, that to which it is called, that possibility of being which the Spirit has already given it, even in its poverty and imperfection.

'The wall of the city had twelve foundations,
and on them the twelve names of the twelve apostles of the Lamb' (Rev. 21.14)

# 10

# The Sacrament of Order: Ministries in the Church

*Now there are varieties of gifts, but the same Spirit;*
*and there are varieties of service, but the same Lord;*
*and there are varieties of working, but it is the same God who inspires them in everyone.*
*To each is given the manifestation of the Spirit for the common good.*

*For just as the body is one and has many members,*
*and all the members of the body, though many, are one body,*
*so it is with Christ.*
*For by one Spirit we were all baptized into one body*
*and all were made to drink of one Spirit.*

*If all were a single organ, where would the body be?*
*As it is, there are many parts, yet one body.*
*Now you are the body of Christ and individually members of it.*
*And God has appointed in the church*
*first apostles, second prophets,*
*third teachers, then workers of miracles,*
*then healers, helpers, administrators,*
*speakers in various kinds of tongues.*

I Cor. 12.4–28

The sacrament of order spontaneously evokes the image of the priest ordained to the service of the church to celebrate the sacraments. This image is not wrong, but it is only partial.

- The sacrament of order also includes deacons and bishops.
- It does not just give a power, that of celebrating the mass or hearing confessions, but is rich in meaning.

- It is not limited to the sacramental life and to acts of worship, but includes more complex realities.

Is the priest a man of the mass? Yes, if that signifies that he is at the service of the body of Christ. And the body of Christ, according to St Paul's expression, is not just the 'eucharistic body', the consecrated bread, but also his 'ecclesial body', the community of believers. Christ brings together the baptized as the members of a single body. The service of the body is also the service of the church.

95

# Origins

At the beginning of the church we do not find a single type of organization for the different groups of Christians. In Chapter 3 we saw that the New Testament is the reflection of communities united among themselves but also deriving from different traditions. Going through the Gospels, Acts, and the epistles, we can see three successive distinguishing factors among the members of communities:

- first of all there is a choice, made by Jesus himself, instituting the apostles;
- then there is the Jewish custom of giving responsibility to a group of elders;
- finally there are the necessities of life which lead to a sharing of services.

## The 'Twelve' and the 'Seven'

The group of 'Twelve' has its origins in the choice made by Jesus himself when he instituted his apostles (Mark 3.13–19; Matt. 10.1–4; Luke 6.12–16). And the Gospel bears witness that among them Peter, 'the rock' (Matt. 16.18), is entrusted with 'strengthening' his brothers (Luke 22.32). Furthermore, at the beginning of Acts we can see him acting quite naturally in exercising this primacy (Acts 1.15; 2.14; 2.37; 3.6 . . .).

These are the Twelve, and their very number is symbolic. They are as it were the representatives of the twelve tribes of a new Israel. They bear witness to the universality of the church. Immediately after the ascension, Peter is concerned to complete this group, which the defection of Judas has reduced by one member. The choice falls on Matthias (Acts 1.15–26). On this occasion the book of Acts, through Peter, defines the Twelve as those 'who have accompanied us during all the time that the Lord Jesus went in and out among us, beginning from the baptism of John until the day when he was taken up from us' and are 'with us a witness to his resurrection'.

The church remains for ever based on the witness of these men. That allows the Apocalypse to state: 'The wall of the city had twelve foundations, and on them the twelve names of the twelve apostles of the lamb' (Rev. 21.14). That is why we say in the creed that the church is 'apostolic'. When it claims apostolic succession, it is affirming that it can go back through the centuries to this initial group, chosen by Jesus.

---

### The Twelve

*Jesus went up into the hills, and called to him those whom he desired; and they came to him. And he appointed twelve, to be with him, and to be sent out to preach and have authority to cast out demons.*
*He appointed twelve:*
*Simon whom he surnamed Peter,*
*James the son of Zebedee*
*and John the brother of James,*
*whom he surnamed Boanerges,*
*that is, sons of thunder,*
*Andrew, and Philip,*
*and Bartholomew, and Matthew,*
*and Thomas, and James the son of Alphaeus,*
*and Thaddaeus and Simon the Zealot,*
*and Judas Iscariot, who betrayed him.*

Mark 3.13–19

---

*In those days Peter stood up among the brethren (the company of persons was in all about a hundred and twenty) and said: 'Brethren, the scripture had to be fulfilled, which the Holy Spirit spoke beforehand by the mouth of David, concerning Judas who was guide to those who arrested Jesus. For he was numbered among us, and was allotted his share in this ministry . . . So one of the men who have accompanied us during all the time that the Lord Jesus went in and out among us, beginning from the baptism of John until the day when he was taken up from us – one of these men must become with us a witness to his resurrection.'*

*And they put forward two, Joseph called Barsabbas, who was surnamed Justus, and Matthias. And they prayed and said, 'Lord, you know the hearts of all, show which of these two you have chosen to take the place in this ministry and apostleship from which Judas has turned aside, to go to his own place.' And they cast lots for them, and the lot fell on Matthias; and he was enrolled with the eleven apostles.*

Acts 1.15–26

---

They are given first of all the title of 'apostle', which means 'sent', emissary, ambassador. Jesus said to them, 'As the Father has sent me, so I send you' (John 20.21). And the author of the letter to the Hebrews states that Jesus himself is the apostle of God (Heb. 3.1). We can see that at the beginning of the church this title was not always restricted to the college of the Twelve, but was used in a wider sense. Paul claims it for himself (Rom. 11.13), while confessing: 'I am the least of the apostles, who am not worthy to be called apostle because I persecuted the church of God' (I Cor. 15.9). He does not consider himself inferior to those many others who deck themselves out in a title which does not belong to them. He calls them ironically the 'super apostles' (II Cor. 11.5, 13; 12.11). But at the same time he uses the term 'apostle' quite simply for Silvanus, Timothy (I Thess. 2.7) and Barnabas (I Cor. 9.5).

---

### The sacrament of order

Why was this name given to the sacrament which concerns ministries? There is a simple reason, but it is not immediately seen by many people, and one could say that the name is the source of much confusion in catechesis.

The members of the clergy are not responsible for keeping order in the community, as children often think.

Nor does the name mean that it is for the pope, bishops and priests to give orders which all should obey.

Nor does it indicate that those concerned are of the first order, i.e. have a quality superior to the rest.

Order means 'a group of persons subject to certain professional, moral or religious rules'. The name is also used for the main religious congregations when one says that a person has become a member of an order.

Originally the elders, in the Christian community, formed a group responsible for government. When someone was chosen for this role he entered the 'College of Elders', in Latin *ordo presbyterorum*, i.e. order of priests.

Ordination is the ceremony in which the sacrament of order is celebrated.

---

However, it seems that after a certain development the name of apostle was reserved in a privileged way for the restricted circle of the Twelve.

But the Twelve were not sufficient for the task. The book of Acts tells how the needs of the Jerusalem community led them to take on colleagues. 'It is not right, they said, that we should give up preaching the word of God to serve tables' (Acts 6.1–7). Hence the choice of the 'Seven'.

Tradition has seen this episode as the first indication of the diversity of ministries. The task of these 'Seven' was not limited to administrative duties, since Stephen also devoted himself to the proclamation of the word (Acts 6.8–7.60), and Philip founded the communities in Samaria and baptized an official of the queen of Ethiopia (Acts 8).

Though the name 'deacon' is not explicitly given to these new colleagues of the apostles, it does appear twice in the New Testament. The deacons are mentioned at the beginning of the letter to the Philippians (1.1) and are spoken of at greater length in I Timothy (3.8–13). We see there that they are charged with a well-established ministry. They are mentioned in both cases immediately after the *episcopoi*, the name from which bishop comes. We should not conclude too hastily that the communities were already structured as they were to be in subsequent centuries. In neither case do we find any allusion to the elders, though they held an important place in other churches. Several systems of organization which emerged in the earliest days were subsequently reduced to a single model.

### The 'elders'

The elders appeared very soon. There is nothing surprising about that, since the Jewish communities customarily had elders at their head. The Bible itself mentions the elders of Israel, and this word denotes distinguished figures, counsellors and wise men.

When Paul and Barnabas returned for the first time to the communities which they had founded on leaving for their first apostolic journey, 'they appointed elders for them in every church, with prayer and fasting, and committed them to the Lord in whom they believed' (Acts 14.23). Here they were simply imitating a practice already established in the Jerusalem church, in which a group of elders played an important role alongside the apostles (Acts 11.30; 15.2, 4, 6; 16.4; 21.18).

And I Peter exhorts the elders to 'tend the flock of God that is in your charge', without exercising too authoritarian a power (5.2). It adds, 'I as a fellow elder and witness to the suffering of Christ'. Similarly, Paul gives his last counsel to the elders of Ephesus when he meets them in the port of Miletus (Acts 20.17–36).

When we speak of elders, we always use the plural, and that should be noted. To be an elder is not a personal honour; it is to be a member of a group, a 'college', the members of which seem to have corporate responsibility for directing the life of the community. This perspective has been preserved down to our day, and that is why the very name of the sacrament is 'sacrament of order'.

'Elder' in Greek is *presbyteros*, hence our word priest. We already stressed in Chapter 8 that this Greek word is not part of sacerdotal vocabulary and does not say anything about the possibility of exercising a sacred function.

However, I Timothy speaks of elders who 'exercise the presidency', doubtless presiding at the liturgical assembly. By virtue of this fact some are charged with preaching and teaching (I Tim. 5.17).

The letter of James also gives elders a role: going to pray with the sick and anoint them with oil (5.14).

Alongside the elders, we can see *episcopoi* appearing in the last writings of the New Testament. It seems that there was only one in each community (I Tim. 3.5–9), and that he was chosen from among the elders (Titus 1.5–9).

It was not until the end of the apostolic age that there was generally a community structured around the bishop, priests and deacons.

## The 'services' of the community

The letters of St Paul bear witness to a more complex organization. In Ephesians, he speaks of the plurality of the members of the community and their unity in the body of Christ (Eph. 4.1–16). All Christians must fulfil their tasks in a way worthy of the calling to which they have been called, so that the whole body grows and upbuilds itself in love. This diversity of ministries has its foundation in the multiplicity of the gifts of the Spirit that the first Christians called charisms.

We can find four passages in which these gifts are listed. They can be compared through the table opposite. Organization varied from one community to another. It is not always easy to specify the particular role to be played by someone to whom a service has been entrusted or who has been endowed with a charism. To what degree would this correspond to permanent or institutional ministries? We have too little information to judge.

The tasks to be accomplished are numerous: some concern the proclamation of the word (apostles, prophets, teachers, evangelists), and others the direction of the community (pastors, administration, wisdom); others ensure mutual service (help and healing). As St Paul says, it is the same Spirit which acts in all.

The key word in this structuring of the community is 'service'. No Christian can dispense with it. We might recall the gesture of Jesus on the evening of Maundy Thursday when he washed the feet of his disciples. When he had done this he said to them: 'I have given you an example, that you should also do as I have done to you.'

We might recall St Paul's expression, 'You are the body of Christ and you are its members, each in turn.' That is the conviction which motivated the first Christian communities and which distinguished them radically from all the religious groupings around them. The image is a powerful one and provides the model for the organization of the community.

All the members are responsible in solidarity. Each makes his or her contribution to the progress of the whole. The Spirit is given to all and to each, for the good of all.

But at the same time this body is the body of Christ. He remains its head. Risen, he is alive. He is present, with an active presence. As head of his body he animates it and communicates to it his life. He leads all his body along the ways of the world to continue his mission. 'I came that they may have life, and have it abundantly' (John 10.10). 'And this is eternal life, that they know you, the only true God, and Jesus Christ whom you have sent' (John 17.3).

The major features which allow us to understand the existence of the different ministries in the life of the church are:

The solidarity and complementarity of the members of the body;

The presence of the head, which animates all with a view to mission.

## The significance of the ordained ministry

From the beginning, a sign has marked the existence of certain ministries, that of the laying on of hands for the giving of the Spirit. It is there that the roots of the present-day celebration of the sacrament of order are to be found.

Only Christ is a priest, and his priesthood is exercised by the whole community of the baptized. But at the heart of this community there is a group of people who have been entrusted with a particular service, that of the priestly ministry.

It is a service of the church so that this can in truth be the church of Christ, the body of which he is the head.

It is a service which unites in an inseparable way the service of the community as the body of Christ and the service of Christ as head of the body.

---

### Diversity of ministries

| *I Cor. 12.8* | *I Cor. 12.28* | *Rom. 12.6* | *Ephesians 4.11* |
|---|---|---|---|
| Gift of wisdom | Apostles | Gift of prophecy | Apostles |
| Gift of knowledge | Prophets | Gift of service | Prophets |
| Gift of faith | Those who teach | Gift of teaching | Evangelists |
| Gift of healing | Gift of miracles | Gift of exhortation | Pastors |
| Gift of miracles | Gift of healing | | Those who teach |
| Gift of prophecy | Gift of helping | | |
| Discernment of spirit | Gift of administration | | |
| Gift of tongues | Gift of tongues | | |
| Gift of interpretation | | | |

### The service of the community as the 'body of Christ'

We can note three main roles:
    the service of communion,
    apostolic witness,
    action in the name of Christ.

#### The service of communion

First, there is a ministry of communion. The Lord is 'the head from whom the whole body, joined and knit together by every joint with which it is supplied, when each part is working properly, makes bodily growth and upbuilds itself in love'.

This is first of all the role of the bishop responsible for bringing together the local church, and in a quite special way that of the bishop of Rome who has the care of all the churches.

It is necessary to create communion between the members of the assembly which meets in the same place. It is not an aggregate but a body: 'The bread which we break, is it not communion in the body of Christ? Since there is only one bread, we all are one body', says St Paul in his first letter to the Corinthians.

But it is also necessary to create communion between the assembly present in one place and the universal church gathered in all times and all places.

The episcopal college, in union with the pope, has this care for the universal church. Similarly, the college of priests, members of the same diocese, have this charge in union with their bishop, to whom they are attached as to the centre of unity.

But the same concern must preoccupy all those who are officially charged with a ministry. That is the case with catechists or responsible members of the community in the young churches. Their regular meetings make them aware that they are at the service of a single church.

#### Apostolic witness

Communion between Christians takes place around a living person, the risen Lord present in the midst of his own. 'Where two or three are gathered in my name, I am in the midst of them.' The faith of the church in this presence is based on the witness of the group of the Twelve. From the beginning, they were the first witnesses to the resurrection.

Since then, through the centuries of history, the witness of the Twelve has been handed down from generation to generation by the college of bishops, who have been given charge of the apostolic tradition.

The apostles received their mission from Christ. They were pillars of the church and remain so. The priestly ministry is at the service of the apostolicity of the church.

The message of these first witnesses has been handed down to us in the writings of the New Testament. The priestly ministry is responsible for the living word in the midst of the community. It follows the work of the sower who went forth to sow (Mark 4.14).

#### Action in the name of Christ

When the community is gathered together, it does not act in its own name but in the name of the Lord.

It is in a way dispossessed of its own action so as to enter into that of Christ.

So when we gather to pray, each of us comes with his or her own intentions, or personal desires. However, common prayer will be far more than the sum of all our prayers. We have to die to ourselves to enter into the prayer of Christ. It is the role of the minister who presides to show that the prayer of all is the one prayer of the Lord.

Similarly, at the time of a baptism, the whole community acts, but does so as a single body of which Christ is the head. That is why one person speaks, not in the name of all but in the name of the body of Christ. He does so 'in the name of Christ'.

In the sacrament of reconciliation we are invited to forgive one another mutually, to show the forgiveness of God, but only one gives absolution 'in the name of Christ'. We can say the same thing for each of the sacraments. They are celebrated 'in the name of Christ' and a particular role is reserved, in the celebration, for the person who serves as president.

As the servant of the community, the president of the assembly is also the servant of the Lord. The two are linked. He cannot perform the one service without being faithful to the other. He shows that the body is that of Christ; he manifests that Christ is the head of this body. It is said that he is the 'sacrament of Christ the head'.

The church is 'convened' by Christ; the apostolic ministry convenes it.

The church is 'sent' by Christ; the apostolic ministry sends it.

The ministry is a sign that the initiative comes from God through Christ. For it is God who is first. We did not love first, but he first loved us. It is not we who chose him, but he chose and called us.

---

# Baptism, Eucharist, Ministry

## A document of the World Council of Churches, 1982

4. The church is called to proclaim and prefigure the Kingdom of God. It accomplishes this by announcing the Gospel to the world and by its very existence as the body of Christ.

5. The Holy Spirit bestows on the community diverse and complementary gifts. These are for the common good of the whole people and are manifested in acts of service within the community and to the world . . . All members are called to discover, with the help of the community, the gifts they have received and to use them for the building up of the church and for the service of the world to which the church is sent.

7. The word *charism* denotes the gifts bestowed by the Holy Spirit on any member of the body of Christ for the building up of the community and the fulfilment of its calling.

The word ministry in its broadest sense denotes the service to which the whole people of God is called.

The term ordained ministry refers to persons who have received a charism and whom the church appoints for service by ordination through the invocation of the Spirit and the laying on of hands.

8. In order to fulfil its mission, the church needs persons who are publicly and continually responsible for pointing to its fundamental dependence on Jesus Christ and thereby provide, within a multiplicity of gifts, a focus of its unity.

9. The church has never been without persons holding specific authority and responsibility.

11. As Christ chose and sent the apostles, Christ continues through the Holy Spirit to choose and call persons into the ordained ministry. As heralds and ambassadors, ordained ministers are representatives of Jesus Christ to the community, and proclaim his message of reconciliation. As leaders and teachers they call the community to submit to the authority of Jesus Christ, the teacher and prophet, in whom law and prophets were fulfilled. As pastors, under Jesus Christ the chief shepherd, they assemble and guide the dispersed people of God, in anticipation of the coming Kingdom.

12. All members of the believing community, ordained and lay, are interrelated. On the one hand, the community needs ordained ministers. Their presence reminds the community of the divine initiative, and of the dependence of the church on Jesus Christ, who is the source of its mission and the foundation of its unity. They serve to build up the community in Christ and to strengthen its witness. In them the church seeks an example of holiness and loving concern. On the other hand, the ordained ministry has no existence apart from the community.

13. The chief responsibility of the ordained ministry is to assemble and build up the body of Christ by proclaiming and teaching the Word of God, by celebrating the sacraments, and by guiding the life of the community in its worship, its mission and its caring ministry.

14. In the celebration of the eucharist, Christ gathers, teaches and nourishes the church. It is Christ who invites to the meal and who presides at it. In most churches this presidency is signified and represented by an ordained minister.

In every sacrament there is as it were a reversal of the situation. We come on our own initiative, and we discover that the Lord has got there first. We come to ask forgiveness, and Christ has already forgiven us. We come to receive the eucharist, and another has already set the table.

It is the role of the minister constantly to show forth this prevenience of God. When the priest welcomes, he is the sign of the welcome of Christ. In their communal relationship the assembly and the priest have to bring out the primacy of the one Lord and High Priest.

---

# A history of the ministries

We have already described the birth of the ministries as it has appeared in the writings of the New Testament.

## Second and third centuries

The great variety of ministries in the first century, and above all of names for them, continued. However, at the beginning of the second century, with Ignatius of Antioch, a hierarchical organization appeared. This comprised the three degrees of the 'ordained ministry': the episcopate, the presbyterate and the diaconate. Since that time they have constituted the three degrees of the sacrament. From then on stress was placed on the responsibility and authority of the bishop:

> Make sure that no step affecting the church is ever taken by anyone without the bishop's sanction.
> The sole eucharist you should consider valid is one that is celebrated by the bishop himself, or by some person authorized by him. Follow your bishop, every one of you, as obediently as Jesus Christ followed the Father. Obey your clergy, too, as you would the apostles; give your deacons the same reverence that you would to a command from God (Ignatius, *Letter to the Smyrnaeans*, 8).

Another level of organization soon becomes evident: a hierarchy among the bishops, or more precisely among the episcopal sees. Five cities then came to be recognized for their pre-eminence, four because an apostle had founded the churches there (Jersualem, Antioch, Rome and Alexandria) and the fifth by virtue of its political importance (Constantinople). They are still the seat of a patriarchate. There is the fine expression 'The Church of Rome . . . which presides over the churches in love'.

At the same time, as another characteristic, there appeared what could be called the 'sacerdotalization' of the episcopal and presbyteral ministries. Under the influence of the Old Testament and the religious categories of the other religions, there began to be talk of the priest and the bishop, using the vocabulary reserved for sacred persons (*hiereus* in Greek and *sacerdos* in Latin). The New Testament had never done this, surprising though that might seem. People then tended to forget that the letter to the Hebrews reserved the adjective sacerdotal for Christ himself (he holds his priesthood permanently, Heb. 7.24) and that I Peter speaks of the whole people as priestly (2.5, 9). On this point reference should be made to what has already been said in Chapter 8. Vatican II in its 'Constitution on the Church' and 'Decree on the Ministry and Life of Priests' brought decisive theological clarification.

## The Constantinian church in the fourth century

In 313, by the Edict of Milan, the emperor Constantine gave freedom to the church, and in 381, by the Edict of Thessalonica, the emperor Theodosius declared Christianity the official religion.

These two dates, which are very important for the church, had highly ambiguous consequences. The church was free, but it increasingly organized itself on the lines of the civil administration. Since the Christian religion was official, it became opportune and no longer risky to be converted to it. The priests had tax exemption, so there was an advantage in being a minister of the church. The opportunity to be at peace and to be able to organize Christian worship freely meant that to some degree the priests became officials and their social position as privileged persons was clericalized. Despite this, the fourth century was a time in which one finds the most extraordinary spectrum of bishops of immense stature: Ambrose of Milan, Athanasius of Alexandria, Basil of Caesarea, Gregory of Nyssa his brother, and Gregory of Nazianzus their friend, John Chrysostom patriarch of Constantinople, Cyril of Jerusalem, Hilary of Poitiers, Martin of Tours, and, right at the end of the century, the beginnings of the episcopate of Augustine of Hippo. What better proof that the church is faithful and solid, despite the risks!

## The Middle Ages

At the beginning of the Middles Ages in Europe, the countryside had almost been evangelized. The number of parishes increased, as did the number of priests. But since evangelization was thought to have been achieved, the priests increasingly confined themselves to their role in worship. On the other hand, the development of the feudal system led to the submission of ministers to the local powers, the bishop to the emperor, and the parish priest to the local lord. One could add that the ignorance of the clergy and their increasing remoteness from authority did not encourage either healthy doctrine or good morals.

In the face of this situation, the eleventh century is seen as an important period of reform:

against submission of spiritual power to temporal power (Canossa in 1077);

against the abuses arising from the link between money and the exercising of ministries;

against the slackening of morality among the clergy.

With Gregory VII in 1073, celibacy became a condition for entering the presbyteral ministry. The monk became an ideal. Monasteries developed at this time, and an increasingly large number of monks were ordained priests.

In the thirteenth century, while cathedrals and universities were being built, it was the religious, Franciscans and Dominicans, who took up the task of pastoral care and preaching which had been neglected by the secular clergy: the apostolate and the ministry of the word.

## The sixteenth century

In a way it is to the power of the development of the religious orders in the thirteenth century that we owe Luther's revolution in the sixteenth century. For the abuses continued: priests were increasingly absent from their parishes; even non-ordained clerics accumulated benefices, and differences between the higher and lower clergy became increasingly blatant; politics rather than faith seems to have been the papal preoccupation.

The Council of Trent was opposed to Luther primarily on a doctrinal level in affirming the priestly character of the presbyteral ministry. But there was also a pastoral concern which in 1563 ended in the promulgation of a decree on the seminaries. This innovation in the training of future priests marked a real change, not in the nature but in the exercising of ministry. It had been at least seven centuries in the coming. The Jesuits who came into being at that time are the best illustration of this. There were also the Lazarists (St Vincent de Paul) and the Sulpicians (Monsieur Olier) who were founded in the seventeenth century to supervise the training of seminarians. They were to be the origin of a 'priestly spirituality' which nurtured diocesan priests until Vatican II.

## Vatican I

Unfortunately interrupted by the Franco-Prussian War of 1870, the First Vatican Council could develop only the first part of its doctrinal statements. So what was stamped on the minds of Catholics was its definition of papal infallibility, which suggests a pyramidal image of the church. This is a curiously unreal conception in which everything is based on the apex of the pyramid. Vatican II went on to complete Vatican I through its Dogmatic Constitution on the Church. The church is made up of the members of the body of Christ, the people of God, in whose service ministers exercise their functions.

## Vatican II

The Dogmatic Constitution on the Church begins by rehabilitating the priesthood of the baptized. Then only does it define the ministerial priesthood and indicate its relationship to the former:

It gives a special role to the priesthood of the one priest, Jesus Christ; in a different way from baptismal priesthood, it is configuration to Christ, head of his body;

it puts the 'minister' at the service of the priesthood of all the baptized;

the preaching of the gospel is the first task of bishops and priests; then come sanctification and the government of the faithful;

there is a diversity of ministries in the church of Christ.

In 1972 Pope Paul VI reorganized the ministerial functions of the Catholic church by:

the suppression of the minor orders and the subdiaconate;

the replacement of the tonsure by a rite of admission to the diaconate and the priesthood;

a distinction between the diaconate as preparation for priesthood and the permanent diaconate; this latter does not carry with it the obligation of celibacy;

the re-establishment of 'instituted ministries' (lay) for the service of the Word, prayer and to assist at the eucharist;

a move towards more varied ministries, but conferred only for a time and in one place.

---

## Today

Nowadays the church is experiencing a great renewal of ministries. Some Christians sometimes seem to fear that the new responsibility given to the laity is obscuring the role of the priest. This fear is unfounded. On the contrary, we can see how in all the communities in which tasks are shared between different members, the specific character of the priestly ministry is being brought out at the same time.

However, it is only to be expected that we should also see some hesitations. History had led the clergy progressively to accumulate all the functions. We must not forget that for a long time the word 'cleric' was synonymous with 'educated person'. So people were accustomed to entrust the

> *As each has received a gift, employ it for one another, as good stewards of God's varied grace: whoever speaks, as one who utters oracles of God; whoever renders service, as one who renders it by the strength which God supplies; in order that in everything God may be glorified through Jesus Christ.*
>
> I Peter 4.10–11

majority of church responsibilities to clerics. A new co-ordination of ministries can come about only if we are attentive to the evolution and the needs of the communities. Vatican II has given a new impulse to the life of Christian communities. And a document from Rome dated 15 August 1972, the *motu proprio Ministeria quaedam*, has established the following distinctions:

There are *ordained ministries*: these are the ministries of bishops, priests and deacons. They are conferred in the course of a sacramental celebration through laying on of hands by the bishop.

Today the Catholic church is experiencing a renewal of the diaconate, which is not just one step on the way to the priesthood. The ancient tradition of the church has been resumed, of ordaining permanent deacons, i.e. people who while keeping their jobs and roles in society, are nevertheless associated in a special and permanent way in the service of the community. Certainly it is too early to define their profile in a definitive way. The direction has been given, but the patterns have still to be worked out in practice.

In this connection reference is always made to the passage in Acts (6.1–6, see above) which describes the institution of the Seven. The 'service of tables' which has been entrusted to them can be interpreted in various ways.

- It can be seen as serving meals: that then includes everything connected with mutual aid and charitable work, the sharing of resources for the most disadvantaged.
- But 'table' (Greek *trapeza*) can also denote the table of the moneychanger or the bank counter (Matt. 21.12; Mark 11.15; John 2.15). In that case the deacons would be the administrators of the financial affairs of the church. In Rome for a long time they were the administrative assistants of the bishop. Hippolytus of Rome in the third century wrote that 'The deacon is ordained to the service of the bishop . . . he administers and indicates to him what is necessary'.
- In Jewish tradition the 'table' is also the table on which was put the 'bread of the presence', the offering of the faithful to the Jerusalem temple (Heb. 9.2). In that case the reference would be to the role given to the deacon at the celebration of the eucharist.

There are *instituted ministries*: these are stable ministries. The institution, conferred during a particular liturgical celebration, gives the Christian a permanent function. The Roman document expressly envisages two ministries:

- 'the service of the word', which can include a catechetical mission and preparation of the faithful to receive the sacraments;
- the 'service of common prayer and the eucharist'; this can be understood as a particular responsibility for the Sunday assembly and for taking communion to the sick.
- However, in addition there is a clear indication that episcopal conferences can give those in other instituted ministries, like catechists, real responsibility for small communities in particular countries.

There are also *ministries conferred for a time*; these can relate to the different services needed for the life and activity of the community. The General Instruction of the Roman Missal speaks expressly of those related to liturgical celebration, in particular the office of reader or the person who distributes communion. This amounts to an official form of delegation which can be made by the priest in charge of the community.

The development is not complete. It is a sign of the times that the problem of ministries is usually on the agenda of diocesan synods which take place in various places. They contain the following items:

### A new stress on baptism

The impulse given by the Council began from a new stress on the responsibility of all Christians by virtue of their baptism. Baptism makes them members of the body of Christ. The Spirit distributes its gifts to each for the good of all. So Christians have solidarity in their action, and the totality of gifts can be found only in the whole of the body.

### Building up the church

St Paul, in the great text of the letter to the Ephesians on ministry, speaks of the whole body which 'joined and knit together by every joint with which it is supplied, when each part is working properly, makes bodily growth and upbuilds itself in love' (Eph. 4.16).

Since it is the whole body which operates, there can be no question in any reflection on ministries of opposing the priesthood to the laity; rather, we have to see the complementarity of the task accomplished by each person for the upbuilding of the whole. It is not correct to suppose that the laity are concerned with the world and that priests are responsible for the community. It is the church as a whole, priests and laity under the movement of the Spirit, which has to live as the body of Christ so as to continue the mission of its Lord.

---

Participators in the function of Christ, priest, prophet and king, the laity have an active part of their own in the life and action of the Church. Their action within the Church communities is so necessary that without it the apostolate of the pastors will frequently be unable to obtain its full effect.

Bishops, parish priests and other priests of the secular and regular clergy will remember that the right and duty of exercising the apostolate are common to all the faithful, whether clerics or lay; and that in the building up of the Church the laity too have parts of their own to play. For this reason they will work as brothers with the laity in the Church and for the Church, and will have a special concern for the laity in the apostolic activities of the latter.

Vatican II, *Decree on the Apostolate of Lay People*, 10, 25

---

The apostolate of the laity is a sharing in the salvific mission of the Church. Through Baptism and Confirmation all are appointed to this apostolate by the Lord himself.

Thus, every lay person, through those gifts given to him, is at once the witness and the living instrument of the mission of the church itself 'according to the measure of Christ's bestowal' (Eph. 4.7).

Vatican II, *Lumen Gentium*, 33

---

## A new way of being the church
### The experience of Zaire

There is a great variety of experiences in the conception and implementation of community services. At Bukavu, for example, the archbishop put forward a list of eleven possible ministries, and this was not exhaustive. But he made an important qualification: a community will create as many ministries corresponding to its needs as it has specific charisms among its members. There are the following ministries: presidency, secretariat, catechesis, liturgy, auxiliaries at communion, youth education, consolation, social development, reconciliation, hospitality, funerals. In fact there are several criteria for establishing ministries: parochial needs, the needs of the local community, and the existence of charisms among the members. This last qualification presupposes that there has been a true discernment of charisms and implies that people are not nominated to services for which they are not fitted, or which do not correspond to the present expectations or needs of the communities.

---

Since it is the whole body which operates, the community must show solidarity with those who perform a ministry within it. These last make visible and operational the preoccupation of all. Some are responsible for catechesis, but it is the whole body which has to be concerned for the transmission of faith. Some have a role of mutual aid, but they do so in the name of all. Others have to see to co-ordination, but all are concerned with communion.

### *A single mission*

'I came that they might have life and have it abundantly', says the Lord. The church has no other *raison d'être* than to continue the mission of Jesus Christ. All reflection on ministry has to begin from a concern for mission. But this is vast. It is easy to understand that it requires all Christians to take part in it.

There is a need to begin from necessary tasks for the church to fulfil its mission and do so in its fullness. Where mission is concerned, there can be no opposition between one group and another; all need to be co-ordinated. Together, priests and laity have to bear witness to Jesus Christ before the world. Together, their task is to proclaim the Gospel. Together, they create communities which are to be places of welcome for the Spirit and which seek to live in the light of the Word of God. Together, they direct the world towards God in praise and thanksgiving.

New tasks may emerge, and new services will have to be invented. In our day we have seen many initiatives towards the development or health of the church in countries where development has been limited. We have also seen arrangements made for Sunday assemblies in the absence of a priest. Lay Christians have been able to take charge in areas which have been without priests.

The case of Sunday assemblies without a priest has been a particularly tricky one. We can certainly rejoice that the dynamism of communities has enabled them to respond to a need. However, it has to be noted that this is a theologically abnormal situation, in the precise sense of the term, i.e. deviating from the norm. It is not normal for the celebration of the eucharist not to be regularly at the centre of the life of a community. This is a limited instance, though quite a widespread one, above all in the young churches, and in countries which have few priests, like Latin America and Africa. We must hope that the Spirit will raise up sufficient youth in our church to provide a solution which conforms with true fidelity.

There are certainly new needs and new services, but tension must be maintained between two kinds of faithfulness. There is faithfulness to the church in its vocation and its very being: is it not the body of Christ, sent into the world like its Lord? And there is faithfulness to the world and to history: in Jesus Christ the word was made incarnate in the village of Nazareth and in Judaea, but incarnation is a work which must constantly be pursued. The church is faced with the problem of its inculturation in human, geographical or cultural sectors which it has yet to touch on. If it is to grow constantly and to renew its way of being and acting it will have to maintain these two kinds of faithfulness.

'Repent, and be baptized every one of you' (Acts 2.38)

# 11

# Christian Initiation:
# Baptism, Confirmation, Eucharist

*But you shall receive power when the Holy Spirit has come upon you, and you shall be my witnesses in Jerusalem and in all Judaea and Samaria and to the end of the earth.*

Acts 1.8

## Christian initiation

'You shall be my witnesses' are Jesus' last words. His mission accomplished, that of the apostles begins. In their turn they are to accomplish the work entrusted to them. They recall their Master's prayer, 'I have accomplished the work which you gave me to do . . . I have manifested your name to the men whom you gave me out of the world . . . And this is eternal life, that they know you the only true God and Jesus Christ whom you have sent.' They are sent out along the roads of the world to proclaim the gospel.

To accomplish this mission they have to transcend their human point of view and enter into the mystery of the death and resurrection of Christ, so as to live by his Spirit and have communion in his eucharist.

Following them, all who discover in faith the presence of the Risen Lord will have to take a similar course. They will always experience a transition, a cross and resurrection which are both painful and exalting, a conversion which has to be taken up again and again, a renunciation of self to be reborn in Christ (see Chapter IV, p. 25).

For those who are born into a Christian family and are baptized at birth, this slow transfiguration of existence can begin as life begins. It can be the fruit of a later encounter, a discovery of Christ at a more advanced age, as happens with the baptism of an adult. It always presupposes an initiation, an introduction into the community of the witnesses to the Lord Jesus.

Such an initiation takes time. The rites which mark its course gradually reveal the different aspects of life in Christ. Adults often take several years to be integrated in this way. Children baptized at birth pursue their Christian initiation during the years of instruction. Then in their burgeoning freedom they have to undergo the inward conversion necessary for all the Lord's disciples.

So Christian initiation always involves the three sacraments of baptism, confirmation and eucharist. They are as it were three aspects of the same mystery. None of the three can be understood unless we envisage its relationship to the two others. They are all already present in embryo in baptism, but the fullness of baptism unfolds in the later stages.

Baptism is the sacrament mentioned most often in the New Testament. In connection with it we shall remind ourselves of the witness of the first Christians. That brings out three major themes:

Christian life is a new exodus;

People are baptized in the Spirit and in fire;

It is the birth of a new people.

---

## Baptize

The word comes from the Greek *baptizein*, which means immerse. Originally, for baptism it was not enough to pour a little water on the forehead. The baptisteries of the first centuries were quite large cisterns, often in the form of a cross. The catechumen went down one side by a series of steps, was immersed in the water, and came out the other side. That helps us to understand better how baptism is both:

- immersion in the death of Christ and a resurrection;

- a passing, like that of the Hebrews through the sea at their departure from Egypt under the leadership of Moses.

---

### The way of the exodus

The earliest Christian text to speak of baptism appears in the first letter of Paul to the Corinthians, as does the first text about the eucharist. That was doubtless written around 56, more than twenty years before the final redaction of the Gospels. The comparison which comes quite naturally from the pen of the apostle is with the departure from Egypt at the time of the exodus under the leadership of Moses. Thus baptism appeared as a departure on a new exodus.

The central mystery of Christianity is in fact that of Jesus' Pasch, experienced in his death and resurrection, into which one enters by baptism. But Christian Easter has its roots in the Jewish passover, the origins of which go back to the exodus.

The exodus is the foundation event. A new people was forged in the crucible of life in the desert. It was a long way from Egypt, the land of slavery, to the Promised Land. Forty years is a human lifetime. This way ran through two crossings of water: the Red Sea had to be crossed at the beginning and the Jordan at the end. Between the two was the long march, the time of 'trial', the time when the faithfulness of the people had to be tested. God went with his people and gave them food and drink. The covenant was concluded on Sinai and the word of God became the rule of conduct for the tribes of Israel.

The evangelists loved to draw parallels between the life of Jesus and the adventure of the Hebrews during the exodus:

- Jesus was baptized in the Jordan, at the place where the tribes entered the Promised Land;
- then the Spirit drove him into the desert, where he spent forty days. That was the time of the temptation;
- Jesus spoke of the new baptism which he had to receive, alluding to his death (Mark 10.38);
- at the time of the Transfiguration he spoke with Moses and Elijah of his exodus which he was to accomplish at Jerusalem (Luke 9.31);
- in the Gospel of John, Jesus is the new Moses who gives the living water (John 4.10) and the true manna (John 6.31).

Paul too, finds no difficulty in saying of the departure from Egypt: 'These things are examples for us . . . they were written down for our instruction, upon whom the end of the ages has come' (I Cor. 10.1–11). For him the life of the baptized Christian has to be seen as a new exodus. So baptism is a departure, and the route it makes us

---

*Our fathers were all under the cloud, and all passed through the sea, and all were baptized into Moses in the cloud and in the sea, and all ate the same spiritual food and all drank the same spiritual drink. For they drank from the rock which followed them, and the rock was Christ . . . These events took place as examples for us . . .*

I Cor. 10.1–6

take is that of true freedom. 'For you were called to freedom, brethren' (Gal. 5.13). Like a new Moses, Jesus goes at the head of the new people of God. 'For freedom Christ has set us free; stand fast, therefore, and do not submit again to a yoke of slavery' (Gal. 5.1).

As with Jesus, our life unfolds like a long march between two baptisms:

- the first is celebrated in the rite of water (like the passage through the Red Sea);
- the second takes place at our death: that is the ultimate Pasch which brings us into the kingdom;
- between the two comes the desert time, when we have to prove our faithfulness;
- we live out the covenant in the light of God's word; the Spirit is given us to lead us; it is the source of living water;
- we are strengthened on our way by the true bread of the eucharist.

That is a dynamic vision of a baptism which is no longer considered as a destination, as 'what has to be done to set oneself right', a simple purification of sins. I Peter says: 'Baptism now saves you, not as a removal of dirt from the body, but as an appeal to God for a clear conscience, through the resurrection of Jesus Christ . . .' (3.21).

### Baptism in the Spirit and in fire

It is important not to confuse Christian baptism with the baptism given by John the Baptist. The latter is as it were the prehistory of our baptism. During the last period before the capture of Jerusalem by the Romans in AD 70, there were a number of baptist sects in Palestine. In particular we know a good deal about that of the Essenes, who lived near to the 'monastery' of Qumran. Excavations have uncovered numerous cisterns which served for ritual purification. We should not forget that John baptized not far from there, on the bank of the Jordan. John was not an Essene, but there may have been contacts and similarities between the group of his disciples and the Qumran group.

According to the Gospel, the rite performed by John was a 'baptism of repentance for the forgiveness of sins' (Mark 1.4). Jesus himself came to be

---

## The Blessing of the Water

Father,
you give us grace through sacramental signs,
which tell us of the wonder of your unseen power.

In baptism we use your gift of water,
which you have made a rich symbol of the grace
you give us in this sacrament.

At the very dawn of creation
your Spirit breathed on the waters,
making them the wellspring of all holiness.

The waters of the great flood
you made a sign of the waters of baptism
that make an end of sin
and a new beginning of goodness.

Through the waters of the Red Sea
you led Israel out of slavery
to be an image of God's holy people,
set free from sin by baptism.

In the waters of the Jordan
your Son was baptized by John
and anointed with the Spirit.

Your Son willed that water and blood should flow
    from his side as he hung upon the cross.
After his resurrection he told his disciples:
'Go out and teach all nations, baptizing them in
    the name of the Father, and of the Son, and
    of the Holy Spirit.'

Father,
look now with love upon your Church
and unseal for it the fountain of baptism.

By the power of the Holy Spirit
give to this water the grace of your Son,
so that in the sacrament of baptism
all those whom you have created in your likeness
may be cleansed from sin
and rise to a new birth of innocence
by water and the Holy Spirit.

Christian Initiation of Adults, 222 A

# The Pasch

## From the exodus from Egypt to our baptism – from slavery to freedom

| *The exodus from Egypt* | *Jesus' Pasch* | *Our baptism* |
|---|---|---|

### A. The Pasch is 'a passage'

| | | |
|---|---|---|
| From slavery to freedom. | Jesus passes from this world to the Father. | Free from sin and from the law. |
| From Egypt to the Promised Land. | He passes from death to life. | We pass from sin to life. |

### B. It is a departure

| | | |
|---|---|---|
| Towards the Promised Land. | He goes to his Father and our Father. | We go towards the kingdom. |
| It is a beginning, the birth of the people of God. | The new life of the Risen Christ. | It is a new birth. |
| It is a new creation. | The firstborn of creation. | We are a new creation. |

### C. It is a long journey

| | | |
|---|---|---|
| Forty years in the desert. | Jesus spends forty days in the desert. | |
| Forty years is a lifetime. | | Our whole life is an exodus. |
| The desert is the time of trial, when faithfulness is tested. | Jesus is tempted by the devil and shows his faithfulness. | We have to have our faith tested. |
| The desert is the time of providence; God guides his people. | Jesus is led by the Spirit. | God is with us and gives us the Spirit. |
| God gives food for the journey. | His food is to do the will of his Father. | We have the bread of the eucharist. |

### D. Lived out in a covenant

| | | |
|---|---|---|
| The concluding of the covenant on Sinai. | Jesus inaugurates the new covenant. | We enter into covenant with God. |
| God gives his word, the law. | Jesus is the living Word. He gives the new law in the Sermon on the Mount. | We walk in the light of the Word of God. |
| The people commit themselves to God. | | Baptism is the commitment of all of our life. |

### E. The entry into the Promised Land

| | | |
|---|---|---|
| The crossing of the Jordan marks the end of the journey. | Jesus, baptized in the Jordan by John is also baptized into his death. | The end of our course is baptism into death, and entry into the kingdom. |

baptized by the forerunner, and to John's amazement replied, 'Let it be so now; for thus it is fitting for us to fulfil all righteousness' (Matt. 3.15). Despite this scene, the evangelists always insist on stressing the great difference between the two baptisms: 'I baptize you with water for remission of sins, but he who is coming after me is mightier than I, whose sandals I am not worthy to carry: he will baptize you with the Holy Spirit and with fire' (Matt. 3.11).

In fact, while it is easy to see that 'baptism in water' is a rite of purification, 'baptism in the Spirit and in fire' is something quite different. Besides, Jesus said to the apostles before leaving them on Ascension Day: 'John baptized with water, but you will be baptized with the Holy Spirit not many days hence.' He was alluding to the gift of the Spirit on the day of Pentecost.

'Where the Spirit of the Lord is, there is freedom' (II Cor. 3.17). To be baptized in the Spirit is to experience a completely new freedom. It is to banish fear and shame and set out along the world's roads to be a witness to Jesus Christ. Much more than being a purification, this is a new birth. It is as it were a call to another dimension of life.

A curious episode related in Acts is a good illustration of the importance that the first Christians attached to the difference between the baptism of John and what they practised themselves. When Paul arrived in Ephesus, he found a group of disciples there. They were believers, yet when he asked whether they had received the Holy Spirit, they replied, 'We haven't even heard of the Holy Spirit.' 'Then what baptism did you receive?' asked Paul. .They replied, 'The baptism of John.' So Paul had them baptized again. This is the only known case in which rebaptism was allowed in the primitive church, so what was at stake must have been important. Everything is judged on the gift and the reception of the Spirit.

So baptism in the name of Jesus seems to be the realization of the vision of the new covenant which Ezekiel already hailed. This is a new people brought into being by baptism; it is a people of the Spirit.

> *Jesus said to Nicodemus, 'I say to you, unless one is born from above, he cannot see the kingdom of God.' Nicodemus said to him, 'How can a man be born when he is old? Can he enter a second time into his mother's womb and be born?' Jesus answered, 'Truly, truly I say to you, unless one is born of water and the Spirit, he cannot enter the kingdom of God. That which is born of the flesh is flesh, and that which is born of the Spirit is spirit. Do not marvel that I said to you, "You must be born from above." The wind blows where it wills, and you hear the sound of it, but you do not know whence it comes or whither it goes. So it is with every one which is born of the Spirit.' Nicodemus said to him, 'How can this be?'*
>
> John 3.1–9

### A new people

To talk of the Spirit is to talk of the church. The Spirit of the Risen Christ takes hold of believers in the act of baptism which attaches them to the church. Baptism in the Spirit put a distance between John and Jesus, but it also put a distance between Israel and the church. In fact a new people is born on the day of Pentecost. We enter into it by faith in the risen Christ and by baptism.

All the nations are called to enter into this people! No religion, not even that of the Old Testament, had hitherto wanted such universalism. There are no more barriers. All are invited. The walls which separate races and people are to come down: 'You who were once far off have been brought near in the blood of Christ. For he is our peace, who has made us both one, and has broken down the dividing wall of hostility, by abolishing in his flesh the law of commandments and ordinances . . . for through him we both have access in one Spirit to the Father' (Eph. 2.13–14, 18).

Even after two thousand years of history, in which the wear and tear of time could have blunted easy enthusiasms, it is easy for us to imagine the joy of the new believers, faced with such a horizon which had been opened up by the resurrection of Jesus. That is what is proclaimed by baptism in the Spirit.

Realization began at Pentecost, a real anti-Babel. Here was the Spirit at work: people talked in different tongues, but they understood one another and each 'heard the wonderful works of God' in their own tongue (Acts 2.11).

It is not surprising to rediscover three times, in the letters of Paul, as it were an echo of what must have been the joyful acclamation of the liturgy of baptism in certain communities:

> For by one Spirit we were all baptized into one body – Jews or Greeks, slaves or free, and all were made to drink of one Spirit (I Cor. 12.13; cf. Col. 3.9–11).

or in a slight variant:

> For in Christ Jesus you are all children of God, through faith. For as many of you as were baptized into Christ have put on Christ. There is neither Jew nor Greek, there is neither slave nor free, there is neither male nor female; for you are all one in Christ Jesus (Gal. 3.26–28).

The human reality which underlies the sacrament of baptism is not just a part of our existence, as is the case with marriage, reconciliation or the sacrament of the sick. In baptism, the whole life of human beings becomes a sacrament of Christ. But it only becomes that when it is lived as:

a departure for a new exodus,
animated by the breath of the Spirit,
directed towards the birth of a new humanity.

What an extraordinary dimension baptism had for this first Christian generation!

Is that not how we must define the new people which is born in the water of baptism?

---

### A new heart

*For I will take you from the nations,*
*and gather you from all the countries,*
*and bring you into your own land.*
*I will sprinkle clean water upon you,*
*and you shall be clean from all your uncleannesses,*
*and from all your idols I will cleanse you.*
*A new heart will I give you,*
*and a new spirit I will put within you;*
*and I will take out of your flesh the heart of stone*
*and give you a heart of flesh.*
*And I will put my spirit within you,*
*and cause you to walk in my statutes*
*and be careful to observe my ordinances.*
*You shall dwell in the land*
*which I gave to your fathers;*
*and you shall be my people, and I will be your God.*
Ezek. 36.24–28

---

### The four rivers

The Bambara of Mali say that the whole of human life is the crossing of four rivers.

We come into the world through our parents. Our fathers and mothers make us what we are. We take after them. Human beings exist through others, and each comes into the world by crossing this first river.

But each of us has a role of our own. Success and failure in our lives depends finally on us and on us alone. We have to develop what we have been given and make it our own. Human beings exist through themselves. That is the second river that they have to cross.

But to find happiness human beings have to be able to relate to others outside the family circle. They are not fires to crackle and burn others, but should respect them and be of service to them. We make our way together: that is the third river that each one has to cross.

But to become a Bambara Christian, says Monsignor Sidibe, Bishop of Segou, there is a fourth river to cross. 'I sought for a long time this fourth river that Jesus asks us to cross. And I found the answer in Matthew 25.31–46. It is that of the solidarity of the Master with men and women, with all men and women. To live as a Bambara Christian, one has to extend to men and women of every race the solidarity we have with our own people'.

## The laying on of hands

From the first days of the church, as recorded in the Acts of the Apostles, the rite of baptism has been completed by that of the laying on of hands for the gift of the Spirit.

So when the deacon Philip evangelized Samaria:

When the apostles at Jerusalem heard that Samaria had received the word of God they sent to them Peter and John, who came down and prayed for them that they might receive the Holy Spirit, for it had not yet fallen on any of them, but they had only been baptized in the name of the Lord Jesus. Then they laid their hands on them and they received the Holy Spirit' (Acts 8.14–17; cf. Acts 19.5–6).

Doubtless there were many ways of doing this, depending on the communities. In Acts, baptism of water is above all for the forgiveness of sins, and the rite of laying on hands relates to the gift of the Holy Spirit. The two would seem to be intimately connected; they are the two complementary aspects of introduction into the Christian community.

The practice of the church subsequently became established over the centuries, keeping a certain diversity, as we can see from the history of the sacraments of initiation. But from the start the duality of the rites prepares for the distinction that the Latin Catholic Church has maintained between baptism and confirmation.

## The breaking of the bread

The 'breaking of the bread' is an ancient name given to the eucharist, which became part of the regular life of the community. Acts mentions it immediately after the event of Pentecost:

'So those who received his words were baptized, and there were added that day about three thousand souls. And they devoted themselves to the apostles' teaching and fellowship, to the breaking of bread and the prayers' (Acts 2.41–42).

Participation in the eucharistic table is what shows complete integration into the community of believers. It is the last stage of Christian initiation.

---

# A history of the sacraments of Christian initiation

## The institution of baptism

### The baptism of Jesus

By having himself baptized, Jesus gives to the baptism of John a meaning which it did not have in itself, namely 'baptism of repentance for the forgiveness of sins' (Mark 1.4). What Jesus adds is:
- a character of incorporation which St Jerome defines like this: 'In entering into the waters of the Jordan, Jesus immersed all of humanity';

- a character of filiation: the phrase 'This is my well beloved Son' (Mark 1.11) shows that the Father recognizes his eternal Son in the man Jesus;
- a character of confirmation: the word of the Father about the Son confirms that the man Jesus is the Messiah, the one sent; Jesus is going to be able to begin his public life.

## The Pasch

The true baptism of Jesus is his Pasch, when he is 'immersed' in death and resurrection from the dead. 'Can you drink the cup that I shall drink or be baptized with the baptism with which I shall be baptized?' (Mark 10.38), Jesus asked his disciples.

St Paul, the first theologian of baptism, deduced from this: 'Do you not know that all of us who have been baptized into Christ Jesus were baptized into his death.' We were buried therefore with him by baptism into death, so that as Christ was raised from the dead by the glory of the Father, we too might walk in newness of life' (Rom. 6.3–4).

## Mission

Before leaving his disciples, the Risen Lord sends them on mission, saying to them, 'Go and make disciples of all nations, baptizing them in the name of the Father, and of the Son, and of the Holy Spirit' (Matt. 28.19).

# Christian initiation

## The beginning of the church

The church begins with the proclamation of the resurrection of Jesus and baptism, on the day of Pentecost (Acts 2.14–41).
- This is a collective baptism of Jewish adults;
- The baptism of the Ethiopian eunuch by Philip, one of the seven, is the first case of individual baptism (Acts 8.20–39);
- Soon, however, non-Jews will also be baptized: Cornelius and his followers (Acts 10.47–48);
- In line with the social principles of the period, when Acts tells us that Paul's gaoler received baptism 'with all his family' (Acts 16.33), there is every reason to suppose that this expression indicates that small children were also baptized.

## The organization of the catechumenate from the second to the fifth centuries

From the middle of the second century, with Justin Martyr, we have evidence that preparation for baptism and its celebration were being organized.

The increase in the number of candidates and the risks of apostasy or heresy as a result of persecutions or sects led the church to strengthen its demands for the training of catechumens. The pattern of Christian initiation derives from this:

*Long-term preparation*

Investigation of the life and occupation of candidates;

admission of candidates in the presence of sponsors who were their companions during the two or three years of their preparation;

catecheses: a series of lessons on the history of salvation from one of the clergy or a lay person; participation in the liturgy of the Word at the Sunday assembly.

## Immediate preparation

When Easter approached, the catechumen would undergo the last stage of preparation (the basis of our Lent) in an intensive series of meetings:

inscription of the name: candidates were presented to the bishop by their sponsors and chosen by the bishop in the name of the Lord;

catechesis on scripture and the creed by the bishop; presentation of the creed (the tradition of the symbol) and the Our Father, which had to be learned by heart.

## The final preparation

In the hours preceding the Easter vigil, the last acts of preparation took place:

the recitation (*redditio*) of the creed and Lord's Prayer;

the *ephphetha* (a Hebrew word meaning open), recalling the healing of a deaf-mute by Jesus (Mark 7.32–35);

renunciation of the devil;

anointing with pre-baptismal oil, a sign of strength for the fight;

prayer over the water pronounced by the bishop;

baptism.

The catechumens descended the three steps which led to the bottom of the pool, in the water up to the waist. The celebrant then baptized them, putting his hand on their heads and plunging them into the water three times, saying the trinitarian formula. The newly baptized then climbed out of the water of baptism.

## Complementary rites

Chrismation, being anointed with holy oil as a sign of consecration;

the laying on of hands by the bishop for the gift of the Holy Spirit (confirmation);

presentation of a white robe which the baptized person would keep for a week;

the eucharist: all the assembly (newly baptized, faithful, priests, bishop) then went from the baptistery to the cathedral church, there to celebrate the paschal eucharist, in the course of which the newly baptized would complete their initiation by receiving the body and blood of Christ, of which they had just become members through their baptism.

You were harvested at the time you entered the catechumenate; during the catechumenate you were milled by fasts, exorcisms, conversion, and you came to the baptismal fountain, where you were moistened with water. You became a kind of dough which has been baked in the fire of the Spirit; so you are the bread of the Lord. Be sure, then, that you see and receive what you are! (St Augustine to the newly baptized).

## The case of confirmation (see Chapter 7, p. 56)

During the first three centuries of the church, Christianity was essentially urban (Jerusalem, Antioch, Rome, Alexandria, Lyons . . .) and the communities were quite small, particularly because of persecutions. The bishop was rather like each person's 'parish priest': he was there, and he was close. At Easter he baptized the catechumens, presiding over, or himself performing, all the rites which preceded and followed the actual baptism. So too, after baptism, he anointed with oil and laid hands on the newly baptized, calling upon the Holy Spirit. It did not occur to anyone to think of baptism and confirmation as two separate operations, far less two celebrations.

But when after the peace of Constantine in 313, Christianity began to spread freely in the cities and into the countryside, the bishop came to be increasingly remote from the communities, which were becoming increasingly numerous. The custom was then established of the priest baptizing the catechumens of the community for which he was responsible and they waited for the arrival of the bishop for the laying on of hands. It was in 465 that Faustus bishop of Riez spoke in this connection of 'confirmation'.

# The later history of baptism

## From the sixth to the twelfth centuries

As the years passed, more and more adults were Christians. Gradually there were only children left to be baptized.

First of all adjustments were made to the ritual of Christian initiation: the time of preparation was reduced; catechesis, which had fallen into disuse, was replaced by the 'tradition of the Gospels'; the role of the sponsor was changed to become that of the one speaking for the infant.

However, the principle of collective celebrations of baptism ending with eucharistic communion continued (if the child was too young to eat, the priest would dip his finger in the blood of Christ and touch the baby's tongue).

## From the thirteenth century to Vatican II

Infant mortality, along with the 'great fears' of the Middle Ages, led to baptism taking place increasingly soon after birth.

For reasons of convenience, baptism by immersion was gradually abolished and replaced with baptism by infusion (water poured on the head) (fourteenth century).

Since there was no longer any time for preparation, the catechumenate disappeared and all the rites were performed in a single celebration (from the fourteenth century).

From the thirteenth century onwards the custom developed of delaying first communion till the child was old enough to understand, then even to eleven or twelve. Confirmation followed the same course, so that it came to be administered only after the first communion: the consequence of this was to reverse the primitive order which put the eucharist as the culmination of initiation.

That is virtually the situation which existed at the beginning of Vatican II, though it should be noted that first communion was brought forward to seven (under Pius X).

---

## Today

Following the liturgical reform proposed by Vatican II, there are three rites for baptism, or to put it differently, three ways of proceeding to Christian initiation:

the rite for the baptism of adults;

the rite for the baptism of children old enough for catechesis;

the rite for the baptism of small children.

### The baptism of adults

An encounter between two beings always begins with a mysterious exploration. Something has begun to spring up in the depths of each of them. Something has begun to sing in the heart. And then there is mutual discovery; there are the first tentative approaches, moments of happiness and questions, sometimes doubts. Adults who encounter Christ go through a similar process.

A friend, a partner, a happy or sad event, professional or social life, reading, a personal quest, may have given someone a glimpse of the Risen Christ. A seed has been planted, and like all seeds, has to develop. The church tries to guide its growth without damaging its spontaneity.

Often, nowadays, a small group of Christians commits itself to helping those who are to be baptized. They help such persons to find a way towards discovering the riches of Christian tradition as they have been developed over the centuries. They read the Gospel together. Bonds of friendship are established. The life of the group is interspersed with times of prayer. For more important celebrations they join up with the parish or perhaps other baptismal preparation groups. Thus with those to be baptized the church relives its youth, when for the first time people discovered the presence of the Risen Lord.

Since the first centuries of the church, the time during which the church celebrates the stages of baptism has been called the catechumenate. The number of months or weeks which separate the celebrations cannot be fixed in advance. This interval is too dependent on individual freedom in the slow germination of faith which is the work of the Spirit. But the number and significance of the major stages are fixed by the official rite.

### Entering into the community

This is the official welcome by the church. After a few weeks, which have made deeper mutual knowledge possible, those who are to be baptized take their place in the community. They receive the first Christian sign, and are marked with the sign of the cross.

Preparation for baptism then goes forward. Just as on the Emmaus road the Lord re-read events with the disciples in the light of the Word of God, so each person preparing for baptism goes over the great texts of scripture. In this dialogue his or her view of the world changes progressively; life is transformed and the riches of faith are discovered.

### The decisive call of the church

Once the decision has finally been taken, the date of the baptism can be fixed. Now comes the second great celebration, that of the 'call', which is generally put at the beginning of Lent.

With those who are to be baptized the whole church enters into Lent so as to take the way towards Easter, which for some of its members will be the first Easter. The bishop is present and calls those to be baptized one by one. He receives the testimony of those who have been with them, and this becomes the guarantee of the seriousness with which those to be baptized commit themselves. At the same time he is the witness of the Christian community which welcomes the new members. So their human volition becomes the church's decision.

---

## The great signings

I mark your forehead with the sign of the cross. It is the sign of Christians; let it remind you always of Christ and how much he loves you.

I mark your ears with the sign of the cross:
hear the words of Christ.

I mark your eyes with the sign of the cross:
see the works of Christ.

I mark your lips with the sign of the cross:
speak as Christ would speak.

I mark the sign of the cross over your heart:
make your heart the home of Christ.

I mark your shoulders with the sign of the cross:
be strong with the strength of Christ.

I mark your hands with the sign of the cross:
touch others with the gentleness of Christ.

I mark your feet with the sign of the cross:
walk in the way of Christ.

I place you entirely under the sign of Christ's cross in the name of the Father, and of the Son, and of the Holy Spirit.

## Great prayers and traditions

Look at the gospels for the Sundays in Lent (year A): Christ's temptations, the transfiguration, the conversation between Jesus and the woman of Samaria, the conversation with the man born blind, the raising of Lazarus. From the first centuries of the church these passages have been chosen to illuminate the last weeks of preparation for baptism. They are calls to conversion, and reveal the action of God through Jesus Christ.

Even now, these Sundays are marked by a time of prayer for catechumens. They are called to 'scrutinies', since according to scripture 'God scrutinizes the reins and heart'. To accept his gaze on our life is to accept the triumph of light over darkness. That is conversion: 'He who does the truth comes to the light' (John 3.21).

With the 'scrutinies' come the 'traditions'. 'I deliver to you that which I also received', said St Paul. The church hands on and entrusts to the catechumens two great riches of tradition: the symbol of faith and the Lord's Prayer, 'I believe in God' and the 'Our Father'. On the day of baptism the new Christians will repeat these two great liturgical proclamations with all their brothers and sisters in the faith.

## The Easter vigil

The Paschal night is the night of the resurrection, the night of this liberation which comes to us over the ages, the night of the departure from Egypt, the exodus, the night of the luminous cloud which led the people through the desert, the night of the presence of the Lord who feeds his people and quenches their thirst. For twenty centuries the church has celebrated the baptism of adults on this night. What night could be better? The community is gathered in the faith, and the newly baptized become its prophets. They tell all their brothers and sisters that even now the Lord is taking human ways for his presence to be recognized.

## Confirmation

The whole of Christian life is already contained in baptism, but the eucharist and confirmation reveal new approaches to the infinite riches of God. And human beings need a variety of signs. They need to take time to live at more depth.

Why are there two sacraments, baptism and confirmation, when originally they formed one? They are like the two wings of a diptych. Like two complementary approaches, two stages of the same thrust, they fit experience well.

Most of the time a baptism involves a wrench. There is a battle to be fought; there are choices to be made. Often rifts open up, friends look at you with amazement, not to say incomprehension and disapproval. By baptism God really calls people to a death in order to arrive at resurrection.

But things cannot be left there. Having taken the way of Christ in his death, it is necessary to welcome the Spirit. It is necessary to leave for the journey on the wind of Pentecost, open oneself up to a new life, have the courage to proclaim to the world the joy that God gives us. The apostles experienced the Easter of their Lord. But it was Pentecost which revealed their true dimension as disciples. They took a new step forward. The Spirit was in them and they could fulfil their task in the world and continue the mission of Christ: proclaiming the Good News.

It is the same today. Confirmation celebrates the mystery of Pentecost. The Spirit is raising up a church in the service of humanity. By the Spirit, each person is integrated into the church as into a living body. No member of it is useless, says St Paul (I Cor. 12). Each receives the gift of the Spirit for the service of all. Each is invited to discover the particular role he or she might exercise, what might be her or his 'ministry' for the common mission.

In the hope of a new life, confirmation appears as the future dimension of baptism. Because those who are baptized are people of the future, the church grows in them. It recognizes that Christ charges each of its members to help the whole body to increase. If we want to rediscover the riches of the sacrament of confirmation today, we have to rediscover in the church the wind of Pentecost.

Confirmation can be administered by the priest who baptizes, in the course of the celebration of baptism. In that case it consists of laying on of hands and an anointing. But for pastoral or personal reasons sometimes there is a preference for a longer interval between the two sacraments. Often baptism is celebrated at parish level, and the bishop then brings together all the newly baptized in another celebration on a diocesan scale. In confirming them he thus gives a more universal dimension to their baptism.

## The baptism of children

The Christian initiation of an adult takes several months or years; similarly, that of a child unfolds throughout his or her growth until he or she has reached the 'adult stature in Christ' of which St Paul speaks and which is reached only in the fullness of life.

The rite of water in which baptism is performed is only the first stage, which is already the hope for the whole process of initiation. This process takes place first at home, then over the years in catechetical instruction. It is during this time that the child will experience the other sacraments of Christian initiation: confirmation and eucharist.

---

**Hippolytus of Rome** (third century):
Children will be baptized first. All those who can speak for themselves will speak. As for those who cannot, their parents or one of their family will speak for them.

**Origen** (third century):
The church has received from the apostles the tradition of baptizing even children.

**Tertullian, at Carthage** (beginning of the third century):
It is preferable to delay baptism, above all in the case of children . . . Certainly the Lord said 'Let the little children come to me.' Let them come, but when they are older; let them come when they are of an age to be instructed, when they have learned to know that towards which they are going. Let them become Christians when they are capable of knowing Christ! Why, at this innocent age, is it so urgent to receive remission of sins?

---

*Should very small children be baptized?*

This question often comes up in family discussions at the time of a birth. Parents are well aware that their responsibility is involved in this choice.

Every sacrament is an event of the Christian community. It is not enough to enquire into the reasons for a baptism, to consider only the significance of the action for the one to be baptized. In performing a sacrament the church celebrates the manifestation of the face of God in our lives. The birth of a human being, the emergence of a new life, is a manifestation of God.

From the first centuries, the church received the children of Christian families for baptism. By acting in this way it announced to the world that in loving us, God does not wait for the time when we can recognize this love. It is very significant that the church baptizes children whom the accidents of life will prevent from achieving full development. It baptizes those who, for one reason or another, to human eyes will always have a deficiency or a handicap. God does not know the same frontiers as we do.

By its birth, a child belongs to a family with which it has solidarity: from this family it receives its name, race, language, customs – all part of the diversity of human riches. When its parents have experienced faith in the church, they want their child in turn to enter into the knowledge and love of the Risen Christ. This baptism is a hope, a way which is opening up.

However, one day the newborn child will have to choose for itself. He or she will have to choose whether or not to ratify the gifts that have been received. Only the children themselves, individually, step by step, within the church, can appropriate the baptismal life and turn it into truth. Hence the need to allow them to take part in the years of catechetical instruction.

Other parents make a different choice. They think that the child will have to make up his or her mind to be baptized on reaching a certain degree of maturity. That does not mean that they are shedding their responsibility; rather, they count on being able to give their children a chance of making a choice in all sincerity, and believe that they will be

121

able to do that when the children are old enough for instruction.

The church has always known this diversity of positions. To indicate this it is enough to quote some early Christian writers. (see the box on p. 121).

### The baptism of children old enough for instruction

Nowadays some children may come to catechetical instruction without having been baptized. Sometimes they are brought by friends; more often the parents themselves have wanted them to receive instruction, although they did not have their children baptized at birth.

The church has provided a ritual especially for their age. They are not baptized like little children, because they are capable of committing themselves. But the role of those who support them is still great, and the children are not as responsible as adults.

There are four stages. The first celebrations are very simple. They are intended to be undergone with friends who are at the same stage in catechesis.

First of all comes the rite of welcome, which corresponds to enrolment. The children then themselves say that they have come to join their friends in order to know Jesus.

After a certain time, sometimes the first year of instruction, the child begins to discover the content of the faith. He or she knows some passages of the Word of God and knows what the Gospels are. It is then good to bring together all the children of a year with their parents and more adults than the catechists. This is the celebration of entry into the catechumenate. As with adults, those who are to be baptized are solemnly marked with the sign of the cross of Christ.

Another stage takes place some weeks before the day fixed for baptism. This has a more penitential aspect. It corresponds to the discovery made even by children of the difficulty of being faithful in friendship to the Lord.

Finally comes baptism, which has its normal place at the Easter vigil. It takes place during a mass and it is expected that the newly baptized will join in the eucharist of their baptism.

Confirmation can be administered in the same ceremony as baptism, by the priest himself. But often the newly baptized will simply rejoin their friends, who will be confirmed during the course of the next year.

In a catechism group the baptism of a friend is a great richness to all the children. It allows each of them to rediscover their own baptisms.

Whether it is for adults, for young children or for babies, baptism, as we have just seen, takes on its full significance only when it is given a place in the whole of Christian initiation. Through it human beings become fully members of the body of Christ. They then become part of the priestly people, the people whom God has chosen to proclaim the mighty acts of him 'who has called us from darkness to his glorious light'. That is how we receive the mission to participate in the Pasch of the universe to make this world a new creation to proclaim the praise of its creator.

# 12

# The Sacrament of Reconciliation

*Therefore, if anyone is in Christ, there is a new creation; the old has passed away, behold, the new has come. All this is from God, who through Christ reconciled us to himself and gave us the ministry of reconciliation; that is, God was in Christ reconciling the world to himself, not counting their trespasses against them, and entrusting to us the message of reconciliation. So we are ambassadors for Christ, God making his appeal through us. We beseech you on behalf of Christ, be reconciled to God.*

II Cor. 5.17–20

## Under the sign of forgiveness

Human, truly human, life is possible only under the sign of forgiveness. In fact there is no life without conflicts; conflicts are inherent in existence. Sometimes they are the source of truth and lead to fertile confrontations, more often they are a cause of destruction.

One might think of conflicts which set countries against each other, of wars which never end; one might think of divisions in families, of social struggles, of tensions in the world of work, of failures of understanding between generations, of religious struggles, of opposition within the church. Everywhere reconciliation seems so difficult to realize.

Yet we feel confusedly that reconciliation is necessary. There is a need for:

- Reconciliation with oneself; how many beings destroy themselves because they cannot bear themselves!
- Reconciliation with others; how many people destroy others because they make them suffer!
- Reconciliation with the world; how many people are always rebelling against their environment or live in dread of forces which are too much for them!

The hope of reconciliation that the gospel proclaims goes right to the heart of the world. We believe that reconciliation is possible. But this is more than a matter of words. To proclaim reconciliation is to take the way of a reconciled life.

One can be reconciled with others only if one is first reconciled with oneself; and that often seems to us to be impossible as long as there is no one there first to tell us that he or she loves us as we are, in spite of what we are. This other allows us to reconcile our energy and our sluggishness, the dream and the reality within us.

For believers, God is this other. God's look is on us, a look of friendship and trust. But often we turn our backs on God. Whereas we have to turn towards him, to be *converted*. Then God reconciles us with ourselves, not in self-satisfaction with the past, but on a journey forward. He sets us on a road

> Who is a God like you pardoning iniquity
> and passing over transgression
> for the remnant of his inheritance?
> He does not retain his anger for ever
> because he delights in steadfast love.
> He will again have compassion upon us,
> he will tread our iniquities under foot.
> You will cast all our sins
> into the depths of the sea.
> You will show faithfulness and steadfast love,
> as you swore to our fathers
> from the days of old.
>
> Micah 7.18–20

which we can take in company with brothers and sisters with whom we must constantly be reconciled.

## At the heart of the gospel

Reconciliation is not just one of the aspects of salvation; it is its heart. Jesus came to reconcile human beings among themselves and with God. Three words from the New Testament will together illuminate our way forward: forgiveness, conversion and reconciliation.

## Forgiveness

This is the most important word. So many pages of the Bible speak of forgiveness, and Yom Kippur, the Day of Atonement, the day of forgiveness, is one of the greatest annual festivals in Judaism.

When Mark begins his Gospel, he announces: 'John the Baptist appeared in the desert, proclaiming a baptism of repentance for the forgiveness of sins' (Mark 1.4). And at the Last Supper, Matthew makes Jesus say: 'This is my blood, the blood of the covenant, shed for many for the forgiveness of sins' (Matt. 26.28).

It is surprising how rarely the theme of covenant appears in the Gospels. It appears in only two places: in the song of Zacharias, who proclaims that 'God has remembered his holy covenant' (Luke 1.72), and in the account of the institution of the eucharist in the passage which has just been quoted. The theme of forgiveness replaces it quite naturally. How could a covenant be lasting if there were not this will to keep reviving it in spite of unfaithfulness? The prophets clearly understood that God himself came to act on the human heart to renew it in his covenant. Is not that true forgiveness? Is not that the work fulfilled in Jesus Christ?

## Yom Kippur

Yom Kippur is the 'Day of Atonement'. It is also called 'the Day', because it is the holiest day in the Jewish calendar.

This festival dates from the last centuries before Jesus Christ. So it is one of the latest of those mentioned in the Bible. Its ritual is given in Leviticus 16. It is celebrated in autumn, ten days after the festival of the New Year, Rosh Ha-Shanah.

Before the capture of Jerusalem by the Romans and the destruction of the Temple, it was the only day of the year on which the high priest penetrated behind the curtain which shut off the most hidden part of the sanctuary, the Holy of Holies. That day he performed a rite of renewing the covenant with the blood of an animal offered as a sacrifice.

St Paul in Romans alludes to this rite when he says that God destined Jesus to be the new place of forgiveness, when he shed his blood on the cross.

The Talmud affirms: 'The Day of Atonement blots out sins between man and God; but those sins which are between man and man the Day of Atonement does not blot out unless they are reconciled with one another.'

Even now, in Judaism, it is a great annual festival. On that day the doors of the synagogue have to remain open so that everyone can return to God.

### Conversion

Forgiveness lies at the end of a way of conversion. What does that mean? God's faithfulness does not fail. Forgiveness exists in God before we have asked God for it. We can see this from the parable of the prodigal son, where the father waits each day for his absent son to return. But the joyful reunion could only take place when the son had set off home to his father.

To be converted is to change one's course. Ezekiel already made God say: 'Thus says the Lord: I do not want the death of the sinner, but that he may turn from his wickedness and live' (Ezek. 18.23).

Conversion means 'return'. The great image has been that of the return from exile, when the people, remote and lost in a foreign land, took the way back to Jerusalem. That corresponded at the same time to a renewal in the life of faith, and was as it were the rediscovery of a friendship with God.

### Reconciliation

The word does not appear in the Gospels. It comes from St Paul. It is a good indication of the mutual relationship between two partners. It also indicates that forgiveness comes at the end of a process which evokes the peace that has been rediscovered. It announces a change of attitude both towards human beings and towards God. For reconciled existence has to be lived on both planes.

## At the heart of human life

Nowadays it is a fact that people seldom go to confession. The sacrament of reconciliation is said not to enjoy a good press. There are doubtless many reasons for this, some of them arising out of the profound cultural change with which we are confronted.

The first effort needed is to rediscover the true meaning of the reconciliation announced by the gospel. It is certainly reconciliation with God. That is the necessary foundation. But it affects the many

> *But now in Christ Jesus*
> *you who once were far off*
> *have been brought near.*
> *For he is our peace,*
> *who has made us both one,*
> *and has broken down the dividing wall of hostility,*
> *by abolishing in his flesh*
> *the law of commandments and ordinances,*
> *that he might create in himself*
> *one new man in place of two,*
> *so making peace,*
> *and might reconcile us both to God in one body*
> *through the cross,*
> *thereby bringing the hostility to an end.*
> *And he came and preached*
> *peace to you who were far off*
> *and peace to those who were near;*
> *for through him*
> *we both have access in one Spirit*
> *to the Father.*
>
> Eph. 2.13–18

activities of human life. It lies at the heart of the very way in which we think of ourselves as 'human beings' in our time.

We shall focus our next thoughts on three pairs of words, each of which evokes a very specific sphere of human life:

Freedom and destiny, which relates to human experience of relationships with the world;

Responsibility and guilt, which affects relations with oneself;

Conflict and society, which affects relationship with others.

Relations with the world, with ourselves and others are the three intermediaries or, to use a more technical term, the three mediations which allow us to experience our relationship with God.

For each of the pairs of words we have chosen we shall try to show briefly:

how the problem arises;

what significance it has today;

what aspect of the biblical revelation correlates with it.

## Freedom or destiny?
## Reconciliation with the world

For the psychologist Carl Jung, consciousness and civilization are interconnected. The dawn of consciousness creates culture. By a profound, almost Promethean movement, humanity strives to emerge from the unconscious. It is the conscious human being who conquers the earth. Now all the evidence is that two reforms (the Protestant Reformation and the Catholic Counter-Reformation) created in a massive and unprecedented way a surplus of consciousness, a considerable development in the sense of responsibility. Carl Jung wrote: 'Nothing tends more to provoke consciousness and awakening than discord within oneself. One cannot imagine any more effective way of arousing the whole of humanity from a state of irresponsible semi-sleep.' If Jung is right, the sense of guilt brought out by Christianity will have been beneficial to Western civilization' (J. Delumeau, *Christianisme va-t-il mourir?*).

These remarks by Jean Delumeau well bring out something that is involved in the sacrament of reconciliation. It could be said that Western civilization was born in the confessional. The confessional leads people to look at their lives and evaluate their share of responsibility. To do this they have to accept that they are not just playthings in the hands of a destiny which is beyond them. They have to recognize the existence of their freedom.

### 1. Stating the problem

Are we beings whose lives are already entirely written out in advance, or do we have some possibility of personal creation within the framework in which we are placed?

Our first experience is that of arriving in a world that we have not made. We are born in a country, in a region, and we speak the language of our parents. We do not provide the framework of our own existence. However, within this framework we seek to become ourselves. We can do this by only perpetual negotiation between our concern to be and the limits within that is exercised.

Sometimes we come to consider our surroundings and the world as a hostile element. That involves a rejection on our part. For some people that is a passing matter, but others imprison their being in this fight against everything around them. Yet others refuse to fight, and are crushed and fatalistic. They can no longer say more than an eternal 'What's the point?'

Given the problems posed by underdevelopment, we can understand that some people need courage to get up and stand upright in a struggle against conditions which encircle them on every side. We can see the drift of Jung's remark, 'It is the conscious person who conquers the earth.'

In the world in which we live, we must either wait with our arms crossed or suppose that there is always something to do. The message of the gospel conveyed by the sacrament of reconciliation is one to seize our conscience. It makes us responsible, makes us 'stand up'.

---

### The new covenant

*Behold, the days are coming, says the Lord,*
*when I will make a new covenant*
*with the house of Israel . . .*
*I will put my law within them,*
*and I will write it upon their hearts;*
*and I will be their God,*
*and they shall be my people . . .*
*And they shall all know me,*
*from the least of them to the greatest,*
*for I shall forgive their iniquity,*
*and I will remember their sin no more.*
Jer. 31.31–34

*I will cleanse you from all your uncleannesses,*
*and from all your idols.*
*A new heart I will give you,*
*and new spirit I will put within you;*
*and I will take out of your flesh the heart of stone*
*and give you a heart of flesh.*
*And I will put my spirit within you,*
*and cause you to walk in my statutes*
*and be careful to observe my ordinances . . .*
*You shall be my people,*
*and I will be your God.*          Ezek. 36.25–28

## 2. The topicality of the problem

The progress of science seems made to increase the possibilities of freedom. Human beings are liberating themselves in space and time. We are increasing the speed with which we get about (planes, trains and cars), and are capable of escaping gravity. The conquest of space is a fine image of the progress of freedom.

We might also recall other spheres: medicine frees us from certain ailments: we are no longer obliged to spend all our time, as in the ancient civilizations, in the quest for food; we are discovering leisure time. All that represents free spaces.

But in parallel to these new freedoms, we sometimes get the impression that inner freedom is contracting. Is not the Pyreneean shepherd more free than a worker on a factory conveyor belt? The human sciences make us dizzy. Psychoanalysis discloses the influences that have marked our unconscious. Genetics is capable of manipulating genes. The techniques of propaganda and brainwashing can make robots.

So what does it take to be someone 'standing upright'? How do we win true freedom? Do not some of our brothers and sisters from the Gulags give us an example? Are not prisoners and those subjected to all kinds of pressure truly free people? Adolpho Perez Esquivel, the Nobel Peace Prize winner, said one day when speaking of the time when he was shut up in a cell smaller than a table: 'If I did not go mad it was because during that time I tried to reconstruct the whole of the Gospel by putting one after another the passages that I remembered.' Is that not an illustration of those people who take their lives in their hands and win their freedom?

## 3. Who is our God?

The revelation of God in the Bible comes to the help of our doubts and our timidity and helps us to discover the sphere of our freedom.

First of all we are shown the God who calls. This is the God of 'vocation'. We might remember the calls of Abraham, Moses, David, the prophets. The call of God is handed on in a personal relationship and recognizes the freedom of the person addressed. Each has his or her way of responding, and also the freedom to refuse. There are no robots among the figures of the Bible.

And God calls into being. 'Let us make human beings in our image and likeness,' says God in the first chapter of Genesis. From this beginning of the Bible, human beings have been presented as having to rule over creation; they themselves are creators in the image of God. The rest of the world has been dedivinized, losing its oppressive magical power. It is no longer the garden of which human beings are the gardeners (Gen. 2.15). Nothing of what is around us is God; we are entirely freed from the idols which we are all too ready to make.

We have experience of this. How many times have we been able to bear witness that we know those who have received the call of the gospel,

---

### Penance

The Latin word *poenitentia*, regret, repentance, change of mind, is equivalent to the Greek word *metanoia*, which is frequent in the New Testament, and translated 'conversion'.

In the first centuries of the church, it denoted the behaviour of Christians who asked forgiveness for their sins. They did *penance*. They were then asked to perform a certain number of works to show the truth of their intention to be converted. These could be works of charity, pilgrimages, or times of fasting and prayer.

Doing penance was painful, and tasks could often be harsh. The word penance then became synonymous with mortification, and subsequently with punishment. To make children do penance was to inflict punishment on them.

When a priest gave a penance at confession, many people thought that this was a punishment proportionate to the gravity of their sins. And the expression 'sacrament of penance' suggested above all a degree of punishment. People lost sight of the fact that this was a return towards friendship with God. That is why nowadays people prefer to talk about the sacrament of reconciliation, thus rediscovering the thought of the New Testament.

when many around them were doubting their capacity truly to become human. The gospel set them on their feet. 'Therefore, if anyone is in Christ, there is a new creation; the old has passed away, behold, the new has come. All this is from God, who through Christ reconciled us to himself' (II Cor. 5.17).

God calls to the service of others. God entrusts people with a mission. So they have the power not only to change their individual destinies but also to become agents in the development of the world and society. 'I have seen the affliction of my people, and have heard their cry; I know their sufferings . . . and I am sending you to free my people', says God to Moses (Ex. 3.7).

The first story which talks of forgiveness in the Gospel of Mark is that of the healing of a paralysed man at Capernaum. It unfolds like a liturgy: the crowd gathers, Jesus 'proclaims the word', a man is brought to him on a stretcher, and Jesus says, 'Your sins are forgiven.' He adds 'Get up and walk.' What a splendid image! For the first disciples someone saved, someone forgiven, is someone standing upright.

---

### Psalm 51

*Have mercy on me, O God,*
*according to your steadfast love;*
*according to your abundant mercy*
*blot out my transgressions.*
*For I know my transgressions,*
*and my sin is ever before me.*
*Against you, only you, have I sinned,*
*and done what is evil in your sight.*
*Behold, I was brought forth in iniquity,*
*and in sin did my mother conceive me.*
*You desire truth in the inward being;*
*therefore teach me wisdom in my secret heart.*
*Cleanse me from my sin, and I shall be clean;*
*wash me, and I shall be whiter than snow.*
*Fill me with joy and gladness;*
*let the bones which you have broken rejoice.*
*Create in me a clean heart, O God,*
*and put a new and right spirit within me.*
*Restore to me the joy of your salvation,*
*and uphold me with a willing spirit.*

---

Still today the Christian community is the 'sacrament of salvation'; it reveals the face of the God of reconciliation each time it raises someone up. It gives birth to freedom when it puts human life under the sign of God's call and not just under that of the law and the commandments. It gives birth to freedom when it commits itself to human dignity in the face of all the Gulags, when it struggles for development. The church pursues the work of the Lord.

### Responsibility and guilt: Reconciliation with oneself

Responsibility and guilt are two difficult words, and one is often taken for the other. However, it is important to distinguish between them.

#### 1. Stating the problem

Responsibility is the capacity to answer for one's actions. That presupposes that one has a real part in performing them. We can even accept being responsible for actions committed by those who are bound to us or who are under our orders. A leader is responsible for the actions of his subordinates, and parents for those of their children.

Guilt is bearing the responsibility for a fault, recognizing that one is to blame. The fault is an evil action in which our conscience and our freedom are involved. Someone can cause a car accident through an illness which affected him while driving; he is responsible, but he is not guilty.

Here we have two ideas which are so close that many people find it difficult to distinguish them. One only has to look at surveys or newspaper cuttings to see this. We all want a world in which human beings are increasingly responsible, yet we do not want them to be overwhelmed by their guilt. We have to accept our responsibilities, but too strong a feeling of guilt can destroy us.

When people feel guilty, a forgiving look saves them and raises them up. That is how God's forgiveness works. But if we are to be truly welcomed in the depths of our being, it is good that this should also be shown by the forgiveness of our friends or neighbours.

## 2. The topicality of the problem

There are two contradictory tendencies today.

An attempt is being made to explain human behaviour in terms of factors that lie beyond freedom: heredity, environment, the influence of the stars. In that case there is no such thing as guilt.

Others, by contrast, create an oppressive climate which tends to exaggerate guilt. A bad sense of guilt creates neuroses . . . which psychotherapists try to cure.

The pastoral work of reconciliation lies at the heart of this debate. It teaches people to look at themselves honestly, without false complaisance and without masochistic severity. It is necessary to recognize one's responsibility and accept being freed from one's guilt.

## 3. Who is our God?

We have to direct towards our brothers and sisters a look like that of God himself. God condemns the evil act, but not the person of the sinner.

We might recall the attitude of Jesus to the woman taken in adultery. The very scenario has great symbolic value. The woman is in the midst of the circle of her accusers. Each one picks up a stone to throw at her; it is a circle of death. This woman is thus imprisoned in her past, and has no future. What does Jesus do? He does not deny the crime. He does not even seek to start a trial. He breaks the circle around the woman. He opens up a future for her. 'Let him who is without sin cast the first stone' (John 8.7). And immediately each person goes his way, beginning with the eldest. What has changed is the way in which the others look at this woman, and also the way in which they look at themselves. Then Jesus can say, 'Nor do I condemn you. Go and sin no more' (John 8.11).

---

*Peter came up and said to Jesus, 'Lord, how often shall my brother sin against me, and I forgive him? As many as seven times?' Jesus said to him, 'I do not say to you seven times, but seventy times seven.'*

Matt. 18.21–2

---

The Christian community lives out the sacrament when it has an attitude like that of Jesus. It has to take the side of people against their sin. It has to open up a future. At every age of life, after all sins, however serious they may be, there is always a call which can ring out. And when it does, it offers the possibility of changing course and being converted.

But we do not have to take this way which opens up before us alone. Our brothers and sisters are travelling companions. Like us they recognize that they are sinners, and like us they hear the call to conversion. In the face of sin, ours as well as that of others, without doubt there is a need for severity and strictness, but also for much love and faith in the person of the sinner. That is God's attitude.

## Conflict and society: Reconciliation with others

### 1. Stating the problem

Conflict and sin must not be confused. Without conflict, it has been said, there is no life. The smaller the society, the more intense the relationship and the more painful the conflict, though it is inevitable. The human couple is the smallest social unit, so it should not be surprising that it can be the place of conflict which gives rise to much suffering.

The real question is: Is conflict going to engender death or lead to a new birth? The latter option is the one chosen by any approach towards reconciliation. But it is not easy, since this conflict habitually leads us to deny the other.

Reconciliation passes through three stages:

Discovering that the other person exists is the first stage. In many international conflicts nowadays one party acts as though the other did not exist, and recourse to terrorism is sometimes had by certain groups as the ultimate means of proving their existence.

Discovering the other as being different from oneself is the second stage. There is in fact a real way of killing the other person which consists in wanting him or her to be completely like oneself. No more conflict is possible, but there is no longer any 'other'!

Finally, there is a need to discover the difference as riches. That is often very difficult. However, there is communion only in acceptance of otherness . . . and of complementarity.

We can see why conflicts take so long to resolve.

### 2. *The topicality of the problem*

Each generation knows different conflicts. The difficulty of 'being together' depends on numerous historical, geographical, psychological and cultural factors. In our time, in our sphere, it is easy to discover the habitual source of the negation of the other. We can see a rebirth of racism. Economic difficulties lead to rivalries and differential claims. We are involved in the rifts which come from the division of our world into North and South, rich countries and developing countries. We ignore one another, we fight one another, we deny one another. And in his encyclical on 'The Problems of Society' (30 December 1987) Pope John-Paul II was not afraid of talking in this connection of 'structures of sin'.

### 3. *Who is our God?*

God created human beings in his own image and likeness. That is true of every human being, regardless of race or degree of development. That is the source of human dignity; and human diversity is simply an image of God's riches.

Our God is the God of the covenant. Covenant means partnership. God willed it between himself and human beings. He willed it between men and women. He calls on us to live it out among ourselves. The covenant is always the place of necessary reconciliation.

Our God is the God of Jesus Christ, the 'righteous sufferer'. Violence leads to violence. There is always a chain of vengeance. In our world bombs are met with bombs, and that remains true, in a less apparent way, in our everyday life. This chain must be broken. That is what Jesus did: 'On the cross he killed hatred', and he addressed God, saying, 'Father, forgive them, they do not know what they are doing' (Luke 23.34).

Living out covenant and forgiveness are the two sources of life which are opposed to everyday conflicts. That is what we are called to by the sacrament of reconciliation.

## Communities of forgiveness

From the start, Christian communities have sought to be communities of forgiveness. That is so much part of the message of the gospel that the Lord's Prayer teaches us to say, 'Forgive us our trespasses as we forgive those who trespass against us.'

Today the church does not just live out the sacrament of reconciliation during its liturgy. In the name of faith, by reason of its discovery of God, it calls on Christians to bear witness:

- that there is a place for human beings where their freedom can grow;
- that human beings can seek responsibility without being crushed by their guilt;
- that the 'other' is not a danger but a source of wealth.

# *A history of the sacrament of penance and reconciliation*

## Origins

Jesus gives first to Peter (Matt. 16.16–19) and then to the disciples (Matt. 18.15–18) the power to 'bind and loose': rabbinic terms which denote the exclusion and reintroduction of a member of the community.

But to understand the meaning and tenor of the sacrament, we need also to see:

The Jesus who calls for conversion at the beginning of his ministry (Mark 1.15);

The Jesus who distinguishes uncleanness from sin, for example in:
   the episode of the man who was born blind (John 9.1–13);
   his remark to the Pharisees (Mark 7.17–21);
The Jesus who forgives and reconciles the adulterous woman, to whom he says, 'Nor do I condemn you: go and sin no more': he forgives her sin but also reconciles her with God and with the community, preventing her from being stoned (John 8.1–11);
   The Jesus who is himself reconciliation: his blood is the blood of the covenant shed for the many for the remission of sins' (Matt. 26.28).

## The time of the apostles

Both penance and conversion (*metanoia*) appear on the day of Pentecost: 'Repent and be baptized every one of you in the name of Jesus Christ for the forgiveness of sins' (Acts 2.37).

Baptism is the first sacrament of penance and reconciliation, as we acknowledge in the creed. There is no trace of another sacrament for a century, but that does not mean that the communities did not have to decide whether to exclude or reintroduce some of their members (see Matt. 18.15–18; Acts 5.1–11; I Cor. 5.1–13).

## Ancient penance from the second to the fifth centuries

Apart from a phrase in the book called *The Shepherd of Hermas* (around 150), it is only from the third century that we have information about ancient penance, which is also called canonical, ecclesial or public penance.

The church faced a real problem. Baptism is for the remission of sins, but what does one do with a Christian who commits a serious sin after baptism (apostasy, murder, adultery) and then repents? Has the church the right to remit sins other than by baptism?

Eventually, after numerous debates, the church recognized the possibility of another remission than that of baptism, but this remission only related to serious sins and could take place only once – hence its name 'second baptism' or 'second penance'.

Foreseeing the pernicious wiles of the devil, God has allowed access to remain open even after forgiveness has been given and the lock of baptism has been fastened. He has put in the vestibule a second penance which can open to those who knock. But only once, since in fact this is already the second time. And never again, since the previous penance has proved useless. And is not once enough? (Tertullian, 155–220).

The Christian who had committed a grave crime confessed it to the bishop in secret.

The bishop put the sinner 'in penance', imposing a special status in the community on him, in the course of a ceremony which gave rise to our Ash Wednesday liturgy.

Penitents were excluded from the eucharistic community to indicate that their sins had cut them off from God. They only participated in the liturgy of the Word, in special dress, at the back of the church and on their knees. After the universal prayer, in which the assembly prayed for them, the bishop laid hands on them and sent them away.

In their everyday life, penitents were obliged to do penance: fasting, prayer, mortification, abstention from marriage or intercourse, a ban on holding public office.

It is from all these practices that penance in antiquity derived its name of public penance, and not from the confession, which was always made in private.

When the bishop thought that penitents had shown sufficient desire to 'change their lives', he decided to reconcile them and reintroduce them into the community. This celebration, which took place on Maundy Thursday, took the name *sacramentum reconciliationis*. It is from this that Vatican II derived the new title for the sacrament of penance and reconciliation.

Five comments may be made on this period:
- The elements of the sacrament follow the order confession, penance, reconciliation. The church never reconciled sinners before they had shown their conversion by doing penance;
- The sign of the rift between the sinner and God was exclusion from the community;
- This practice of penance was admirable, but so hard that sinners ended up waiting until the moment of death to resort to it. Moreover the church was well aware of this difficulty. Cassian bears witness to it in the fifth century by making a list of ten substitute remissions: charity, alms, tears, recognizing oneself to be a sinner before God, the acceptance of suffering, amendment of life, intercession for the brethren, mercy and faith, the conversion of a sinner, forgiving offences;
- In the fifth and sixth centuries we can see a progressive diminution in public penance. And since it only related to serious sins and no one resorted to it for slight sins, this period has been referred to as a 'penitential void'.
- The fact that the majority of Christians did not resort to the sacrament does not mean that a penitential attitude did not exist. St Augustine reminds his faithful:

> I have said that in scripture there are three ways of envisaging penance. The first is that of the catechumens who have a thirst for baptism . . . There is another daily penance. Where do we find it? There is no better passage in scripture than the daily prayer in which the Lord taught us to pray, showed us what to say to the Father, and expressed it in these words: 'Forgive us our debts as we forgive our debtors' (Matt. 6.12) . . . There remains the third kind of penance. This is a more serious and more grievous penance' (St Augustine then talks of public penance).

## Tariffed penance from the seventh to the twelfth century

The monks of St Patrick, evangelizing Ireland, became aware that they could not introduce the ancient form of penance there since it had already fallen into disuse on the continent. They created a new form, combining some forms of ancient penance with some monastic practices of fraternal correction.

When the Irish monks arrived on the continent, they brought their new practice with them. This met with strong opposition from the bishops, but pastoral concern that penance should be experienced in the church finally won the day, in favour of the new form, which was more approachable than the old.

The confession remains secret, but the penance also becomes secret. There is no longer public penance.

This penance can be repeated. One can resort to it as often as one wishes, and to make access easier, it is no longer just the bishop who is its minister, but also priests.

The bishop preserves a certain authority over it by setting up lists of penances (hence the name tariffs of penance) which guide the monk who is a confessor. These are the *Penitentials* (so many days fast for such and such a sin).

For the tariff to be applied, the penitents need to specify what sort of sin they have committed, in what circumstances and how many times.

Absolution, which was originally given after penance had been done (as in ancient penance), comes increasingly close to the confession, to the point of being given immediately after it, and therefore before penitents have fulfilled their time and acts of penance; this is so that the sinner does not wait too long for forgiveness.

In spite of everything, the tariff of penance was still heavy: the addition of days of penance could surpass the duration of a life. So we see the multiplication of remissions of sins by other means than sacramental penance:

pilgrimages to Rome, St James of Compostella, the Holy Land;

participation in the building of a church;

offerings for mass to be celebrated;

a penitential tariff to be replaced by a financial tariff.

## Private penance from the twelfth century to Vatican II

This was the situation when, at the beginning of the twelfth century, the left bank of the Seine in Paris became the scene of a great intellectual and particularly theological ferment.

Abelard, not without some insight into the gospel, attacked external practices of penance by tariff, recalling that the essence of penance was within the heart. For him, the contrition that sinners must have took precedence over the penances that they had to perform.

Around 1250, Peter Lombard arrived at a precise definition of the seven sacraments (see Chapter 7, p. 59).

The formula of forgiveness changed from the deprecative (May God forgive you) to the declarative form (I absolve you).

Eucharistic communion had become so rare that the Fourth Lateran Council (1215) prescribed that it should take place at least once a year, at Easter. The mentality of the age, expressed by this council, also required of all the faithful that before receiving communion they should have confessed 'all their sins'. The question is whether by 'all their sins' the council meant only serious sins, or absolutely all sins, both serious and slight, and even just the slight sins if there were no serious ones. Though the theologians tended towards the first solution (only the serious sins), piety increasingly brought in the second, as is shown by the third commandment of the church (fifteenth century): 'Confess all your sins at least once a year,' and the fact of systematic confession before the Easter communion.

The ritual of 1614, promulgated by the Council of Trent, defined the norms of private confession, but it further increased its individual and secret character by prescribing that a grill should separate the priest from the penitent. These confessionals increasingly came to be set up in churches.

It only remained for devotion to insist to ardent Christians that they should make their confessions as often as possible, to arrive at the practice of the sacrament of penance as it existed on the eve of the Second Vatican Council.

The rites and formulae of Penance are to be revised so that they more clearly express both the nature and effect of the sacrament (Vatican II, *Constitution on the Sacred Liturgy*, 72)

---

## Today

The new rite which has emerged from Vatican II is particularly rich. It was inspired by the long tradition to give reconciliation the place that it should occupy in the Christian communities. Three main directions can be stressed.

The Council took up again the old name which used to denote the sacrament.

The Council wanted the restoration of a proclamation of Holy Scripture in the celebration of all the sacraments, and the rite suggested it for reconciliation.

The Council desired that 'the rites which are meant to be celebrated in common, with the faithful present and actively participating, should as far as possible be celebrated in that way rather than by an individual and quasi-privately' (*Constitution on the Sacred Liturgy*, 27). So the rite has provided for a diversity of celebrations.

## Reconciliation

People used to talk about the sacrament of penance or confession. That put the stress on the human approach more than that of God: 'God was in Christ reconciling the world to himself' (II Cor. 5.19). Christians have now become used to talking of reconciliation.

## The place of the word of God

The reading of the word of God was notably absent from the rite of reconciliation. Where is it to be put from now on?

For communal celebrations the solution is easy enough. The first part is a liturgy of the word. The chief role of the main reading is to proclaim a God who loves and forgives us; at a secondary stage it is a revelation of calls of God and an invitation to conversion. Thus it becomes the mirror which reveals our defects.

For individual confessions, the introduction of a reading of the Word of God might seem a novelty. In preparing their confessions, penitents themselves can choose passages of the Bible which seem suited to their situation. So they could begin their confession by saying: 'I have chosen such and such a passage from scripture. In the light of it I accuse myself of such and such sins.' When the penitent has not chosen a text, it is up to the priest to suggest a passage from scripture at whatever moment seems best to him.

## Diversity of celebration

None of the forms of celebration suggested by the ritual exhausts the riches of the sacrament. They are complementary.

*Individual confession* is the best demonstration of personal encounter with God. There are moments in life when conversion can only be individual. That is clearly the case when a serious sin causes an important rupture in our relationship with God. But it is also the case before certain important commitments, like approaching marriage, before a religious consecration, or even when we have to take a major decision. A personal approach is also indicated during a retreat when we are trying to take stock of ourselves.

*Communal celebrations* best bring out the ecclesial aspect. The ministry of the priest is set at the heart of the prayer of the community. Here we can understand better that it is not enough to ask God for forgiveness, but that we must also forgive our brothers and sisters and create a world in which human relations can blossom in reconciliation.

These celebrations are also the place where we can become aware that our world consists, to use John Paul II's expression, 'of structures of sin' for which we are partly responsible, each for our part.

They have the great advantage of allowing members of the same community to prepare together for the great festivals like Christmas and Easter. They create a rhythm in the unfolding of the liturgical year. They remind everyone of the need for conversion and disclose specific implications. Though this is not their prime motivation, they bring into play a real catechesis, and often renew the 'examinations of conscience' which otherwise get bogged down in somewhat out-of-date sins.

The usual form includes individual absolution, but for quite specific instances the rite provides for recourse to communal absolution, which is wrongly called 'collective'. It is up to the conferences of bishops to make these rites more precise.

*Celebrations without absolution* Some people have found it strange that a sacramental rite can provide for celebrations of reconciliation without absolution. This is a good way of indicating that the sacrament takes place over time, as we showed in Chapter 2 (see p. 14).

These celebrations involve a liturgy of the word, a call to conversion and a self-examination of conscience. They are only the beginning of an approach which will be pursued in the days or weeks to come. They fit well on Ash Wednesday or another day at the beginning of Lent. People then choose in all freedom the particular point in their lives on which they want to focus their Lenten effort. They sum it all up by subsequently coming to make their confession before Easter.

In small communities, they sometimes take place as the conclusion to a kind of general assembly which allows each of the members to share in a change in the life of the community. In that case, efforts at conversion are fixed in common and all are called on to play their part in implementing them.

They have the great advantage, in a common approach to reconciliation, of providing a place for Christians whom their habitual situations have prevented from participating fully in the sacraments of the eucharist and reconciliation. That is particularly the case with all those who do not think themselves yet ready for a full integration into the church; sometimes in certain countries people with a background in polygamy; also couples who have not yet celebrated their marriage in church, or even remarried divorced persons.

### Each has a particular rhythm

As we have seen, the rhythm in which Christians have had recourse to this sacrament has varied a great deal over the course of the centuries. About forty years ago people used to distinguish three categories of faithful:

Committed Christians who went to confession regularly, every week, every two weeks, or every month;

those who made their confession as a preparation for the great festivals: Christmas, Easter, the Assumption and All Saints' Day;

those who confessed only at Easter.

Nowadays the most committed Christians are often members of teams concerned with lifestyle or sharing the Gospel, which in part play the role once exercised by private confession: this is a confrontation of life with the demands of the word of God. They feel the need for frequent confession less. They adopt the parochial rhythm emphasized by the communal celebrations of their community, which take place three or four times a year. They add a personal approach in certain circumstances special to themselves.

God, the Father of mercies,
through the death and resurrection of his Son
has reconciled the world to himself
and sent the Holy Spirit among us
for the forgiveness of sins;
through the ministry of the Church,
may God give you pardon and peace,
and I absolve you from your sins.

From the Rite of Reconciliation

'This at last is bone of my bones and flesh of my flesh' (Gen. 2.23)

# 13

# The Sacrament of Marriage

*In the beginning God said, 'It is not good that man should be alone; I will make him a helper fit for him.'*

*God formed a woman and brought her to the man. Then the man said: 'This at last is bone of my bones and flesh of my flesh; she shall be called woman, because she was taken out of man.' Therefore a man leaves his father and his mother and cleaves to his wife, and they become one flesh. And the man and his wife were both naked, and were not ashamed.*

Gen. 2.18 . . . 3.20

Marriage, that ancient institution which people fifty years ago would readily have claimed to be universal, is now in trouble. However, the reality still exists and many young people in fact have a high ideal of it. It is the civil or religious institution which is rejected, or at least put in question. Must what is personal intimacy depend on laws and regulations?

Within this chapter we cannot make either a sociological study or a plea in defence of marriage. We cannot even present the whole of the church's doctrine and the basis for its legislation. There are a large number of works on the question; above all you should refer to Jean-Pierre Bagot, *How to Understand Marriage*, in the same series as this book.

The church did not invent marriage. Marriage existed long before the church. And the first Christians married, like those around them, without needing a special religious ceremony. However, from the beginning marriage was considered important in the Christian community, since St Paul could affirm: 'Husbands, love your wives as Christ loved the church' (Eph. 5.24).

Marriage is certainly a 'reality of human life', and it is not too difficult to discover why it has found a place among the signs of the kingdom.

To begin to live as a married couple is an important stage in the development of personality. At that point the husband and wife modify their attitudes towards all around them. As children they have lived in a family circle in which each person had a place. As adolescents they gained the right to be themselves, sometimes with difficulty or pain. But now they have to live an adult life, and those who have received everything have to be a source in their turn. They are no longer solitary beings, but are facing the family environment and the circle of their friends together.

Solitude is a basic human situation. It cannot be denied, and has to be salvaged. And solitude can be salvaged only by being overcome. Paradoxical though it may seem, solitude is necessary if people are to have communion. First one has to be oneself, facing one's own personality, in order to be able to enter into relations with others. One might say that the couple is the crucible in which solitude finally turns to gold, since it shows itself to be capable of communion.

The Bible describes it like this. It shows us 'man',

in the beginning, looking in the universe for his helpmeet. It describes his joy when he has found the 'flesh of his flesh' (Gen. 2.23). It hymns the love that burns at the heart of two beings:

> My beloved is mine and I am his . . .
> Love is as strong as death,
> jealousy is cruel as the grave.
> Its flashes are flashes of fire,
> its fire comes from God.
> Many waters cannot quench love,
> neither can floods drown it.
> (Song of Songs 2.16; 8.6f.)

The word of God is stronger still. It borrows the words of this passion which burns in the heart of lovers to express the marvellous love which unites God to his people.

## Human love, the face of God

We have already said how difficult it is to talk of God, how there is a risk of imprisoning God in our words, the fear of escaping into timeless or unreal talk as we do so. God needs to be the one with whom we live, who calls us to live, rather than the being of whom we speak. God is certainly in everyday life, but he remains a hidden God whose face is difficult to discern, the mysterious God.

And it is precisely there that the sacramental reality is to be found. It comes to birth in the very mystery of human beings, to lead them to the mystery of God. It is none other than everyday life, but lived out in its fullness, to become a witness to the invisible.

> With what shall I come before the Lord,
> and bow myself before God on high?
> Will the Lord be pleased with thousands of rams,
> with ten thousands of rivers of oil?
> He has showed you, O man, what is good;
> and what does the Lord require of you
> but to do justice, and to love kindness,
> and to walk humbly with your God?
>
> Micah 6.6–8

What is more everyday and yet more mysterious than the encounter of two beings who love each other and recognize each other, and yet who never finish discovering each other? That is everyday life in all its poetry, in both its riches and its monotony; it is everyday life which becomes a mirror of the infinite.

In the first page of the Bible, the encounter between man and woman is felt to be one of the places where the invisible is unveiled. God himself wanted to imprint his face on this human couple who appeared on the sixth day as the climax of creation.

> God said:
> let us make human beings in our image,
> according to our likeness . . .
> God created human beings in his image,
> in the image of God he created them,
> male and female he created them.

If male and female become the image of God in their married life, the definition of the sacrament as 'a human reality which proclaims the kingdom because it is a place where it is realized' fits them marvellously.

And among all the sacraments, marriage is one of those in which it appears clearly that one cannot separate human reality and sacramental reality.

The prophet Micah already proclaimed that the real act of worship is not in the offering of goods external to human beings, but in the everyday doing of what is just, in a way of living with humility and – tenderness.

## Love and covenant

One might wonder which way to put it: is marriage a sacrament of love or a covenant sacrament? It might be supposed that the two phrases amount to the same thing. But that is not the case.

The content of the word love is difficult to detect. Sometimes it is a portmanteau word which covers very vague or diverse things. There is passionate love and romantic love. There is the 'love of women' which perhaps has only a distant relationship to 'love of neighbour'. People talk of making love and dying of love . . . What meaning should we give this word?

In its riches, the biblical tradition gives it a content bound up with the making of a covenant. To discover the covenant is to make sense of love.

Nowadays, the fact that many young people fall in love, live together for a number of years and then one day decide to marry is a good indication that for them the word marriage means more than a loving relationship. In their own way they are rediscovering the reality of a covenant.

To replace the word love with covenant is certainly to convey a less ambiguous content, but it is also to put the adventure of two people in a relationship which transcends them and which takes the whole social group of their relations and friends as witnesses.

If marriage were only the sacrament of love, one could say that the sacrament came to an end when love disappeared. But it is not as simple as that. There are days when love is hidden and nevertheless faithfulness to the covenant keeps its greatness. Besides, have there not always been two kinds of civilizations in the world: those in which people marry because they are in love and those in which people are in love because they marry? It is very difficult to say which of the two has guaranteed the most happiness.

## What does covenant mean?

Covenant is so omnipresent in the Old Testament that it is difficult to single out the most significant texts. You really need to re-read the whole of the Bible. The covenant was lived out down the centuries before it became the source of a theology. And it is the same with human couples: theory never takes full account of the life that has to be discovered over the months and years.

In speaking of the covenant, what texts should we choose? Those which reflect joy and suffering, strictness and tenderness, ruptures and reunions? Doubtless all that, but there are a great many of them.

In every covenant there are partners. That is also the case in marriage. One of the audacities of the biblical tradition is to envisage that such a partnership exists between God and human beings. How is that possible? Two words would seem to be particularly important: faithfulness and reciprocity. They are the two which need most to be stressed.

---

### In faithfulness

*And I will betroth you to me for ever;*
*I will betroth you to me in righteousness and in justice,*
*in steadfast love and mercy.*
*I will betroth you to me in faithfulness,*
*and you shall know the Lord.*

Hos. 2.21f.

---

### Faithfulness

In his covenant with his people, God, who is there first, is faithful. By virtue of the reciprocity which gives meaning to all covenants, the prophets constantly summon the people also to live in faithfulness to him.

That is how forgiveness emerges. For there is duration in a covenant only if each partner constantly refuses to imprison the other in a past which is sometimes hard to bear. Forgiveness goes further than the gift. It is that which is constantly renewed. The God of the covenant must also be the God of forgiveness.

But the covenant between man and woman is fragile. Nevertheless, because the human couple is in the image and likeness of God, they are called to live in faithfulness.

It is not wrong to say that in its gospel aim of absolute fidelity, marriage is a 'madness'. Beyond question it is neither more nor less than celibacy for the kingdom, and it is just as demanding.

The apostles understood this well. In the Gospel of Matthew, when Jesus stated that it is not permissible for the husband to repudiate his wife, they retorted, 'If such is the case of a man with his wife, it is not expedient to marry.' And Jesus replied, putting marriage and celibacy in parallel, by saying, 'Not all can receive this precept, but only those to whom it is given' (Matt. 19.10–11).

In marriage more than elsewhere, faithfulness and forgiveness are always linked. Both have the same source. When one partner forgives the other, it is because they remain together, so that tomorrow can be different from yesterday. It is not a matter of forgetting a past and not taking account of it. It is more and other than that. To forgive as God forgives is to love enough to want to go on building the future together.

That is why the married couple, like the nuclear family, is certainly the context within which one can best understand all the riches and all the difficulty of forgiveness. And that again reveals a face of God to us.

### Reciprocity

It is somewhat surprising that reciprocity can be envisaged between God and his people. Is there not too great a disparity between the two partners? Is not God considered above all as the 'master' who gives orders? So how can God become the partner?

---

#### A reciprocal enthusiasm

*I will greatly rejoice in the Lord,*
*my soul shall exult in my God,*
*for he has clothed me with the garments of salvation,*
*he has covered me with the robe of righteousness,*
*as a bridegroom decks himself with a garland,*
*and as bride adorns herself with her jewels.*

*For as the earth brings forth its shoots,*
*and as a garden causes what is sown in it to*
*    spring up,*
*so the Lord God will cause righteousness and praise*
*to spring forth before all the nations.*

*You shall no more be termed 'Forsaken',*
*and your land shall no more be termed 'Desolate',*
*but you shall be called 'My delight is in her',*
*and your land 'Married';*
*and as the bridegroom rejoices over the bride,*
*so shall your God rejoice over you.*
                                    Isa. 61.10–11; 62.4–5

---

In many civilizations the husband or head of the family is virtually a god in his family; so it is not surprising that one finds few human groups in which husband and wife enjoy equal rights. And the husband is not usually ready to give up his prerogatives and privileges. There are so many places where marriage is a contract concluded for the benefit of the husband and his clan!

Is it not surprising that it is St Paul, usually thought to be a misogynist, who was the first to set down equal rights in rigorous terms? Does he not in fact say:

Each man should have his own wife and each woman her own husband. The husband should give to his wife her conjugal rights, and likewise the wife to her husband. For the wife does not rule over her own body, but the husband does; likewise the husband does not rule over his own body, but the wife does (I Cor. 7.2–4).

In the slow evolution of humankind, the pattern of married life is doubtless only at its beginning. And the gospel enters into dialogue with each of us so that the mutations set off in history may become an enrichment and a quest for truth. For it calls on all men and women to bear witness to the God of faithfulness and reciprocity.

### Christ and his church

When Paul spoke of the union of man and wife he concluded: 'This is a great mystery and I take it to mean Christ and the church' (Eph. 5.32). To talk like this was to count marriage among the sacramental realities even before the word sacrament existed.

As in all sacraments, there is interaction: human reality allows us to understand the relationship of God to human beings, and the discovery of God comes to enrich our grasp of human reality. What are we to say of the relationship of Christ to the church if the union of man and woman had not come to unveil it? Conversely, contemplation of the gift that Christ makes of himself to his church shows the demands and the riches of marriage.

## Marriage and celibacy

Human beings are social animals. They become themselves only in relation to others. To reject this relationship is to condemn oneself. To believe that it can exist at less cost, without commitment on either side, is to move towards failure. Here, as in so many spheres, the Gospel maxim applies, 'For whoever would save his life will lose it, and whoever loses his life for my sake will find it' (Matt. 16.25).

But not everyone marries. There are many reasons for this, as Jesus knew well: 'There are those who do not marry because they are incapable of it from birth; there are those who cannot marry because they have been mutilated by men; and there are those who have chosen not to marry because of the kingdom of heaven. He who is able to receive this, let him receive it' (Matt. 19.12). Not

to marry is not necessarily to reject a relationship. In a civilization like ours in which the number of those who are celibate is important, it is often a call to give oneself.

### Marriage and consecration to the religious life

At certain periods of the life of the church consecration to the religious life was considered a sacrament, and not without reason. There are two ways of living out the covenant: there is a choice between marriage and celibacy. Both can be sacraments of the covenant.

Marriage and celibacy are complementary. We cannot exalt one to the detriment of the other, or disparage one to emphasize the other.

Some people, on the pretext of a high spirituality, regard marriage as a second best and consecration to the religious life as superior to it. By contrast, others so exalt marriage as to suggest that celibacy is a mutilation.

In reality, here we have two complementary ways of establishing a place in the world. They should provide mutual enrichment:

both can be ways of giving oneself completely;
both can be a source of fertility,
both demand the same kind of fidelity;
both also know joy and suffering, success and failure.

You cannot choose one and dream unconsciously of the other. One situation is not easier than the other, since it is difficult for everyone to live authentically.

### Celibacy accepted

However, the truth of the covenant is not reserved for those who have made the choice of celibacy in consecration to the religious life. There are celibates, men and women, who are true witnesses to the covenant. They may not have chosen their state, which is often the result of circumstances and other diverse factors. Fidelity, fertility, reciprocity and self-giving are nevertheless not excluded from their life.

We all know those who achieve a relationship with others and a wealth of service for all through their celibacy. They live out their Pasch and thus enter into the mystery of the covenant. We can attest, and they too can attest, the riches that God has put in their hands.

### Failure in marriage

Marriage can get into painful situations which end up in failure. Does that mean that we have to say that the sacrament has not been lived out? Far from it. It is useless to examine the past to see whose fault it was. The couple has to live out their present situation and, moreover, do so in faith and in the light of the word of God. Even in his passion, Jesus bears witness to life. Even in their suffering and failure, the separated partners can still bear witness to the truth of the God of the covenant.

All the Christian churches agree in affirming that the Christian ideal of marriage involves the union of the couple in faithfulness. This is a call of the gospel, and it is unambiguous. However, to many of our contemporaries the legislation of the Catholic church on those who are divorced and remarry often seems too severe. But to show the magnitude of the sacrament it maintains the principle of absolute indissolubility.

In the Orthodox Church and in the Reformation churches a 'principle of mercy' is used in favour of divorced persons to authorize remarriage in some cases. It is impossible to discuss this problem in the present chapter with the nuances that are desirable. It is covered in more detail in *How to Understand Marriage*.

However, it has to be affirmed that those who are divorced and remarry have their place in the Christian community. Though current legislation does not allow them to take part fully in the eucharistic communion, they nevertheless form part of the communion of the church. They participate with their brethren in the liturgical assembly, and with them they feed on the word of God. That is why they should not be said to have been 'excommunicated': that is not the right word to describe their situation.

---

# A history of the sacrament of marriage

## Origins

As we have said, to state that Christ instituted the sacraments does not mean that he fixed their rites and symbolic actions, but that he gave them a meaning and a value that they could not have by themselves. Marriage is a good example of this. Jesus did not invent it, but St Paul explains its new significance well when he affirms that 'This is a great mystery and I take it to mean Christ and the church' (Eph. 5.32).

## Up to the third century

In Roman society, marriage was well enough organized legally (contract, consent) and ceremonially (marriage veil, marriage feast, procession to the husband's house) for the first Christians not to seek to celebrate it in any other way; they were content to add the Christian significance of their union to the ceremonies and to abstain from pagan sacrificial practices.

The first specifically ecclesial act was the obligation to obtain permission from the bishop in certain cases, particularly for the marriage of clergy.

## From the fourth to the eleventh centuries

While keeping to secular practices, Christians gradually came to indicate the particular significance that they attached to marriage by adding a specifically Christian stamp to one of the customary rites which made it up. In this way the nuptial blessing came into being. This took place

in Rome and Milan, when the veil was put back on the young woman;

in the East, during the crowning of the bride;

in Gaul and Spain, when the bridal couple entered the nuptial chamber.

Having begun at Rome, first of all for the marriage of clergy and their children, the habit of giving this blessing during the course of a mass spread throughout Christianity for all bridal couples.

It is very picturesque and revealing of the changes possible in certain disciplines to see how the first example of a nuptial blessing that we have comes from the fourth century, from the marriage of the lector Julian, future bishop of Eclanum and son of the bishop of Benevento, to the daughter of the bishop of Capua!

## Marriage in the Middle Ages

Wars and social troubles led the church above all to secure freedom of consent for the wife and to require marriage to be public: the priest was entrusted with the civil formalities, and the bridal couple tended increasingly to receive the nuptial blessing, which was a way of forcing them to have recourse to the priest. The exchange of consents even came to be shifted, from the house of the fiancée to the door of the church. The couples only entered church after the marriage, for Mass and a nuptial blessing.

At the same time, theologians and canon lawyers worked on the question of the nature and number of the sacraments, among which from the twelfth century they included marriage (see p. 56).

## The Council of Trent

For the West, it was the Council of Trent which, in 1563, imposed what is called the canonical form of marriage, i.e. the appearance of the couple before their own parish priest to exchange consents.

Vatican II maintained its demand, but enriched the ritual:
- a greater possibility of adaptation to local customs;
- an exchange of consent systematically preceded by a liturgy of the word, even if there is no Mass;
- a greater variety and greater richness in the formulas exchanging consent, in nuptial blessings and final blessings;
- the possibility of holding the celebration in the vernacular.

---

### Today

Nowadays those who want to marry are asked to report to their parish some months before the date fixed for the celebration. The actual length of time varies in different countries and even dioceses. This should not be seen as an extra bit of administrative harassment. Certainly, a file has to be put together, and birth certificates and baptism certificates have to be produced. But more importantly, this is an act of the church which has to be prepared for and undergone.

Preparation consists in talks with a priest, but also with other couples, at meetings organized by a team of Christians who undertake to perform this service for the community.

These meetings often give place to fruitful exchanges between the couples themselves. They make it possible to answer very different questions.

143

The whole of human reality is covered: relations between men and women and their different psychologies, the problem of children, marriage difficulties; and also the content of faith and an explanation of the church's thought on marriage.

With the priest the preparation is more personal. The passages from the word of God which will be at the heart of the celebration are chosen. These texts are read together, listened to, reacted to. In a way this is rather like what happened between Jesus and the disciples when they recognized his presence on the way to Emmaus.

The priest is there to ensure freedom, not simply freedom which excludes pressures of all kinds, but freedom which becomes more clear about the act that is being performed.

## The faith of the married couple

Those who come and ask to be married in church are often not practising Christians. Some even find it difficult to say just what their position is on the faith. We should not be too surprised at that. In the life of many young people, recent years have led to rifts with earlier generations, sometimes of major dimensions. Some of what the church says has become alien to them, and they find it difficult to give it a context.

The sacraments are sacraments of faith. The priest is at their service so that they can be lived in faith. But he is also at the service of young people, so that they can be loyal to the course they have chosen. So it is not surprising that the attitude of the church is both welcoming and demanding.

# 14

# The Sacraments of the Sick

*'Is any one among you sick? Let him call for the elders of the church, and let them pray over him, anointing him with oil in the name of the Lord; and the prayer of faith will save the sick man, and the Lord will raise him up; and if he has committed sins, he will be forgiven.'*

James 5.14

## Sacraments for the sick

There is no human life without suffering and death. Unless faith in Jesus Christ can look these in the face, it is vain. However, they still remain the greatest question that is posed to each one of us. Are suffering and death the destruction of life or a 'passage' towards the New Life? Only our brothers and sisters who face them in their flesh can tell us of this way which was opened by Jesus himself.

So it is good that the church has sacraments for the sick. In fact, the rites of the Roman Ritual speak not of one sacrament, but of several sacraments of the sick. Three are listed:

the communion of the sick;
the anointing of the sick;
Viaticum.

We should not be surprised at so close a connection between the world of faith and that of attention to the sick. On the contrary, this is one of the finest discoveries of the gospel. But here, as in many other areas, Jesus asks us to change our approach. The sacrament will play its role as a call to conversion, proclamation of the gospel, and discovery of the true countenance of God. To understand that better we must first turn our attention to Jesus of Nazareth.

## Jesus and the sick

If you look up in the Gospels all the passages in which Jesus encounters sick people, you will be amazed at the importance of the sections that you find.

For example, open the Gospel of Mark and look. After his baptism Jesus leaves for the desert. Then he begins to proclaim 'the gospel of God' and calls his first disciples. Immediately he acts against evil and suffering by driving out an unclean spirit and healing the sick.

| | |
|---|---|
| 1.21–28 | Jesus drives out an unclean spirit |
| 1.29–31 | Healing of Peter's mother-in-law |
| 1.32–34 | Multiple healings |
| 1.35–39 | Jesus goes throughout Galilee |
| 1.40–45 | Healing of a leper |
| 2. 1–12 | Healing of someone who is paralysed |

As though it were a conclusion to all this, we have Jesus' declaration at his meal with Levi: 'Those who are well have no need of a physician, but those who are sick; I came not to call the righteous, but sinners' (2.17).

We find a healing immediately afterwards, on the sabbath, of a man with a paralysed hand (3.1–6) and the arrival of 'all who had diseases' (3.10). The first time that Jesus goes to the Decapolis he heals a

147

demoniac (5.1–20). When he returns to Galilee he heals a woman with a haemorrhage and restores Jairus' daughter to life (5.21–43). He heals the sick even in Nazareth (6.5). His apostles go on a mission and it is specifically said: 'And they cast out many demons, and anointed with oil many that were sick and healed them' (6.13).

The whole of this part of the Gospel ends as it were with a summary: 'And wherever he came, in villages, cities, or country, they laid the sick in the market places, and besought him that they might touch even the fringe of his garment, and as many as touched it were made well' (6.56).

Tension mounts between the authorities and Jesus. The Gospel becomes more dramatic. The Master takes the road to Jerusalem for the passion. Then there is less talk of the sick. However, there are still some healings at key moments, discussions with the Pharisees on 'what is important' and healings of a foreign woman possessed with a spirit and of a deaf-mute (7.24–37). The incomprehension of the disciples and the proclamation of faith by Peter frame the healing of a blind man (8.22–26). The Transfiguration, apart on a mountain, is followed by the healing of an epileptic, in the plain in the midst of a crowd (9.14–29).

As a prologue to the great passion week, we have the healing of the blind man of Jericho who sets out to follow Jesus (10.46–52). But at this moment it is Jesus himself who becomes a man of sorrow, and enters on his passion.

This view is not limited to the Gospel of Mark. As evidence we might look at the scene in the Gospel of Luke when the emissaries of John the Baptist ask Jesus: 'Are you he who is to come, or shall we look for another?' Luke continues the story by noting: 'In that hour Jesus cured many people of diseases and plagues and evil spirits, and on many that were blind he bestowed sight. And he answered them: "Go and tell John what you have seen and heard: the blind receive their sight, the lame walk, lepers are cleansed, and the deaf hear, the dead are raised up, the poor have the good news preached to them' (Luke 7.18–23).

So Jesus constantly showed himself to be concerned for the sick. Even more than today, these

When the church cares for the sick, it serves Christ in the suffering members of the mystical body. And imitating the Lord Jesus who 'went about doing good and healing all that were sick' (Acts 10.38), it obeys his commandment to care for the sick (Mark 16.18).

The church shows this concern in a variety of ways: it visits those whose health is affected; it brings them relief through the sacrament of unction; it restores their strength by the sacrament of the eucharist, either during the course of their illness or when they are in danger of death; finally, it prays for them and entrusts them to God, above all when they come to their last hour.

*Decree at the Promulgation of the Rite*,
Rome, 7 December 1972

were people apart, often banned from society: the lepers in particular lived as outlaws. They were declared unclean. Sickness was always suspected of being the consequence of a sin. Jesus challenged such ideas and declared them false. He was the friend of the sick. One can say that in this way he took the part of the person against the illness, in the same way as he took the part of the person against his or her sin.

He gave precise instructions to his apostles: 'Jesus gave them authority over unclean spirits, to cast them out, and to heal every disease and every infirmity' (Matt. 10.1); and the Gospel of Mark ends: 'Go into all the world and preach the gospel to the whole creation . . . and these signs will accompany those who believe . . . they will lay their hands on the sick, and they will recover' (Matt. 16.15–18).

So it is not surprising that the church has always shown a particular concern for the sick. The first action of Peter and John on the day after Pentecost was to heal a sick man by the Beautiful Gate in the name of Jesus Christ (Acts 3; 4). Similarly, the church started hospitals. How many religious congregations have been founded over the centuries to care for the sick, the infirm and the handicapped? How many thousands of vocations have they produced? And even now we see people like Mother Teresa bringing together numerous groups to work throughout the world to welcome the disinherited.

## God in human suffering

Suffering is non-sense. Suffering is an evil that has to be fought against. However, suffering is unavoidable. It is present in every life. Suffering and sickness are part of human reality. But how is it that there is life only in heartbreak?

What a temptation it is to accuse God then! To accuse God or even to deny God! How can this being exist who is called the Omnipotent One, if his very power fades into impotence in the face of the suffering of those whom he is thought to love?

Some people think that suffering can be explained as a punishment. Are not human beings primarily responsible for the evil that they suffer? We do not know the secrets of human hearts, and those who might seem to us to be upright might have hidden faults which amply justify the hand of God weighing heavily on them. All these fine arguments collapse in the face of the suffering of the innocent child. One can always accuse others and find reasons in the wickedness inherent in human nature. And certainly that is true of the mass of suffering engendered by war and all our egotistic and machiavellian machinations. But in the light of such simplistic explanations, how can we contemplate the child who is born handicapped, the one whom chance strikes and makes a cripple for ever, those young people who seem to bear in their flesh all our sorrows?

From the distant past, scripture has taken the opposite side to these 'windbags'. We might recall the way in which Job replied to the theologians who assailed him:

I have heard many such things,
miserable comforters are you all.
Shall windy words have an end?
Or what provokes you that you answer? (16.2–3).

How then will you comfort me with empty nothings?

There is nothing left of your answers but falsehood (21.34).

As for you, you whitewash with lies,
worthless physicians are you all (13.4).

The book of Job is a drama, and one could still suppose that it merely reports academic discussions. However, it must be remembered that at the source of such a work there is a meditation on the real life of the one who was an authentic servant of God, the prophet Jeremiah. He was the first to cry:

Woe is me, my mother, that you bore me! (15.10).

Why is my pain unceasing,
my wound incurable, refusing to be healed? (15.18).
Cursed be the day on which I was born!
The day when my mother bore me, let it not be blessed.
Why did I come forth from the womb to see toil and sorrow,
and spend my days in shame? (20.14).

Jeremiah the just, Jeremiah the sufferer. His experience and even his words were taken up by the one who left us, a generation later, the great poems known as the Suffering Servant songs:

As many as were astonished at him –
his appearance was so marred, beyond human semblance,
and his form beyond that of the sons of men –
He had no form or comeliness that we should look at him,
and no beauty that we should desire him.
He was despised and rejected by men;
a man of sorrows and acquainted with grief;
and as one from whom men hide their faces
he was despised, and we esteemed him not (Isa. 52.14–53.14).

The Bible does not offer any theory of suffering, but it does give us authentic witness to keep close to. Jeremiah, the servant of God, and Job are both witnesses of God and witnesses of humankind. Their cries of distress are our cries and those of our brothers and sisters. They level an indictment against the atrocity of human suffering.

However, their words of challenge, their complaints verging on blasphemy, are for ever written in the great Book of the Word of God. When human beings cry against suffering, it is God himself who guarantees the authenticity of these words.

These great witnesses bring us to the feet of the Crucified One. In the garden of Gethsemane the mystery of a God who allows suffering and of human beings who undergo it fuse in a single mystery. We have not finished exploring life and discovering how it only gives itself by losing itself. And the blood which brings life flows from a wound at the heart of humankind. Jesus is the great witness to this God who made himself our companion, to bring life out of the death that he accepts. If suffering is written on human destiny, from now on we know that it is not alien to the face of God.

Then we know those riches expressed for all the Christian community by the discovery of the truth of the sacrament of the sick.

### The two faces of the sacrament

If it is true that every sacrament unveils to us part of the face of God manifested in Jesus of Nazareth, it has to be said that for the sacrament of the sick this part has two aspects. First there is the face of the Jesus who is concerned for the sick and cures them, but there is also the face imprinted on Veronica's veil, the image of suffering.

In our mutual relations we are there for others, a sacrament of God in Jesus Christ.

Those who suffer need in their loneliness to know that they are not alone in their struggle. In that case all those who exercise with concern the role of carers or simply companions become the guarantors of God's concern. For the sick they are truly sacraments of the mysterious presence of the one who never abandons his friend in difficulty.

Thus hospital staff, members of the chaplaincy, others who are sick, those who are simply friends paying a visit, are also participants in the sacrament of the sick. They may not perhaps be present when it is being celebrated with the priest, but they are the ones who give it consistency and have rooted it in everyday life.

On the other hand, however, our brothers and sisters in suffering are for all of us the sacrament of Jesus Christ. 'Philip, he who sees me sees the Father.' John tells us that this word was pronounced on the evening of Maundy Thursday. The next afternoon, when Philip saw his master nailed to the cross, did he remember what had been said the previous day? Did he then discover that suffering is also a face of God? This second meaning is more profound. It is always difficult to explain, since only those who suffer have the right to talk of their suffering.

In a sacrament, the one who receives it becomes a prophet for the community. The sick proclaim a face of God to us. They are in a very special way associated with the mystery of Christ. They reveal to us that the mystery of God is as incomprehensible as the mystery of evil and suffering. They are not just the words that they say to us; they give us their lives to contemplate.

---

## A history of the sacrament of the sick

### Origins

In keeping with the practices of the time, the first Christians showed by the laying on of hands and anointing with oil that Jesus Christ was present to the sick among them, as he had been to so many sick and infirm during his earthly life (see the text from St James at the beginning of this chapter). Did not Jesus send his disciples on a mission in order, among other things, to anoint the sick with oil (Mark 6.13) or to lay hands on them (Mark 16.18)?

## Up to the seventh century

The formulas for blessing oil for the sick are evidence that the practice of unction was never interrupted. A letter from Pope Innocent I in 416 makes it clear that if all Christians have the power to perform this anointing, with all the more reasons so do the priests and the bishop.

There is anointing of the sick. The sacrament for the dying Christian at this time seems more to have been the *viaticum* (see the note on this word below, 154).

## From the seventh century

The ritual of anointing the sick was becoming organized, particularly in the monastic sphere. It influenced the ritual for the simple faithful on two points;

The accent slipped from a request for healing towards a penitential act; the consequence of this change was that the sacrament was administered as near as possible to death. Anointing the sick became extreme unction.

The faithful no longer had the right to give unction, but only the priests.

## From the thirteenth century

Celebration so near to death meant that the ritual was abbreviated. It was this ritual, abbreviated in the thirteenth century, which was chosen by the liturgical reform which followed the Council of Trent in 1614.

## Vatican II

The liturgical reform which emerged from Vatican II re-established the intentions and practices of the early church:

Not an extreme unction as near as possible to death, but an anointing of the sick for all those afflicted by serious illness or old age;

Reintroduction of the laying on of hands;

Restoration of the context of anointing the sick to within the eucharist (which can be celebrated at the home of the sick person), particularly so that the sick can communicate in two kinds (see the note on the *viaticum*) and even only with the blood of Christ if their state does not allow them to take solid food (the host);

The inauguration of community celebrations of the sacrament.

## Viaticum

The church has always thought that it should suggest to dying Christians that they should join Christ in the paschal mystery of his death and resurrection, through the paschal sacrament itself, the eucharist which 'proclaims the death of the Lord until he comes' (I Cor. 11.26).

In 325 the Council of Nicaea (after which our Sunday creed is named) stated: 'In the matter of those who are making their departure, ancient and canonical law must also be observed: if someone is making his departure he should not be deprived of the last and very necessary viaticum.' This viaticum was understood as communion under both kinds, for it was unthinkable that the dying Christian could be united in the death of Christ without sharing in the blood which the Lord shed for us on the cross.

After centuries during which viaticum was not abandoned but during which it was 'extreme unction' that passed for the sacrament of the dying, Vatican II sought to restore viaticum as the sacrament of the death of the Christian. The ritual of 1614 put viaticum before the anointing of the sick, but in the case of the continuous rite, the ritual of 1972 resumed the old order: penitence, anointing, viaticum. It also states that 'when possible, viaticum should be received within Mass so that the sick person may receive communion under both kinds' (no. 26).

## Today

'Liturgical actions are not private actions, but celebrations of the church,' states the Vatican II Constitution on the Liturgy. That is why there is a requirement that 'rites which are meant to be celebrated in common, with the faithful present and actively participating, should as far as possible be celebrated in that way rather than by an individual and quasi-privately' (*Constitution on the Sacred Liturgy*, 27).

That is particularly fitting in the case of the sick, since life itself risks cutting them off from the rest of the community.

The new rites of the sacraments for the sick, decreed by Vatican II, are inspired by this concern.

### Communion for the sick

To take communion to the sick is one of the richest ways of showing that they are considered to be fully members of the community. According to the ancient tradition of the church, Christians themselves must have this concern.

That was originally the main reason for part of the eucharist being preserved at the end of the mass. The Roman instruction on 'The Worship of the Eucharistic Mystery' appropriately recalls this (*Eucharisticum mysterium*, no. 49).

Following the new ritual, in many parishes provisions have been made for:

Teams of lay people specially trained to perform this ministry. In visiting the sick, first they can suggest communion, and after having spoken to the parish priest, can be allowed, as happened in the first centuries, to take the eucharist regularly to the people whom they visit;

To make visible the close relationship between communion taken to a sick person and the celebration of the eucharist, the persons who are to administer the communion receive the hosts they need during the Sunday mass in the presence of the whole congregation. For that they go up to the altar, before or after the communion of the faithful, and the celebrant gives them the Holy Sacrament with a formula like, 'Go and help our sick brothers and sisters to participate in the eucharist that we have just celebrated';

To name in the universal prayer or in the eucharistic prayer those who are participating in the celebration through the communion that they are going to receive at home. So it is the community which becomes aware of the moral presence of those who are prevented from attending;

Similarly, at the moment of giving the eucharist to those who are sick, it is usual to read with them the gospel of the mass from which the eucharist comes. They can also be given news of the community and, when possible, have the parish newsletter delivered.

### The sacrament of anointing

Too often, there is hesitation about suggesting that a member of one's family should receive the anointing of the sick. The fear is that such a suggestion might cause a psychological shock and reduces his or her capacity to fight against the illness, or that it might cast shadows on the last moments of lucidity. So people wait until the patient has lost consciousness before appealing to a priest.

Faced with this situation, the new ritual suggests three pastoral efforts:

First of all to rediscover the ancient tradition of the church for the very name of the sacrament. We have seen the custom, since the Middle Ages, of calling it 'extreme unction', as if to suggest that it was administered when a person was at the last extremity. Now it is called the 'sacrament of anointing' or the 'anointing of the sick'.

Secondly, there is a requirement to celebrate this sacrament when the illness becomes a test which calls for courage and lucidity. It can also be administered to those whose advanced age forces them to make marked changes to their usual lifestyle.

So it does not necessarily mark the immediate approach of death. There is even a provision that it can be received several times in the course of a prolonged illness, or when after a cure a person is afflicted by the illness again. The box below contains the exact rules given by the Roman rite.

Finally, the Council has required that the sacrament, like all the others, should be celebrated in a more communal fashion. In a large number of parishes such a celebration is announced each year. Those taking part can prepare themselves for it by a time of reflection and prayer, a brief recollection. The whole community can take part in it.

This way of proceeding has two advantages. It allows a better discovery of the riches of the sacrament for the life of the whole community. It largely contributes towards changing old frames of mind and dispelling the fear felt over this sacrament.

Changing old frames of mind is often difficult. In the case of the sacrament of anointing, the difficulty comes as much from the sick themselves as from those around them. By choosing a communal celebration the church has made a major contribution to this development.

## The rules of the Roman Ritual

Great care should be taken to see that those of the faithful whose health is seriously impaired by sickness or old age receive this sacrament (no. 8).

A prudent or reasonably sure judgment, without scruple, is sufficient for deciding on the seriousness of an illness; if necessary a doctor may be consulted (no. 8).

In public and private catechesis, the faithful should be educated to ask for the sacrament of anointing and, as soon as the right time comes, to receive it with full faith and devotion. They should not follow the wrongful practice of delaying the reception of the sacrament. All who care for the sick should be taught the meaning and purpose of the sacrament (no. 13).

The sacrament may be repeated if the sick person recovers after being anointed and then again falls ill or if during the same illness the person's condition becomes more serious (no. 9).

A sick person may be anointed before surgery whenever a serious illness is the reason for the surgery (no. 10).

Elderly people may be anointed if they have become notably weakened even though no serious illness is present (no. 11).

The sacrament of anointing is to be conferred on sick people who, although they have lost consciousness or the use of reason, would, as Christian believers, have at least implicitly asked for it when they were in control of their faculties (no. 14).

It is especially fitting that all baptized Christians share in this ministry of mutual charity within the body of Christ by doing all that they can to help the sick return to health, by showing love for the sick, and by celebrating the sacraments with them. Like the other sacraments, these too have a community aspect, which should be brought out as much as possible when they are celebrated (no. 41).

### Viaticum

Viaticum is the provision given to someone to allow them to go on a long journey. In the Middle Ages this was money given to a religious for expenses incurred in moving from one abbey to another. Hence came the custom of saying, when one took the communion to a dying person, that he or she was going to receive the eucharist 'as viaticum'. The image is a good one. Death is not the end of a life, but a departure for the real journey.

We all have the experience of this departure. It is non-sense for those who remain behind, since they see only the separation. But for those who go, though they also experience separation and being torn apart, the departure takes on meaning, since it opens up a way.

Look at our lives. Every time that we have done something important, we have had to part. Marrying is parting; taking a job is parting; every major decision is like a new departure. Those who have always been afraid of parting have never done anything. One needs often to have had an occasion to part, in order to discover slowly that every departure opens up a way.

If our departures have found their meaning in the Easter of the Lord, if the law of the grain of wheat has seemed to us to be proved on the occasion of each one of them, then we are ready to welcome death. Despite its apparent absurdity, it is like a departure on a new way. That does not do away with either the anguish or the suffering, but it does allow us to see its true meaning.

The church, the body of Christ, gathers up the experience of all its members who down the centuries have experienced the mystery of death. It announces and welcomes the Lord's Easter in each one of them.

It does this by viaticum, which is a quite special participation in the eucharist:

- When are individuals nearer to the memorial of the passion than in the hour of their agony?
- When will we be nearer to Maundy Thursday than at the hour of our personal Good Friday?
- When is the presence of the Risen Lord more necessary on our way than at the place where night falls?
- When do we best prophesy the drama of faith if not at the moment when we have to fight our last battle?

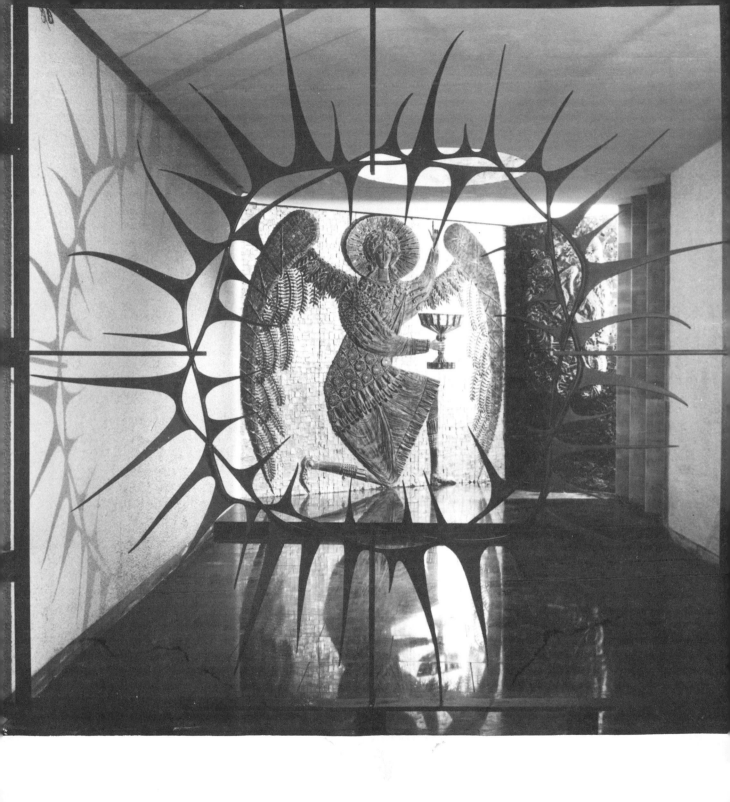

# Conclusion:
# Word and Sacrament

*In the beginning was the Word*
*and the Word was with God*
*and the Word was God.*
*It was in the beginning with God,*
*all things were made by it,*
*and without it was not anything made that was made.*
*In it was life,*
*and the life was the light of men . . .*
*The Word took a body*
*and set up its tent in our midst.*

John 1.1–4, 14

The sacraments are the basic words at the heart of our lives. Not words of information, but those living words which allow two beings to join together.

### The word and humankind

Speaking makes us be, for it is in our language that we emerge. A word exchanged brings each of us out of our cocoons and liberates the capacity to express ourselves.

Even the tiniest children need someone to speak to them, from birth onwards, to rouse them to life. And the child can only say 'I' in a dialogue in which someone has already said 'you'. Children discover themselves only at the moment when someone else addresses them.

Speaking is putting oneself before another and expressing oneself with all one's being; it is entering into dialogue with others both by the sound of our voices and by our behaviour, our attitudes, our very presence.

To speak is to discover a common language which is created only by mutual association. Otherwise words take on different meanings for each person. One thinks that one understands, but is left in ambiguity or is talking at cross purposes.

To speak is to accept an encounter. It is to go part of the way together. It is to create a common route.

In a human relationship faith given and faith received become the most complete expression of dialogue. In this way recognition of the other comes about, not only as part of the scenery which surrounds us but as a being whom one names and by whom one is named in turn.

If God wants to speak with human beings, one might say that there are no other means of communication than in human language.

If God wants to speak with human beings, he can do so only in the daily realities of our life.

If God wants to speak with human beings, he has to come and live with them: 'The Word took a body and set up its tent in our midst.'

## Jesus, Word of God

In many and various ways God spoke of old to our fathers by the prophets; but in these last days he has spoken to us by a Son, whom he appointed the heir of all things, through whom also he created the world (Heb. 1.1–2).

Jesus is the living Word. He is not a preacher or a teacher. He speaks by his life. His words are also his actions. His words are encounter. And those with whom he speaks, whether disciple or adversary, isolated person or the crowd pressing round him, an outcast from society or a leader of the people, scribe or high priest, centurion or Roman procurator, know themselves to be known. The word of Jesus evokes faith, and it is a gift of faith.

His word is forgiveness and it is a call. It is inserted into every life. His word gives a sign and human beings stand upright. When the emissaries of John the Baptist came to question him, Jesus replied: 'Go and tell John what you have seen and heard: the blind receive their sight, the lame walk, lepers are cleansed, and the deaf hear, the dead are raised up, the poor have good news preached to them' (Luke 7.22).

The word of Jesus is living because it encounters human beings at the heart of their lives.

And his word is submission to another, a revelation of this other whom he calls his Father. Jesus is the Word of the Father. He is fond of repeating: 'The words that I say to you I do not speak on my own authority' (John 14.10). 'I have not spoken on my own authority; the Father who sent me has himself given me commandment what to say . . . What I say, therefore, is as the Father has bidden me' (John 12.49–50).

## Word and sacrament

The word of Jesus did not stop with the tragic evening of Good Friday. On Easter morning, Jesus was there in the midst of his own. He gave them his Spirit and his word is always alive.

We saw that the first Christian communities did not claim to speak in their own names. When, after receiving the Holy Spirit on the day of Pentecost,

Peter and John made the lame man at the Beautiful Gate stand upright (Acts 3), they did so in the name of Jesus Christ.

It is in his name that one forgives and baptizes, in his name that one breaks the bread, that one prays and anoints with oil a sick brother or sister.

This is how the sacraments of the church were born, under the impetus of the Spirit. They are the living presence of the risen Lord; they are a 'memorial' of his word and his gestures. They continue to be, in our time, the living encounter of God with human beings, by Jesus Christ his Son.

The sacraments are certainly words. Not magic words which someone external to us, like a magician, a druid or a good fairy, says over us to transform us externally even without our co-operation.

They are life in accordance with the Spirit. They are dialogue in which we discover Jesus of Nazareth as the one who calls, the one who has made himself near to meet us in our very existence and in the realities of our life, the most intimate but also the most everyday. They do not exhaust our dialogue with God, but they are essential elements of it.

In the sacrament God speaks, and his Word is a welcome to what we are and what we experience. In the sacrament, God speaks, and his Word is efficacious.

## Word of God

God speaks and everything happens. His Word is creative. That is what the first chapter of the first book of the Bible has affirmed since ancient times:

In the beginning God created heaven and earth. The earth was without form and void, and the breath of God moved over the face of the waters, and God said . . .

And the world, its organization and all its population, with human beings at the summit, all this is the fruit of ten words! St John recalls this first page of the Bible when he writes, 'In the beginning was the Word'.

God speaks! In the silence of things or in the turmoil of the worlds, God speaks! And his Word makes things be.

We find God so silent. We perceive only the echoes of this Word which resound in human words. The prophets and all the great inspired figures of the Bible have been such voices. The Spirit awakens in them the echo of the Word which they have heard. It is in them like a 'burning fire, impossible to contain' (Jer. 20.9). And the Word takes form in their lives so that we can perceive it in our turn.

The Word of God is the true light which lightens every person who comes into the world. The light can be seen when it strikes an object, when it illuminates something. Similarly the Word of God can be seen only when it comes upon the events of our life. The sacrament is the meeting place between the Word and life.

### Living the faith

Christians are no different from other people. The framework of their lives is the same as that of all those around them. Everyday events, great and small, mark its stages.

But life can become the place of a mysterious dialogue with the one who is its source and becomes its horizon. We still need to learn the words.

Like the child who receives its language from its mother, we too receive the words of our faith from this long line of witnesses who have brought the book of the Word of God down to us. They are the church. And in teaching us to express our faith, they make it be.

The sacraments are sacraments of faith, not just because they need faith to be truly experienced. They are also privileged occasions in which faith expresses itself and is experienced.

They are not monologues, but dialogues in solidarity with the believing community. They are the sacraments of the faith of the church. It is in its faith that our faith is found.

To live the faith is to make one's life a place where the kingdom comes.

To live the faith is to accept that life becomes a sacrament of salvation.

To live the faith is to live the sacraments.

---

*Ho, every one who thirsts, come to the waters!*
*Even if you have no money, come, buy and eat.*
*Why do you spend your money on that which does not*
*    feed you?*
*Incline your ear and come to me; hear and you will*
*live.*
*I will make with you an everlasting covenant.*

*Seek the Lord while he may be found;*
*call upon him while he is near.*
*For my thoughts are not your thoughts,*
*neither are your ways my ways,*
*says the Lord.*

*For as the rain and the snow come down from heaven,*
*and return not thither but water the earth,*
*making it bring forth and sprout,*
*giving seed to the sower and bread to the eater,*
*so shall my word be that goes forth from my mouth;*
*it shall not return to me empty,*
*but it shall accomplish that which I purpose,*
*and prosper in the thing for which I sent it.*
                                        Isa. 55.1–11

# Photo Credits